Theme Reader

The McGraw·Hill Companies

www.WrightGroup.com

Printed in the United States of America.

Send all inquiries to:
Wright Group/McGraw-Hill
P.O. Box 812960
Chicago, IL 60681

ISBN 978-0-07-656839-0
MHID 0-07-656839-3

1 2 3 4 5 6 7 8 9 QWV 16 15 14 13 12 11 10

The McGraw-Hill Companies

Contents

UNIT 1

Common Ground

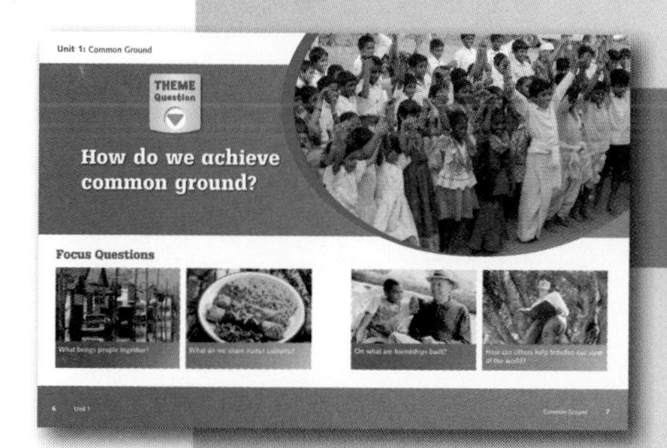

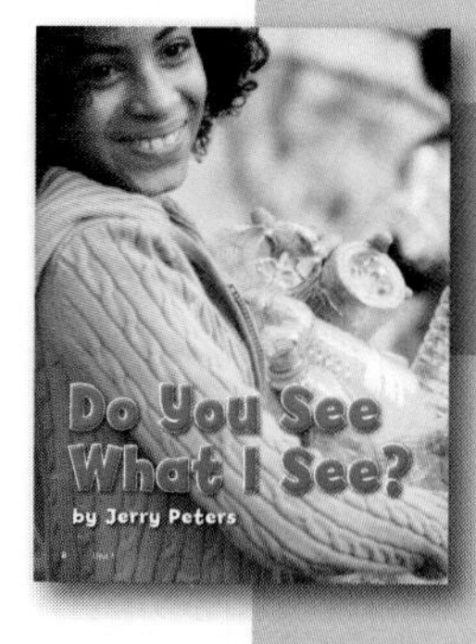

How do we achieve common ground?

Focus Questions

What brings people together?

What do we share across cultures?

On what are friendships built?

How can others help broaden our view of the world?

Do You See What I See?

by Jerry Peters

Contents

Chapter

CHAPTER ONE

Kids Reach Out

People may be from different backgrounds, but when there is a need they come together and **cooperate** to get things done. Here are some ways that a shared interest—wanting to help others—has brought kids and adults together.

Project Backpack

In August 2005, Hurricane Katrina hit the United States, bringing with it terrible floods. Many people had to leave their homes. They lost everything. They needed shelter and vital supplies—things necessary for survival—such as food and clothing.

Many neighborhoods in New Orleans were flooded. This photograph shows flooding along North Broad Street.

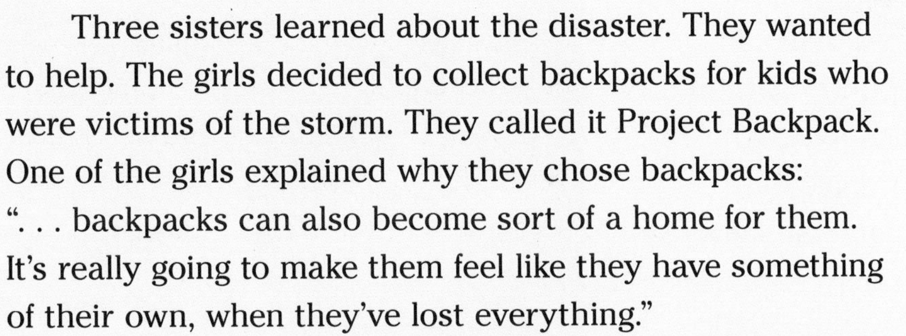

Three sisters learned about the disaster. They wanted to help. The girls decided to collect backpacks for kids who were victims of the storm. They called it Project Backpack. One of the girls explained why they chose backpacks: ". . . backpacks can also become sort of a home for them. It's really going to make them feel like they have something of their own, when they've lost everything."

Project Backpack started with the goal of filling 1,000 backpacks. Working with their parents, the sisters built a Web site and sent e-mail messages. They told people how to participate by donating backpacks, pens, pencils, crayons, books, and toys. In less than two weeks, more than 10,000 filled backpacks were sent to storm victims.

The founders of Project Backpack—Melissa, Jenna, and Jackie Kantor—pose with donated backpacks.

News about Project Backpack soon spread. People in more than 100 communities across the country gathered their own backpacks and supplies to help out. In most cases, these people didn't know the hurricane victims personally. Many of these people had only seen the destruction on television, but they still sent more than 50,000 backpacks. They shared an interest, a goal, and a bit of themselves.

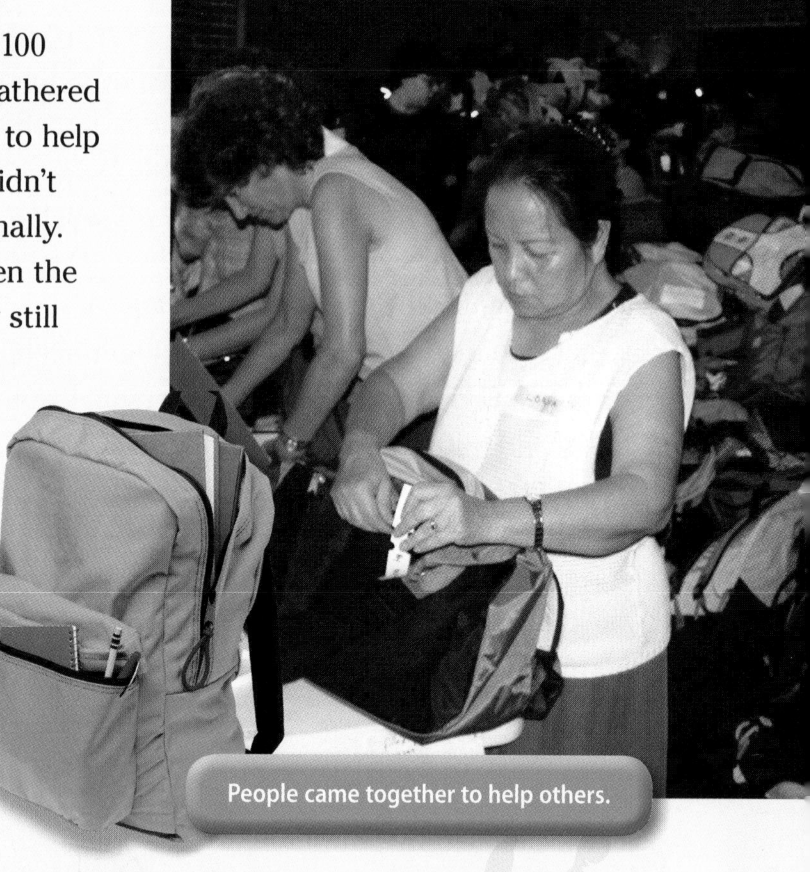

People came together to help others.

When Hurricane Katrina hit, I wanted to help. My friends and I had a lemonade stand and raised money. We had fun picking out the backpacks. We hope you enjoyed the toys and supplies!

Sincerely,
Juan

I am writing to thank you for the backpacks that you sent our school. How excited the kids were to open them! We didn't know how we were going to stock the school, since everything was terribly damaged. Your gifts of backpacks, folders, pencils, crayons, and stickers made a huge difference.

Thank You,
Ms. Allen

Be a Buddy!

What are some other ways kids can reach out? Some kids come together to help others in their own school by being part of a mentoring program. A **mentor** helps someone learn or get along in a new place. For example, a fifth grader and a first grader might be paired as "buddies." Throughout the year, older buddies are mentors. They read to younger buddies, play with them, and help them with homework. The buddies often become friends.

Little buddies like knowing older kids because it helps them feel comfortable, especially in a big school. Big buddies like knowing that they are helping younger kids.

Working with Buddies

- Introduce yourself in a nice way. Smile!
- Be patient and understanding.
- Find interesting ways to explain things.
- Be a good model. Don't show younger buddies bad habits.
- When they do well, tell them so!

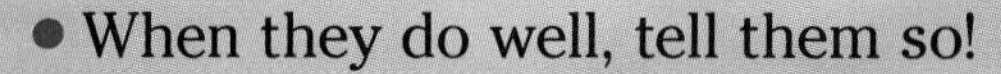

Older buddies talk about good ways to work with younger kids.

Play for Peace

Many children today live in unsafe places. They may live where wars have been fought or where there is a lot of crime. Play for Peace is an organization formed to help these children. It does so by bringing kids and adults together. The goal? To make a more peaceful world.

Places where Play for Peace works include Northern Ireland, India, and Guatemala. Kids from different backgrounds come together to play games. Some of the games encourage them to cooperate and to learn about one another. While playing, kids begin to understand their different ways of thinking and doing things.

Play for Peace kids and leaders gather in Guatemala.

Gatherings in India show how Play for Peace involves kids young and old.

As kids in the program get older, Play for Peace teaches them to be leaders. They become mentors. The older kids lead the games for the younger kids. One leader from a small village in India described her experience: "The first time I realized there was a larger world was when I became involved with Play for Peace . . . . It was a big challenge for me. But I grew to feel safe and like them [people from dissimilar backgrounds] even though they were different than me."

Play for Peace works because it brings kids together. They have fun and learn how to get along. Many kids who participate find that they have much in common—and they become friends!

CHAPTER TWO

Do You Like It?

Solve this riddle.

Which food . . .

- is grown on every continent except Antarctica?
- is eaten by many people around the world, often at every meal?
- can be baked, boiled, steamed, fried, or microwaved?
- is used in soups, main dishes, salads, and desserts?

Did you guess *rice*? Correct! Along with wheat, rice is one of the most important food crops in the world. It is a nutritious, healthful food. Rice is vital for many **cultures**—groups of people with the same backgrounds and ways of thinking about and doing things.

Each year, farmers grow millions of tons of rice. Most rice is grown in Asia. Along with growing rice for their own people to consume, many countries export rice, selling it to other countries.

Top Five Rice-Producing Countries

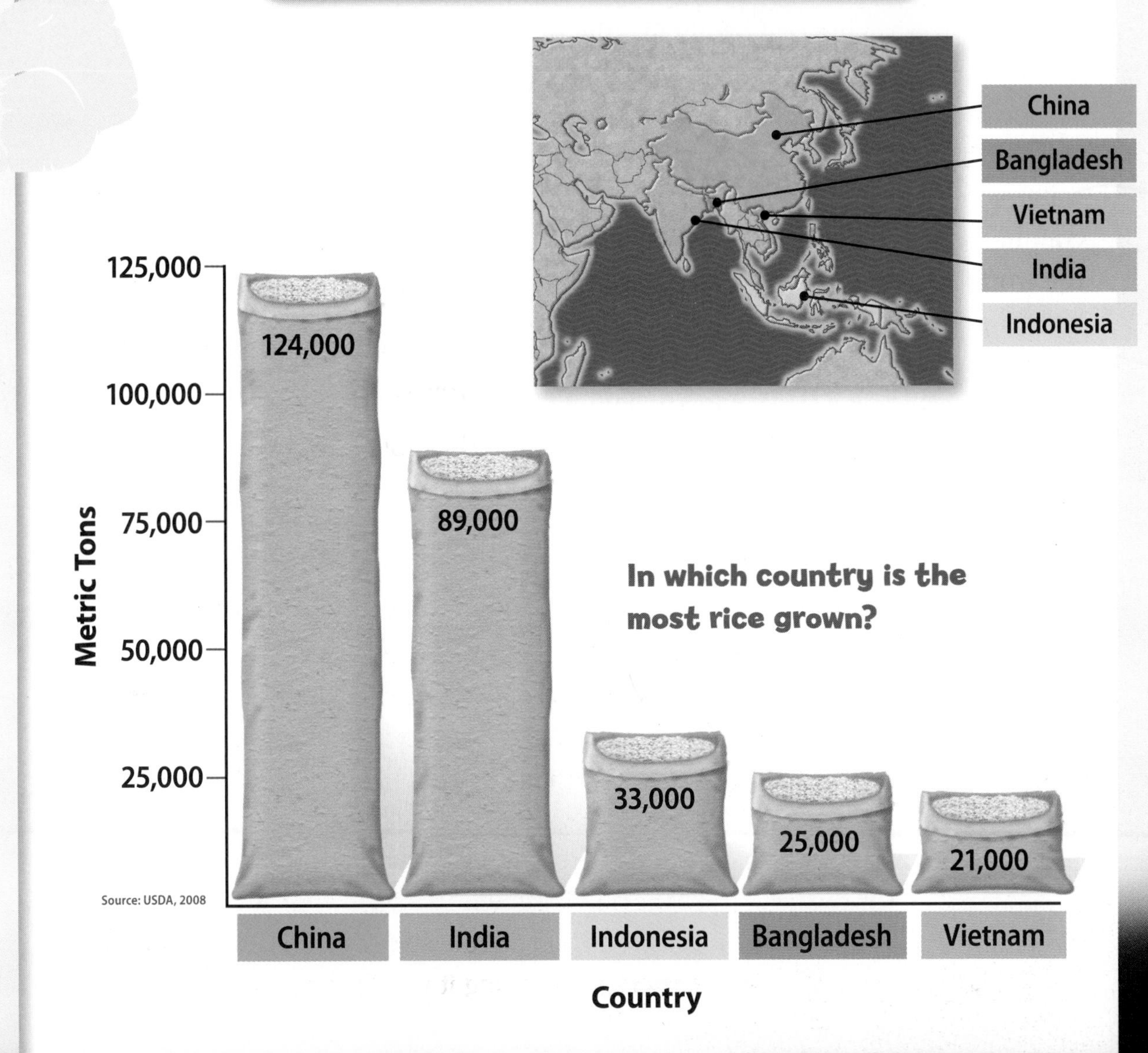

Growing Rice

Have you ever seen a rice paddy like the one shown here? In the United States, only farmers in California, Missouri, Texas, Arkansas, Mississippi, and Louisiana have the ideal soil, climate, and water conditions to grow enough rice to sell commercially. Together, they grow about 2% of the world's rice each year. This means about 16 million pounds are grown in the U.S. each year. Across the world, however, farmers in more than 110 countries grow a total of nearly 800 million pounds of rice each year! In China and India, they grow more than half of the world's total crop.

Many farmers in China tend rice by hand. They also use animals such as water buffalos to pull plows.

Some farmers use mechanical harvesters to collect rice.

Farmers in different countries grow different kinds of rice. A few types of rice are long grain, short grain, black, brown, and white. Farmers in different countries also have different ways of growing rice. How rice is grown depends on the land and the weather. Some farmers use machines to raise crops. Much rice cultivation, however, is still done by hand. Farmers plant rice along small hills in rows and then flood the hills with water. During the growing season, the water may be drained for weeding.

When the grains of rice are ripe, they hang down from the top of the plant. Farmers then go into the fields to cut and tie the stalks. When the stalks are dry, the rice grains can be shaken out and collected.

Rice and Culture

Many people depend on rice. They eat rice regularly. Some even use rice plants to make mats and clothing! In a few cultures, people have depended on rice in these ways for centuries.

The importance of rice is shown in one ancient Chinese tale. According to the story, there was a **famine** in a village, so people were starving. A dog came to the village and shook grains of rice from its tail. Once the people grew this rice, they were never hungry again.

In some cultures, rice is part of everyday talk. When you greet a friend in the United States, you might say, "How are you?" In Bangladesh, though, you might greet a friend by saying, "Have you eaten your rice today?" A Chinese person might wish you a Happy New Year by saying, "May your rice never burn."

During Chinese New Year, people sometimes refer to rice in their holiday greetings.

Eating Rice

People around the world eat rice. In our country, people enjoy rice in many different dishes. Have you tried any of these dishes?

▼ Indian biryani

▲ Japanese sushi

▲ Mexican beans and rice

CHAPTER THREE

Tell It Your Way!

What stories do you like to tell? People of all cultures have told stories for **generations**! Parents have shared folktales, fairy tales, legends, myths, and other stories with their children. Later, the grown-up children share these same stories with their own children.

Some of these stories teach important ideas about a culture. For example, they might tell how a group of people learned to use fire. Other stories show why it is important to be generous or kind or patient.

Because people around the world have **similar** hopes and dreams, some stories sound alike. Do you know the story *Cinderella*? People of many cultures tell some version of this tale. The setting and characters differ a bit, but the story is very similar. However, *Cinderella* is not the only story shared by people of different cultures. Can you think of any others?

Looking at Folktales

This chart gives information about folktales, one kind of story that many cultures tell.

Who's Who in Folktales

- Characters are often all good or all bad.
- Many characters are common people.
- A folktale may feature a trickster, someone who enjoys fooling others.

Where and When Folktales Happen

- The setting usually is an ordinary place such as a forest, a fishing village, or a town square.
- The setting in a folktale may be where the people of the culture telling the story are from. This makes the story more familiar to the listeners.

What Happens in Folktales

- Characters might have a problem to solve—for example, how to get others to help make or do something.
- Some folktales explain things, such as why a chipmunk has stripes.
- There is almost always a happy ending!

Other Things to Look For

- The action takes place quickly.
- Events and groups of words may be repeated.
- Good behavior is rewarded; bad behavior is punished.
- The story may present a lesson for listeners.

This folktale presents a lesson about sharing. Like Cinderella, *it is told in various forms around the world.*

All from a Stone

Not so very long ago, at the end of the American Revolution, three Patriot soldiers were walking back to their homes. They looked pitiful! Their uniforms were torn, and their boots were full of holes.

At night, they came to a village. Food was scarce, so the villagers were hiding what little food they had, even from neighbors and friends. The soldiers stopped at one house after another and inquired where they might find a meal. "There's not a bit of food to eat in the whole countryside," people told them. "You should keep walking."

The first soldier finally said, "Well, I guess that it's time for us to make some stone soup. We will share it with all of you." He pulled a large iron pot from his pack, filled it with water, and built a fire under it. The second soldier took an embroidered bag from his pack and pulled an ordinary-looking stone from it. With a flourish, he dropped the stone into the boiling water.

By now, word had spread. Curious villagers came to watch the soldiers who claimed to be making soup from a stone. As the third soldier sniffed the broth, his face wore a smile like sunshine. "Ahh," he sighed as he looked at the growing crowd, "I do like a tasty stone soup. Of course, stone soup with cabbage—that is a dish that's hard to beat!"

Soon a villager approached, holding a cabbage that she had retrieved from its hiding place. "Wonderful!" cried the first soldier as he cut it up and added it to the pot. "You know, we once shared stone soup with cabbage with General George Washington himself. Of course, our soup had a bit of dried beef in it. *That* made it especially delicious!" The village butcher quietly slipped away from the crowd. He quickly returned with a large chunk of dried beef for the soup.

So it went. Other villagers located carrots, potatoes, onions, salt, and collard greens for the soup. Soon there was a rich, nutritious soup bubbling in the pot. The villagers then brought out tables, chairs, bowls, and spoons. They talked and laughed with each other as they shared the soup.

The next morning, the villagers watched as the second soldier reached into the empty pot, retrieved the stone, and put it back into his embroidered bag. The soldiers then said good-bye and started off toward home.

As they came to the edge of the village, the third soldier turned to his friends. With a grin, he declared, "Well, there's another village that's learned the best meals are shared by all."

CHAPTER FOUR

How Does an Artist See the World?

Carmen Lomas Garza

How do we learn what's important to people? We can talk to them or read about them. In the case of artists, we can look at the art they create.

Carmen Lomas Garza is an artist who uses her artwork to show us how she sees the world. Her **perspective**, or way of looking at things, is unique.

Carmen Lomas Garza was born in Kingsville, Texas, in 1948. The paintings in this chapter show scenes from her childhood in a Mexican-American neighborhood. Each painting provides information about Carmen's life. Study the paintings. Then think about your life. How is her life different from yours? How is it similar?

The weather in Kingsville is hot! Sometimes Carmen and her brother Arturo played outside in the hottest part of the day. The painting *Hormigas (Ants)* shows Arturo trying to feed an ant to a lizard called a "horned toad." The artist recalls that her mother and grandmother called Carmen and Arturo "horned toads," because they went out in the heat of the day, like the horned toads.

The details in Carmen's paintings show us what Kingsville looks like. What might you include in a painting set in your hometown?

Hormigas (Ants)

Carmen's family made and ate lots of tamales, a traditional Mexican food. Tamales are corn husks filled with a spicy mix of meat, peppers, and cornmeal dough. After being prepared, the tamales are steamed. In this painting, she shows that everybody participates and cooperates in making the popular dish. Carmen stands next to her grandfather as they soak the dried corn husks.

Many of Carmen's paintings show family members preparing and eating food together. What things do you and your family do together?

Tamalada (Making Tamales)

Cama Para Sueños (Bed for Dreams)

On hot nights, Carmen and her sister Margie would go up to the roof and look at the stars. They shared their hopes and their dreams for the future. One of Carmen's dreams was to become an artist. She has made that dream come true! What do you dream of becoming?

CHAPTER FIVE

What Do Poets Show Us about Ourselves?

Like an artist, a poet can give us different ways to think about something. Artists use colors and shapes. Poets use words. Sometimes these words describe something familiar in a new way. For example, a poet might compare the rising of the sun in the morning to the peeling of an orange or the opening of a present. Something—the new day—soon will be uncovered. What will it be like?

Read the following three poems. What message do you think each poet is trying to give about working with and learning about others?

To You

To sit and dream, to sit and read,
To sit and learn about the world
Outside our world of here and now—
our problem world—
To dream of vast horizons of the soul
Through dreams made whole,
Unfettered free—help me!
All you who are dreamers, too,
Help me to make our world anew.
I reach out my hands to you.

Langston Hughes

We Are Trees	Somos árboles
our roots connect	nuestras raíces se comunican
with the roots of other trees	con las raíces de otos árboles
our branches grow wanting	nuestras ramas crecen deseando
to reach out to other branches	otras ramas alcanzar

Francisco X. Alarcón

A Little Song of Life

Glad that I live am I;
That the sky is blue;
Glad for the country lanes,
And the fall of dew.

After the sun the rain;
After the rain the sun;
This is the way of life,
Till the work be done.

All that we need to do,
Be we low or high,
Is to see that we grow
Nearer the sky.

Lizette Woodworth Reese

Sum It Up

People are unique! We see that in poetry, in art, and in everyday life. Yet, when people come together, they often find common ground. They see that they have similar hopes and dreams. They also learn about one another's cultures—and begin to understand one another (and themselves) better. Best of all, they often share a goal and cooperate to help others.

What hopes and dreams are common to kids your age?

How can sharing a goal make a difference to someone else—and to yourself?

JULIA ALVAREZ

HOW TÍA LOLA CAME TO ~~VISIT~~ STAY

illustrated by S.G. Brooks

"Why can't we just call her *Aunt* Lola?" Miguel asks his mother. Tomorrow their aunt is coming from the Dominican Republic to visit with them in their new home in Vermont. Tonight they are unpacking the last of the kitchen boxes before dinner.

"Because she doesn't know any English," his mother explains.

"*Tía* is the word for aunt in Spanish, right, Mami?" Juanita asks. When their mother's back is turned, Juanita beams Miguel a know-it-all smile.

Their mother is **gazing** sadly at a blue bowl she has just unpacked. "So you see, Miguel, if you call her Aunt, she won't know you're talking to her."

"That's fine, Miguel thinks, I won't have much to say to her except "*¡Adiós!*" Goodbye! But he keeps his mouth shut.

Miguel and Juanita's parents are getting a divorce, and Mami has been hired to be a counselor in a small college in Vermont. Papi is a painter who sets up department store windows at night in the city.

Mami does not like the idea of Miguel and Juanita being alone without an adult, and that in large part is why she has invited Tía Lola to come for a visit.

◆ ◆ ◆

Miguel cannot believe how much luggage his aunt has brought from the Dominican Republic!

Two big suitcases, covered in plastic wrap. "*Para más seguridad*," Tía Lola explains. For more security. She raises her eyebrows as if the crown jewels are packed inside.

A box with a piñata, which Tía Lola says they should save for a special occasion.

A duffel bag full of gifts from their cousins, aunts, and uncles.

A tube with a rolled-up Dominican flag inside.

A flowered carpetbag with Tía Lola's *cositas*, her thises and thats.

Tía Lola unpacks her bright summer dresses and her black hat with a veil. She unpacks a half-dozen pairs of high heels to match all the different colors of her outfits, and a dozen bright *pañuelos* to wrap around her head like a turban. Her closet looks like a midsummer flower garden.

She upacks her maracas and *tambor* to make music in case there is a fiesta. She puts on her castanets and clacks around the room, stomping her feet as if she is throwing a tantrum. Their mother and Juanita join in, acting goofy. "Isn't she fun?" his mother keeps asking Miguel.

"I guess," Miguel mutters, and then, because his mother is looking straight at him, he adds, "She's *lots* of fun, Mami."

◆ ◆ ◆

One afternoon, two of Miguel's classmates show up at the front door. In the car, the mother of one of the boys waits, peering up at the old, gabled house. The boys are collecting money for the town's Little League team. Come spring, they will need equipment and uniforms.

"Wow!" Miguel says. "I'd really like to be on that team."

"You should try out," one of the boys says. The taller one's name is Dean. He has bright blue eyes that Miguel's father would call ultramarine and a wide grin his mother would call trouble with a capital T.

As the boys stand in the mudroom talking, Tía Lola walks by in her spiked heels and white turban.

"Wh-wh-who's that?" the smaller boy, Sam, asks. His fine blond hair stands on end naturally from electricity. But now he looks as if he has just had a terrible fright.

Miguel turns his head and looks, then shrugs as if no one is there. As the boys hurry down the front steps, Miguel hears Dean say, "I bet it was a ghost. My mom says this old house is haunted."

Miguel shuts the door and leans against it, his face pale as if he *has* seen a ghost. When he looks up, Tía Lola is looking back at him.

◆ ◆ ◆

That night, a snowstorm blows in. When Miguel glances out the window the next morning, flakes are still falling in the light by the front porch. Downstairs, Tía Lola is not at breakfast.

"Good news," Juanita says as Miguel sits down. "No school today!"

"I do have to go to work," their mother reminds them. "I'm so glad Tía Lola is here so I don't have to worry about you. Where is she anyhow?" Their mother glances up at the clock. "She's usually up at this hour. She seemed a little sad last night."

"She wouldn't tell us a story," Miguel admits.

"Did you hurt her feelings?" Since she is a psychologist, their mother always guesses everything that happens has to do with people's feelings.

"How could I hurt her feelings?" Miguel says, trying not to sound annoyed at his mother. *Her* feelings are awfully sensitive these days. "I don't know enough Spanish to hurt Tía Lola's feelings."

"Tía Lola is a special person," Miguel's mother observes. "She can tell the secret feelings in a person's heart." Miguel's mother gives him a look as if *she* can tell what is in his heart.

The truth is Miguel has mixed feelings about having Tía Lola around. She is fun, but he sure doesn't think having her here will improve his chances of making new friends.

Why can't Tía Lola act more like his teacher, Mrs. Prouty, who speaks without moving her jaw and is so proper that she says, "Pardon me" *before* she sneezes. Or like farmer Becky, their shy next-door neighbor, who dresses in a white pullover sweater as if she wants to blend in with the sheep she shears and tends.

"You have to love people for who they are," his mother is saying, "then they will become all they can be."

That sounds like a riddle, but it makes sense. When Miguel first started playing baseball, Papi would always say, "Great swing, Miguel," or "Nice try," even when Miguel missed the ball. Over time, his playing actually got better because of Papi's encouragement.

"Remember," his mother continues, "Tía Lola might be a little homesick. She needs to feel really welcomed."

Miguel looks down at his cereal. Today he has gotten the blue bowl. He is sorry that he has made Tía Lola feel unwelcomed. He knows what that feels like. At school, an older kid in his class named Mort has nicknamed him Gooseman, because that's what Miguel's last name, Guzmán, sounds like in English. Now other kids are calling out, "Quack, quack!" whenever they pass him in the hall. Maybe they are trying to be funny, but it makes him feel embarrassed and unwelcomed.

"What's the word for welcome in Spanish?" Miguel asks his mother.

"Bienvenido for a man, *bienvenida* for a woman." His mother spells out the words. "Why do you ask?"

"I've got a great idea. Nita, I'll need your help."

Juanita nods. She loves to be included in her brother's Great Ideas. She doesn't even have to know what they are ahead of time.

◆ ◆ ◆

The snow is deep, almost to his knees. Miguel trudges down to the back field, keeping close to the fence line. The sun has broken through the clouds. All around him, the field is fresh and unspoiled by footprints and sparkling with diamonds of light.

He starts by walking in a straight line, kicking the snow to either side. Then he walks in a half circle, out and back to the straight line, and then out and back again. Every step of the way, he has to imagine what each mark will look like from the house.

He thinks of his father in New York. Although he works setting up department store windows at night, Papi's real love is painting. Today, Miguel feels the closest he has felt to his father since his mother and Juanita and he moved to Vermont. He is an artist like his father, but working on a larger canvas. He is trying to create something that will have the same result: making somebody happy.

At one point, he glances up, and he thinks he sees his little sister waving. It is her job to keep Tía Lola from looking out the windows.

The sun is right above his head when Miguel is done.

When they have finished eating, Miguel announces there is a surprise for his aunt in the back field.

"*¿Para mí?*" Tía Lola says, pointing to herself.

Miguel can see the color coming back into her cheeks, the sparkle in her eyes. The beauty mark that was above her upper lip on the right side is now on the left side. Tía Lola tends to forget little things like that. It winks like a star.

Miguel leads the way up the stairs to the landing. They line up at the big picture window and look out at the snowy fields where large letters spell out *¡Bienvenida, Tía Lola!*

Tía Lola claps her hands and hugs Miguel.

"Who says I did it?" Miguel asks.

Juanita and Tía Lola look at him, surprised.

"*¡Ay, Miguelito!*" Tía Lola kisses and hugs him all over again. "*Tú eres tan divertido.*"

"You're fun, too," Miguel says. This time he means it.

◆ ◆ ◆

At school, Miguel starts hanging out with Dean and Sam at recess. Almost every day, they practice pitching and catching in the gym. Miguel wants to be ready for spring tryouts for the town's Little League baseball team.

Dean and Sam have never brought up the **incident** with the "ghost" in the white turban. But Miguel has noticed they are none too **eager** to come over to his house after school or during weekends, which is just as well. How can he explain Tía Lola to them?

It is hard to believe Tía Lola can be kept a secret. She is full of life. She is full of laughter. She is full of stories. And she is full of noise.

Some nights after supper, Tía Lola gives Juanita and Mami dance lessons. They move across the living room, stomping their feet and snapping their fingers, or shaking maracas and swaying their hips to the music of Fernandito Villalona and Juan Luís Guerra and Rafael Solano.

◆ ◆ ◆

Rudy, the owner of Rudy's Restaurant in town, begins his Spanish lessons with Tía Lola.

Mondays, when his restaurant is closed, Rudy drives over in his old red pickup. "Almost as old as me," he likes to joke, patting it, as if the pickup were a barn animal. Rudy is tall and big shouldered, with rumpled gray hair and thick eyebrows and red cheeks. He looks like someone who has lived in the Old West, but has retired to modern times in Vermont. When his wife died five years ago, he opened up a restaurant. "I love eating, but I hate eating alone," he tells his diners. He is always giving discounts and coming out of the kitchen in a white apron, holding a big pot of something he has just "invented" for everyone to try out.

The first night he steps into the Guzmán house, he smells the mouth-watering odors wafting from the kitchen. "Wow!" he says.

From that moment on, the Spanish lessons turn into cooking lessons followed by a cup of espresso and a merengue dance lesson to top off the evening. Sometimes, Tía Lola throws in a little Spanish vocabulary between servings of whatever she has made that night.

"Arroz con habichuelas," Tía Lola pronounces. That is the name of the rice and beans she is piling on Rudy's plate. *"Con un poquito de bacalao."* With a little codfish.

"Sweetheart, honey," Rudy says, between mouthfuls, "I don't care what it's called. This is *magnificat*!" Rudy was an altar boy when he was Miguel's age, and Mami says that sometimes Rudy's Spanish sounds a lot like Latin. "Lola, I just love your cooking! *Adoremus! Adoremus!*"

"He's not learning much Spanish," Mami complains one night after Rudy has left.

"*¿Qué importa?*" Tía Lola says. What does it matter? Monday nights prove her point. You don't have to speak the same language to have fun with other people.

◆ ◆ ◆

"How you doing, *tiguerito*?" His father is on the phone. It is Saturday morning. In five more days, fourteen hours, and fifteen minutes, it will be Miguel's birthday. "What you planning for the big day?"

"Nothing much," Miguel replies. He feels sad. This will be his first birthday without his father. No matter how special it is, it won't be special enough.

"Have you thought about what you want?"

Of course he has. More than anything, he wants his parents to be together. But he can't say that. He has already mentioned a few things to his mom: a new bat; a baseball signed by Sammy Sosa, who also came from the Dominican Republic, like Miguel's parents; Rollerblades; a visit from his best friend, José, once the weather gets nice. "One other thing," he tells his dad, lowering his voice. "I wish Tía Lola . . . I mean, she was supposed to come for a visit . . . and she's still here . . . and she won't even try to learn English . . . ."

"Is that so? Maybe it's good to have your aunt around so you have to practice your Spanish."

"But the kids at school already think I'm different enough," Miguel explains. He is surprised that he is telling his father this much. "They can't even pronounce my last name!"

His father has gone very quiet on the other end. "*Mi'jo*," he finally says, "you should be proud of who you are. Proud of your Tía Lola. Proud of yourself."

It is Miguel's turn to be quiet. He knows his father is right, but he can't help feeling what he feels.

"I know sometimes it's hard," his father is saying softly. "You'll grow into that pride the older you get. *Te quiero mucho*," he adds. "Don't forget."

◆ ◆ ◆

The following Friday morning, when Miguel comes downstairs, his mother is already eating her breakfast.

"*Buenos días,* Miguel," she says, looking up and frowning. "You're going to wear *that* to school today?" She stares at his Yankees shirt as if it has a bad smell to it.

"It's my favorite shirt," he reminds her.

Juanita walks into the kitchen. "Mami, where's my book bag? Oh, hi, Miguel. I thought I left it in the mudroom."

IT'S MY BIRTHDAY!!! Miguel feels like screaming.

Tía Lola has been outside feeding the birds. The minute she enters the room and sees Miguel, she throws her arms around him and gives him ten kisses, one for each year since he was born. Then she adds a couple more, which she calls his *ñapa.*

His mother stares pointedly at Tía Lola, the way she does when she wants to remind her of something without saying it out loud. "That's right, big boy," she says, play-punching him in the arm, "you're in the double digits now. Gotta run," his mother adds, glancing at her watch. "Staff meeting." She rolls her eyes.

"Guess I'll be catching the school bus today, the thirty-first of March, the anniversary of my first decade on planet Earth," Miguel says.

"We'll celebrate later. Promise!" his mother calls as she heads out the door with her coat half off, half on.

All morning at school, Miguel feels gloomy. His friends are acting funny. No one wishes him "Happy birthday," though he has been dropping hints for the last few weeks.

"Want to hang out after school?" Miguel asks Dean as they head back for their classroom after recess.

"Can't today," Dean explains. "My mom's, um, picking me up early. Got . . . uh . . . uh . . . uh . . . a dentist appointment."

"I got . . . uh . . . a dentist appointment, too," Sam says when Miguel turns to him.

Nice friends, Miguel thinks. José would have hung out with him on his birthday instead of going to some stupid dentist. Maybe these new friends are not real friends, after all.

Miguel grows even gloomier as the school day wears on.

That afternoon, Miguel comes out of school, head bowed, dragging his feet. His friends have run off early. The school bus is gone. Just as well, he would rather walk home than ride the noisy bus with his sister and her friends on his birthday.

When he looks up, he can't believe his eyes!

Just ahead stands his father in his jeans and leather jacket, holding Juanita's hand, a great big smile on his face. "Happy birthday, *tiguerito!*" he calls out.

Miguel drops his book bag and runs into his father's arms. This is the best birthday present ever. He hugs his father and then holds on a little longer while his moist eyes dry up.

They get in the rented car his father has driven from New York, and Juanita and Miguel give their father directions. It takes forever to get home.

When they finally pull up at the house, Miguel's mother's car is already in the drive, as is Rudy's red pickup.

As Miguel steps in the door, Sam and Dean spring out from behind the couch. "Surprise!" they shout. The table is piled high with gifts. Just above it hangs the parrot piñata Tía Lola has brought with her. Rudy is standing by, holding a hammer. He must have just finished putting it up.

Suddenly, Miguel understands everything. He is about to thank everybody when he hears one last shout coming from the kitchen. Before he can turn around and hide, his top-secret aunt walks in with a big cake in the shape of a baseball, showing off her one word of English. *"Sooprise! Sooprise!"*

Then everyone sings “Happy Birthday”—in Spanish!

“We sort of rehearsed before you came,” Sam explains. “Your aunt taught us.”

“I’ve never had a “ghost” for a teacher before!” Dean adds, poking Miguel in the side.

Miguel feels his face getting red. But when his friend bursts out laughing, Miguel cannot help smiling.

He looks over at his father, who smiles back at him. It's true what Papi has said. Miguel is ten years old today and already feeling ten times prouder of being who he is.

UNIT 2

Seeking the Unknown

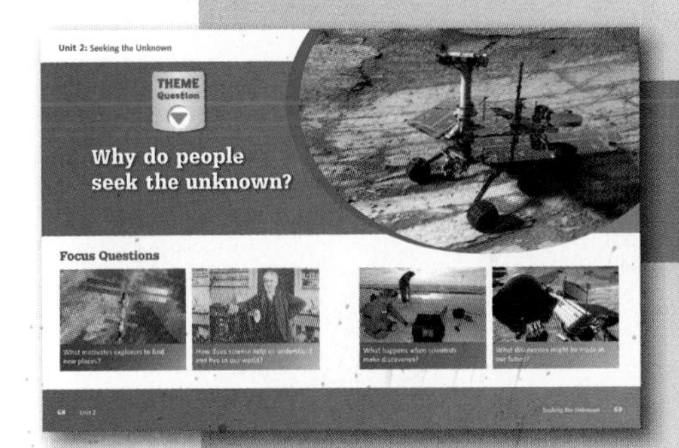

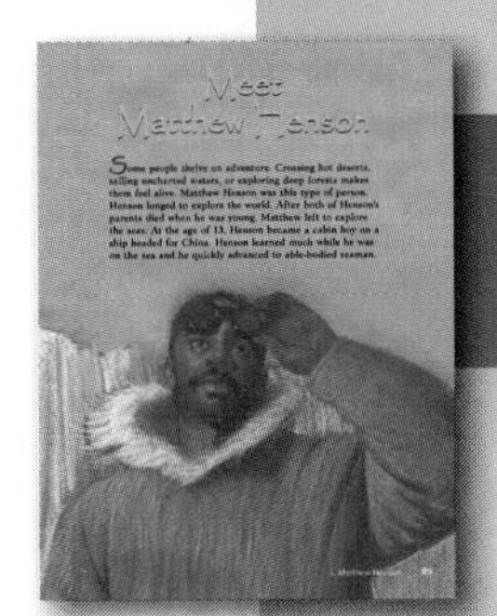

Why do people seek the unknown?

Focus Questions

What motivates explorers to find new places?

How does science help us understand and live in our world?

What happens when scientists make discoveries?

What discoveries might be made in our future?

Questions! Questions! Questions!

by Peter Dooling

Contents

Chapter

Chapter 1

How Do I Get Home from Here?

"This place does not look familiar."
"I thought you had a map. What does it say?"
"I *do* have a map, but it doesn't *say* anything."
"Can't you figure out where we are by using the map?"
"Only if I know where we are now, and I don't know that!"

I can help, thought Alita as she took out her cell phone and loaded the GPS feature. In a few moments, she had their location. Then they used the map on Alita's phone and the family set off again—this time, in the right direction.

How GPS Works

Alita could identify her family's location because she had a GPS receiver on her cell phone. *GPS* stands for "Global Positioning System." This system is based on 24 satellites that always orbit Earth. When Alita turned on the receiver, it went to work. The GPS **analyzed** radio signals from the four nearest satellites. By studying this information, it was able to find the receiver's—and the family's—location.

handheld GPS receiver

Each satellite orbits Earth in a p
The point at which the paths cr
is the location of the receiver.

Bonfires, Birds, Stars, and the Sun

Like Alita and her parents, people have always wanted to explore. People left home to find new markets, to get to new land, and to just to see what was out there. Before the age of GPS, explorers needed ways to travel far away from home and to return safely. How did they do this?

At first, sailors stayed close to shore. They tracked their position with landmarks. Early Greeks lit bonfires at key locations along the shore to guide ships that sailed at night.

Polaris, also known as the North Star, is easy to locate on a clear night. It sits directly above the North Pole. Most people use the Big Dipper and the Little Dipper as a guide to find it.

Like the Greeks, the Vikings traveled great distances. They used various kinds of information to **navigate**, or determine their course. They used the shape of their coastline. They knew how winds would affect their direction. They matched certain kinds of seaweed with certain places. They used the sun to guide them by day and the stars, especially the North Star (Polaris), to guide them at night.

Viking sailors often had a cage of birds with them on a voyage. The birds helped with navigation too. When the captain thought that the ship might be close to land, he released a bird. If the bird flew off instead of staying with the ship, the captain knew that land was near.

Determining Latitude

In the 1400s, most sailors used the position of the sun or the position of the North Star to help them find their way. A sailor would find the altitude, or the height, of the sun (or of the North Star) above the horizon. The angle formed between the horizon and the sun (or the North Star) would allow the sailor to determine the latitude, or the ship's position north or south of the equator.

Sailors used tools such as the cross-staff to find latitude by charting the position of the stars and the sun. These tools were often heavy and had to be held steady, so they were difficult to use on a moving ship. Because of this, sailors sometimes got readings that were not accurate.

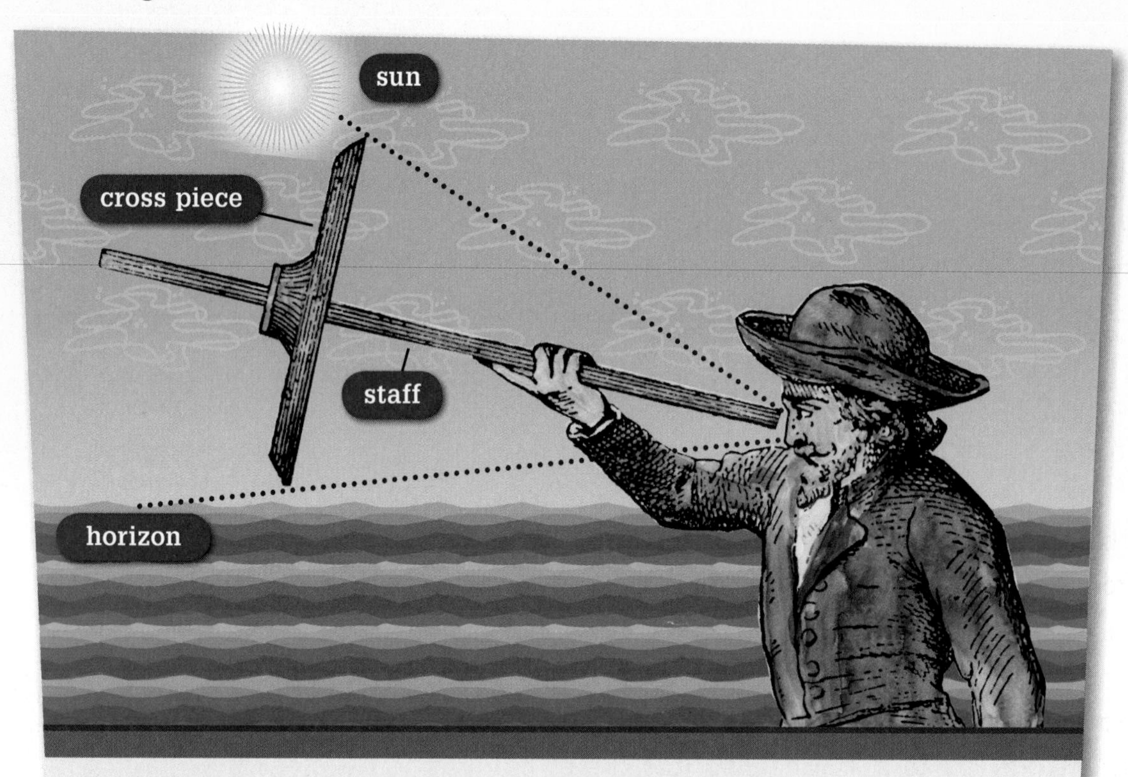

Cross-Staff

A sailor held the cross-staff below one eye. He aimed it so the top of the staff's cross piece pointed to the sun (or to the North Star). Then he moved the cross piece closer or farther from him until the bottom of it pointed to the horizon. The sailor could then check the angle on the cross-staff from the sun to the horizon. This gave him the altitude of the sun (or the North Star). The sailor could then use this information to determine the ship's latitude.

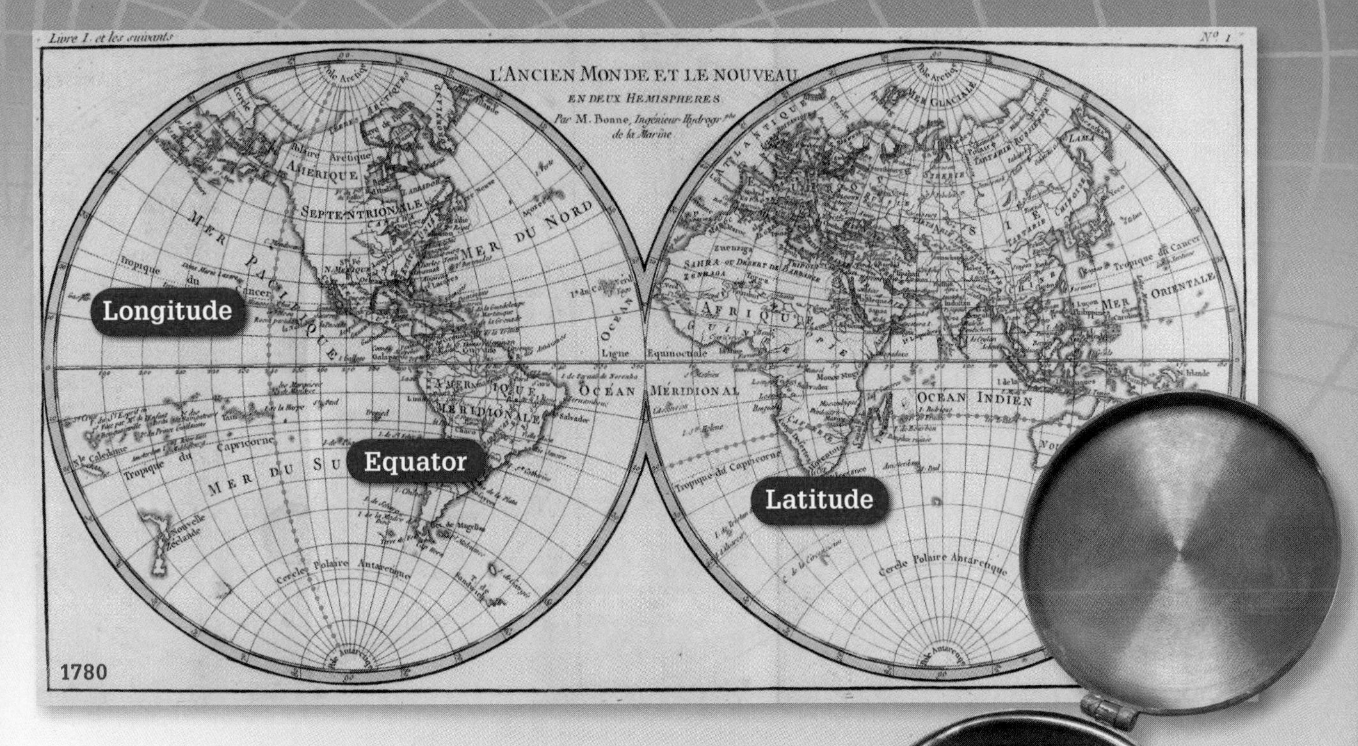

Mapping Earth

Inventors acted to help sailors identify their exact location. People also learned how to find longitude, the position east or west of the prime meridian. Mapmakers began to include lines of longitude as well as latitude on maps. These maps made ocean travel easier.

magnetic compass

An invention called the *compass* made travel easier. The earliest known compass was probably used in China. People there discovered a rock called *lodestone*. They put the rock on a stick and floated it in a dish of water. The stick would always turn until it pointed north and south. This happened because the lodestone is like a magnet, so it is drawn to the Earth's magnetic poles. Later, people learned how to make a compass out of iron. The compass made it much easier for people to travel without getting lost.

Above and Beyond

Early explorers bravely left home to explore their world. They wanted to answer the question: *What's out there?* People today still ask that question. To answer it, explorers are traveling beyond Earth, into space. Some astronauts have been to the moon. Others live and work at the International Space Station. Different kinds of spacecraft, loaded with new and exciting tools, are gathering information about our solar system.

Astronaut Alvin Drew, Jr. has flown missions to the International Space Station.

International Space Station

This photograph shows an artist's rendering of *Opportunity* on Mars.

Some spacecraft have even landed on other planets! The National Aeronautics and Space Administration (NASA) has sent rovers to Mars. The rovers were fashioned to travel across the surface of the planet. Two of the rovers, called *Spirit* and *Opportunity*, sent back valuable photographs and other data. The rovers worked much longer than NASA thought they would!

Scientists who have analyzed the rovers' information are excited. The rovers found rocks and minerals that suggest water once existed on Mars. *When was that time? Might there still be liquid water somewhere on the planet?* Scientists hope that more exploration will answer these questions.

Cindy Oda, a Mars rover mission manager

Missions like these show the power of curiosity. What places make you curious? What places might you explore one day?

Chapter 2

Is My Life Better with Inventions?

Think about your day so far. What inventions have you used? Check out the inventions shown on these pages. How have they improved your everyday life?

Wake Up!

Do you wake up to music from a clock radio? Turn on a light in the bathroom? Make toast? You can do these things—and many more—because of electricity.

Thomas Alva Edison invented a practical electric light bulb, the phonograph, and many other useful items that run on electricity. These early devices used direct current, or DC. Direct current flows in only one direction, moving from the power source to the device that you want to power. A battery is an example of a source that produces direct current.

Thomas Alva Edison, one of the most famous inventors of his time, worked at a laboratory in East Orange, New Jersey.

Other researchers showed that current could flow back and forth through a wire. This is called alternating current, or AC. Unlike direct current, alternating current can be sent long distances so it is more useful. Today, power plants generate, or make, AC. It comes to your house through the power distribution grid found across our nation. The grid **delivers** power to people—and helps you get up every morning!

Power lines distribute electricity across the grid.

Mark Dean and the Personal Computer

Do you use a computer when you do your homework? If so, you should be grateful to Mark Dean. He is one of the inventors who helped make personal computers what they are today.

Mark Dean built his first computer in high school. After college, he helped invent the first personal computer. In 1999, Dean led the team that produced the 1-Gigahertz chip. This chip, about the size of a dinner plate, could perform one billion calculations per second! Today, people like Dean are working to make the chips smaller and faster.

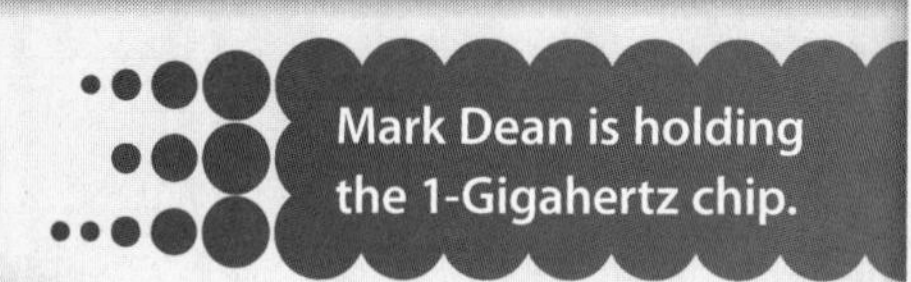

Mark Dean is holding the 1-Gigahertz chip.

Get Dressed!

Have you worn a cotton shirt this week? Was it white, or did it have a color?

Long ago, people hand-spun both white and colored cotton fibers to make clothes. Then machine-weaving became a widespread way to make cotton cloth. The machines only work with long fibers, however, and colored cotton has short fibers. As a result, people could only use white cotton. If they wanted color, they added it later with dyes.

In the 1980s, a plant scientist named Sally Fox began experimenting with colored cotton seeds. Eventually she developed cotton plants with long fibers that can be woven by machine. Fox's first colors were shades of green and brown. She continues to develop new colors.

Because Sally Fox's cotton does not have to be dyed, it is a more environmentally friendly way to make clothes.

Pack Up Your Stuff!

You load your backpack for school. Have you included any inventions? You might be surprised!

Eyeglasses

NASA developed a special coating that keeps the visors of astronauts' helmets from getting scratched. The same coating also makes the lenses in eyeglasses scratch resistant.

Bike helmet

Stephanie Kwolek, a research chemist, invented a new, tough material called Kevlar™. This material is often used in the outer shell of bicycle helmets. Her invention is also used in many other kinds of safety materials such as elbow pads for riders.

Plastic in your backpack

If any of the items in your backpack are made of plastic, you have packed at least one invention. Alexander Parkes was the first person to create a plastic that could be shaped when it was hot and retain its shape when it cooled. Named after its inventor, Parkesine was first publicly demonstrated in London at the 1862 Great International Exhibition.

Chocolate chip cookie

Ruth Wakefield invented this sweet treat when she added chunks of chocolate into cookie dough. She thought that the chips would melt into the dough. They didn't—but people loved the result! Maybe you do too!

Peanut butter sandwich

In the early 1930s, George Washington Carver helped people see that peanuts were a good crop to grow in the southern United States. He developed more than 300 uses for peanuts. And even though a paste like peanut butter had been around for thousands of years, Carver helped make peanut butter a popular spread.

Chapter 3

What Can We Discover When We Work Together?

Exploring with a team can be exciting. You get to work with people who ask interesting questions. You also may get to use some very cool tools.

The Hidden Ocean is an **expedition** that took a team of explorers to the Arctic in the summer of 2005. Team members were looking for answers to their questions. *What is sea ice made of? What kinds of creatures live in sea ice? What does the sea floor look like under all that ice?*

The Hidden Ocean team

The team included 35 scientists and 75 Coast Guard crew members. They went to places along the Arctic Ocean. For one month, the team worked around the clock to study the ice, the water, the sea creatures, and the ocean floor. Team members brought along special clothing and tools to use in their **research**.

Members of the Hidden Ocean expedition collect data from cores they cut from ice.

Ice Diving

Gathering information was a tough job. Ice divers did a lot of this work beneath a ceiling of ice.

Arctic ice is not a solidly frozen mass. It is a collection of ice floes (masses of floating ice) with different thicknesses. Organisms live in pockets within the ice that have water in them. This water is salty, so it does not freeze. In places, the sun shines down through cracks in the ice.

Ice divers collected samples of ice and seawater. They also took videos of the creatures that live on the underside of the ice and in the waters beneath.

Shawn Harper, an ice diver and member of the Hidden Ocean team, "stands" upside down on the ice ceiling above him.

One Explorer's Journal

Explorer Elizabeth Calvert kept a journal during this expedition. Here she describes beginning a dive into the Arctic Ocean.

I sit on the edge of an ice floe, my feet dangling through a hole just large enough for two divers to fit through. I am bundled in layers of thermal underwear beneath my dry suit and with dry gloves on, my head is the only part of my body that will directly feel the 30-degree water. A camera is clipped in on my right side, a collection bag clipped to my left, and a 5-foot tether connects me to my buddy. A second tether clipped to my dive buddy connects us to our dive tender at the surface.

Ice divers Katrin Iken and Elizabeth Calvert are about to descend through a small hole in the ice.

Tools and Technology

Team members used many tools to gather information and samples. These tools included an ice augur, which drilled big holes into the ice. Another apparatus was an ice corer that the scientists used to gather ice samples from locations around the Arctic. The team used nets to collect living things at the surface. Special listening devices helped them pick up the sounds of whales and seals. They used a remotely operated vehicle, or ROV, to collect living things that live at great depths. The ROV also removed chunks of the seafloor for the team to study.

This remotely operated vehicle is capable of reaching depths greater than a mile beneath the water's surface.

Jellyfish, sea stars, crustaceans, and an octopus they named Oliver (below) are just a few of the species of marine life the team encountered in the Arctic's frigid waters.

What Did the Team Learn?

The story didn't end when the team left the Arctic. Months of work examining the samples collected continued in research labs.

Scientists used the samples, videos, and other data to expand our knowledge of living things in the Arctic Ocean. They learned that zooplankton, tiny animals that other ocean animals eat, could live more than a mile below the ocean's icy surface. They also learned many plants and animals actually live in the sea ice. Team members might have discovered several new **species** of ocean animals—including three new species of bristle worm. By finding a wider range of plant and animal life than expected, the scientists learned more about the Arctic food web. Their work answered many questions about the Arctic. Arctic exploration continues today, as teams of scientists dive deeper into discovering the unknown in this chilly and remote location.

What Questions Will I Answer?

Watch an adventure show on television, or pick up a science magazine, and you will see that people are still asking questions and going out to find the answers. People have ideas for new ways to travel, new ways to help people, and even new places to live.

Medicines from Frogs

The Chocó people of western Colombia hunt with blowguns and darts. The tip of each dart is coated with a poisonous **substance** that is given off by a tiny frog.

What is this substance? How does it work? Dr. John Daly, a scientist for the National Institutes of Health, has spent years studying these frogs. He and his team have identified the substance in their skins. They are learning how the substance acts on human nerves and muscles. Could it be used in medicines for people? Dr. Daly and his team have discovered that the answer to this question is yes—they have developed the poison into a painkiller for people. What other kinds of medicine might we discover from frogs?

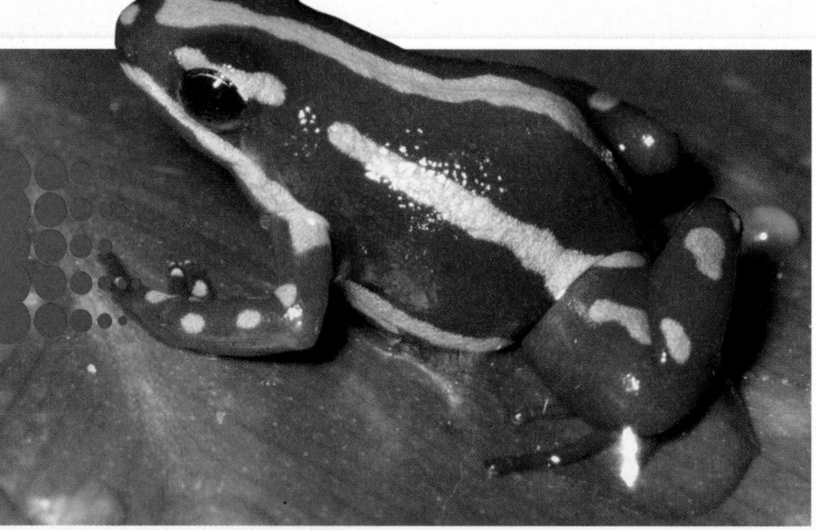

The venom released by the poison dart frog helps protect it from predators.

Two of Paul Moller's flying cars

Flying Cars

Can you picture getting around town in a flying car? One engineer is trying to make that happen! Paul Moller has worked for more than 40 years to make a safe, affordable, and reliable vertical takeoff and landing vehicle, or VTOL. Since the government is strict about how airspace is used, Moller made a model that flies at a height of only ten feet. This means you do not need a pilot's license to fly it! The car can reach 50 mph and travel for 90 minutes on a tank of fuel.

New Artificial Limbs

People in many areas of science work to develop improved prosthetic, or artificial, limbs. Some scientists are using electrical energy to make robotic limbs that work more like a natural arm or leg. How do these limbs work? When you contract your muscles by flexing, you create a small electric signal. These limbs take that energy, make the signal stronger, and then use small motors to move the artificial arm or leg.

Artificial limbs allow people to do their everyday activities and pursue their hobbies.

Most current prosthetic arms and legs are made of tough plastic. This can rub and hurt soft body tissues. Scientists wonder, what material can do the job best?

The best material is one that has some flexibility. For ideas, some scientists are studying the giant squid. That's because a giant squid has a hard beak that is sharp enough to attack a whale. However, the beak gets softer and more flexible around the squid's mouth. It doesn't rub against the softer part of the squid. Could we make a similar material that gradually changes from hard to soft, like a squid's beak? If so, how else could we use that material? Time will tell!

At Home on the Moon

Today, people who go on space missions come home to Earth. Tomorrow? "Home" may be the moon, our next-door neighbor.

NASA plans to send future missions to the moon. The goal is to build a base there and to eventually have people live there! A base on the moon could be just the beginning. From there, missions could go out to explore farther areas of space, searching for new discoveries.

An inflatable habitat similar to this could represent part of an outpost, a first step to a permanent inhabited lunar base on the moon.

Like many new ideas in science, building a moon base is controversial. Opponents say that money for the project should be spent in other ways. They think that it is wiser to focus on missions that use robots, not humans. Some people argue that the money should be spent on problems that affect our planet. What do you think?

Questions for Tomorrow

As you can see, the future is yours. What questions will you ask? How will you help answer them?

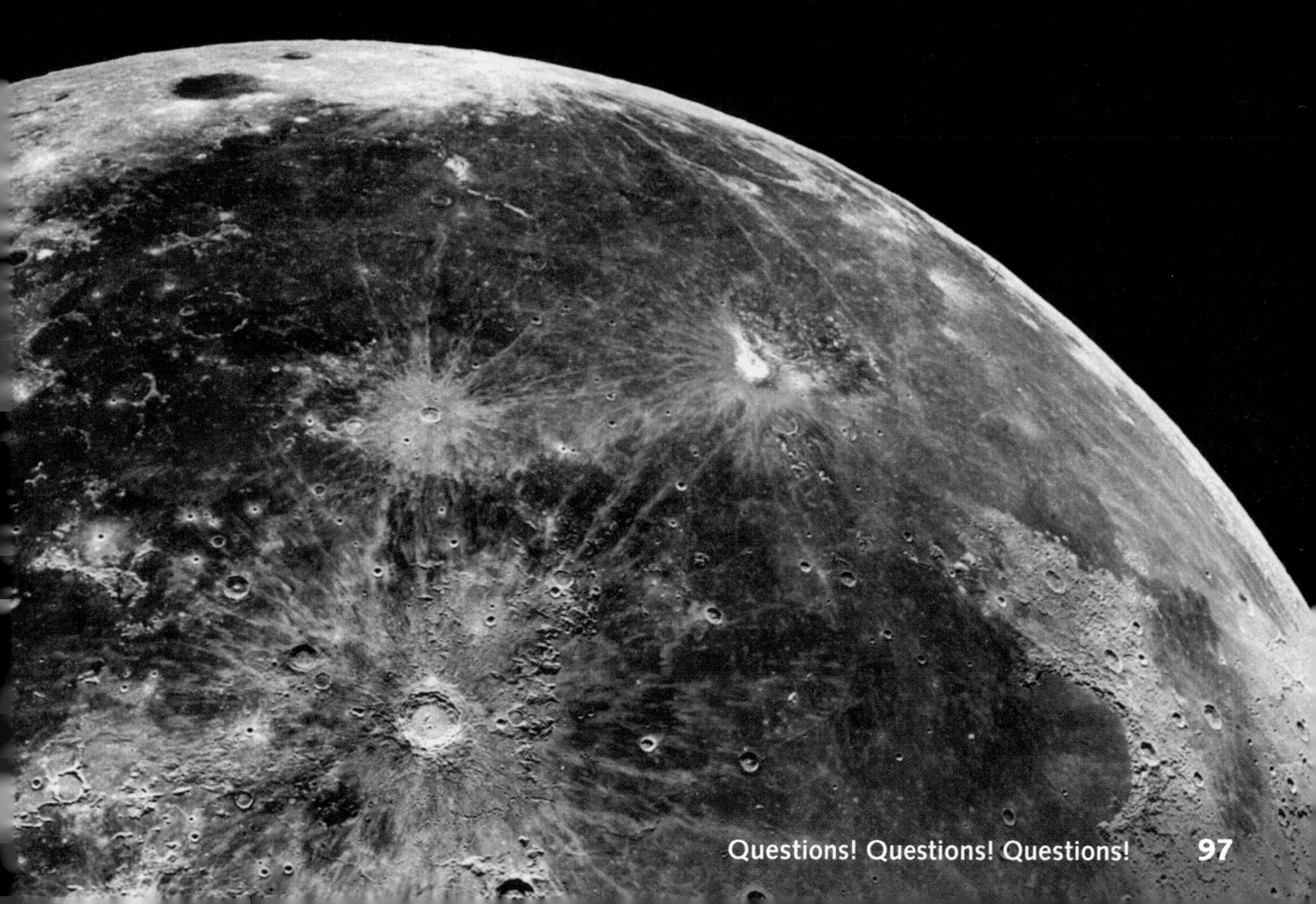

The Big Ideas

People have always been curious. We have wanted to study the world and see how it works. Today we are also exploring the wide expanse of space.

- People have many reasons for exploring the world. Over the centuries, we developed tools to help us find our way.
- Scientific discoveries and inventions can be very helpful. Some inventions make everyday life easier. Other inventions save lives.
- People often work in teams to explore the world. New discoveries may answer some questions—and raise even more. These questions make further exploration possible.
- Many people are thinking ahead—looking for ways to make life better and sharing new ideas. There is still room in the world for explorers—like you!

Meet Matthew Henson

Some people thrive on adventure. Crossing hot deserts, sailing uncharted waters, or exploring deep forests makes them feel alive. Matthew Henson was this type of person. Henson longed to explore the world. After both of Henson's parents died when he was young, Matthew left to explore the seas. At the age of 13, Henson became a cabin boy on a ship headed for China. Henson learned much while he was on the sea and he quickly advanced to able-bodied seaman.

After five years at sea, Henson returned to Washington, D.C., and met Lieutenant Robert Peary. Peary hired Henson as his valet for a Nicaragua Canal route survey. This was just the beginning of Henson's adventures with Peary. Henson and Peary made several attempts to reach the North Pole together. Each attempt brought them more experience which allowed them to prepare and attend to every detail necessary for making the final expedition a success. Henson learned much from the Inuit people he met in Greenland: how to make and fix sleds, how to drive a dog team, and the best way to build camp. Henson played a leading role in the success of finally reaching the North Pole.

Henson's feat in reaching the North Pole is great among adventurers. Many countries and explorers had been involved in the "race" to the Pole for hundreds of years. Each had dreamt of being the first to step foot at the North Pole. Henson and Peary spent almost two decades themselves trying to reach this goal. Despite adversity, both men's strength and courage helped them to never give up. The following story recounts the events in Henson's life that led to the expedition of a lifetime.

I, Matthew Henson

POLAR EXPLORER

CAROL BOSTON WEATHERFORD

Illustrated by
ERIC VELASQUEZ

I did not walk forty miles
from the nation's capital
to Baltimore's busy harbor to eye
ships from a dock. Though just thirteen,
I yearned for a taste of the adventures
that I had heard old sailors speak of,
to explore the seven seas
and somehow find my calling.

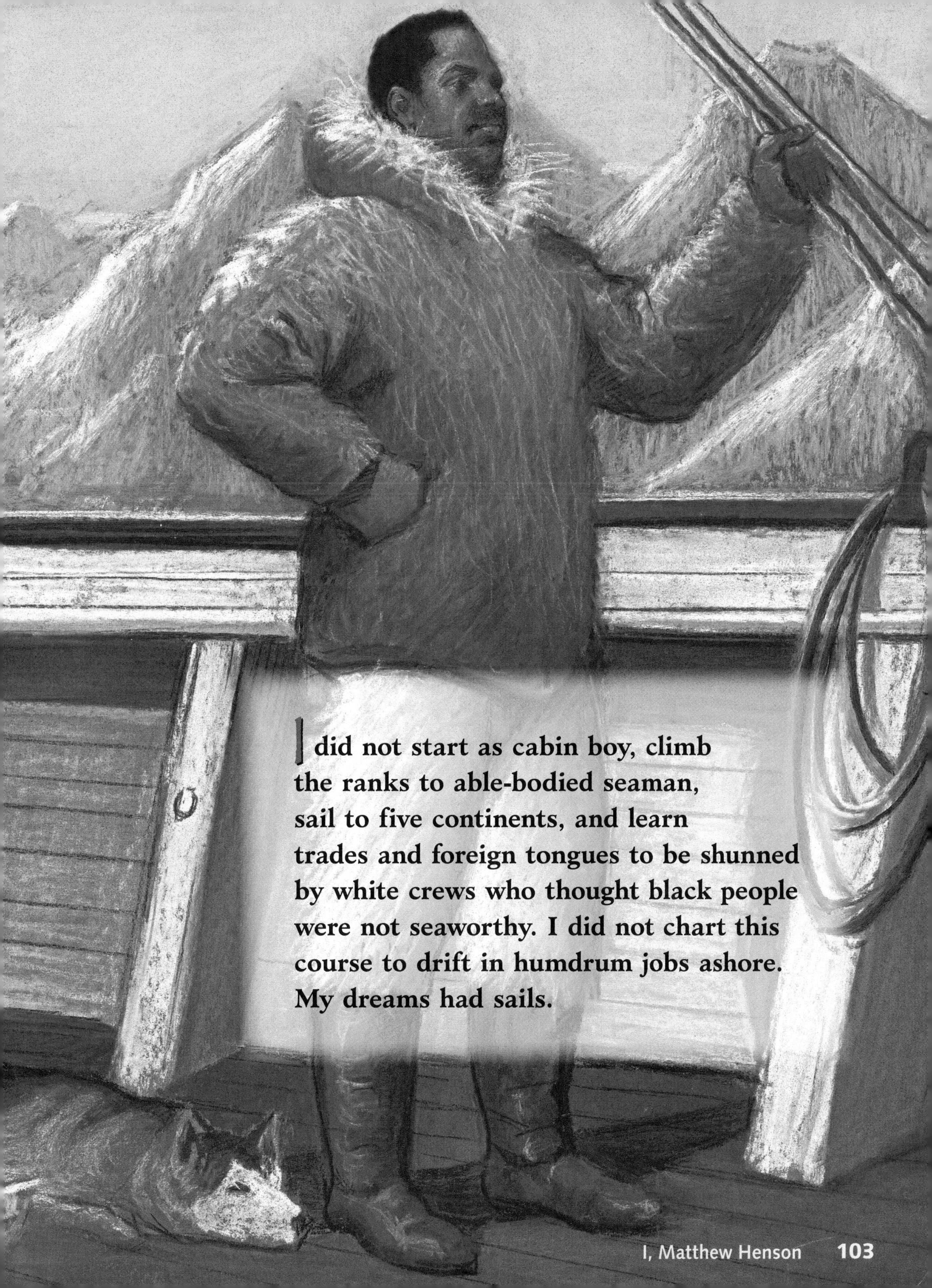

I did not start as cabin boy, climb
the ranks to able-bodied seaman,
sail to five continents, and learn
trades and foreign tongues to be shunned
by white crews who thought black people
were not seaworthy. I did not chart this
course to drift in humdrum jobs ashore.
My dreams had sails.

I did not take a job as a stock boy
at a men's store to work my way up
the ladder to clerk. I yearned for wind
at my back. So when a customer,
a naval officer, said he needed
a manservant for an expedition
to Nicaragua to map a canal,
I signed on without a second thought.

I did not sail to the tropics just to launder
shirts and cook meals. I meant
to prove myself as an explorer.
That chance came when the chainman
fell ill and I joined the survey crew.
In the swampy jungle, I learned Peary
as well as I knew the ropes. And he leaned
on me like his right-hand man.

I had not earned Peary's trust to part ways
and turn my back on adventure. *Next trip,*
he said, *you'll have to work like three men.*
On the *Kite* with five others, we sailed
to Greenland. I alone learned Inuit,
the Eskimo language, and built our base camp
while Peary charted a journey to the North Pole.
To go *there,* I would work like a horse.

I did not **befriend** the Inuit, learn
to build a sledge, handle a dog team,
track and hunt on ice, and kill a polar bear
to let an Inuit legend freeze me with fear.
Kokoyah, the Devil of the North, guards
the ice cap, the Inuit warned. *He is not real,*
I told them. After they danced and drummed,
I played the accordion and sang hymns.

I did not sail north with Peary again and again
through the frozen sea, charting
the ice cap, inching toward the Pole,
where no man had stood,
for frostbite to halt our mission.
When ice took most of Peary's toes,
I carried him back alive—Kokoyah
on our heels, howling in the wind.

We had not braved the frozen wilderness,
going miles beyond the last village,
only to starve because new snow
hid our store of food. We tracked
hare and musk ox until the hunting
was poor and we were skin and bones.
Then, we ate our dog team—all
but one. Kokoyah churned in our guts.

We had not survived the frigid cold
that broke some and killed others
to let our dream melt when hope
and cash ran low. While others gave up,
we returned to the polar region
and, guided by Inuits, fetched
a prize from the ice cap—a meteor,
which Peary sold to raise funds.

I did not explore the Arctic to sit still between voyages while Peary planned. I became a railroad porter and explored my own land. In the South, I met hate face-to-face. And in New York, I met Lucy, who loved me though I didn't have a cent. I promised her the Pole as a wedding gift. Before we could marry, I had to set sail.

Peary and I had not sailed the *Roosevelt*,
a new ship built to cut through icy seas,
only to set out on foot from our base camp
and have our path blocked by melted ice.
But turn back we did, tricked by Kokoyah again.
Back home, we both knew our next trip
would be our last. I now had a wife,
and we were no longer young men.

Peary had not handpicked seven men—
and timed our trip so I had the six-month winter night
to build sledges, train dog handlers, and enlist
Inuit guides—for our last try to fail.
In the long daylight of spring, two dozen men
and 130 dogs struck out like teams in a relay,
pushing across the ice to store food and supplies
for the team that would go farther.

We had not faced sudden storms, frozen peaks
and ridges, and shifting iceberg castles
to let leads, patches of open water, swallow us.
With a quarter ton of supplies and an often-lame
Peary on a sledge, we crossed twenty miles
in as many hours. Snow pricking our faces,
fingers burning with cold, we built igloos
each night and dared Kokoyah to stop us.

I had not stuck by Peary for two decades, sharing the same goal, only to reach a fork when our journey was on its last leg. Tasks completed, team after relay team returned to base camp. In the end, Peary picked me to go all the way, vowing he could not make it without me. Kokoyah would be no match for us.

We had not trudged on, rushing across
the ice pack with four Inuits,
to let faulty instruments steer us wrong.
I used dead reckoning to guide us north.
Sluggish from the cold, Peary sent me ahead.
Miles later, I stopped the sledge,
wiped my frozen lashes, and scanned
the vast sheet of ice. I was close.

Shortly, Peary arrived and we broke through
the thin ice. He did a sounding, lowered
nine thousand feet of rope into the ocean. Six men—
one black, one white, four Inuits—had reached
the North Pole. *We have found what we hunted,*
I said in Inuit. A camera froze our feat in time.
But we had not come for photos; we came
to plant our flag. And Kokoyah was nowhere in sight.

August 8, 1866
Matthew Alexander Henson is born in Charles County, Maryland.

1877
Matthew leaves home.

1878–1879
Henson meets Captain Childs. Childs takes special care to educate Matt himself, teaching him literature, history, and navigation.

At age 13, Henson is taken on as a cabin boy by Captain Childs of the ***Katie Hines***.

1885
At age 19, Matt leaves the ***Katie Hines*** after Captain Childs's death.

1887
Lieutenant Robert Peary hires Matthew Henson as his valet for a Nicaragua Canal route survey.

1891
Matthew Henson leaves for Greenland with Peary's crew onboard the ***Kite***.

1893–1908
Henson and Peary make several more attempts to reach the North Pole.

February 1909
In what would be their final attempt to reach the North Pole, Peary's party depart their anchored ship, USS ***Roosevelt***, at Cape Sheridan to make the remainder of the journey to the North Pole by dogsled.

April 6, 1909
Matthew Alexander Henson is the first man to reach the North Pole during the Arctic expedition of Commander Robert Edwin Peary. Peary, who arrived 45 minutes later with the rest of the polar party, claimed the North Pole in the name of the President of the United States.

December 1909 / January 1910
Peary's claim to the North Pole is recognized by the National Geographic Society. The Congress of the United States also formally recognizes Peary's claim to the North Pole.

February 1912
The Frederick A. Stokes Co. of New York publishes Henson's autobiography with a foreword by Robert Peary and an introduction by Booker T. Washington.

1850 — 1900

1936
Henson retires as a clerk from the U.S. Customs Service.

1937
Henson is elected to membership in the Explorers Club based in New York.

1938
Henson Gletscher/Glacier (82 degrees, 20 minutes North, 40 degrees, 00 minutes West) in North Greenland is named as a tribute to Matthew Henson.

1948
The Geographic Society of Chicago awards Henson with a gold medal and cites him as "the first Negro in this country to be honored for scientific achievement in the geographical field."

April 6, 1949
The U.S. Department of Defense gives Henson a citation for his contribution to the discovery of the North Pole.

1950

February 9, 1953
The National Association for the Advancement of Colored People presents the Explorers Club in New York City with a bronze bust of Matthew Henson.

April 6, 1954
Henson is commended at the White House by the President of the United States, Dwight D. Eisenhower, for his significant contributions to the success of the discovery of the North Pole.

March 9, 1955
Henson dies in New York City at the age of 88, survived by his wife, Lucy Ross Henson. He is buried in New York.

1959
The Maryland State House honors Henson's accomplishments with a memorial plaque.

1986
A 1986 set of U.S. Postal stamps features Henson and Peary's attainment of the Pole.

1988
Henson is reburied with military honors at Arlington National Cemetery.

2000
The highly coveted and prestigious Hubbard Medal is awarded to Henson's family in his honor.

Afterword

A year after the Civil War ended, Matthew Henson was born in Charles County, Maryland, on August 8, 1866. At an early age, his mother died, leaving him to live alone with his father. In 1867, his family moved to a farm just outside of Washington, D.C. While his father worked, Matthew cared for his uncle. He was not fond of this task. Shortly after Matthew's father died, he decided to drop out of school and leave home. By 1878, he wound up in Baltimore, where he stumbled across a small restaurant. Henson was hired to sweep and mop the floors, clean the kitchen, and wash the dishes. Since he had nowhere else to stay, the owner allowed Henson to sleep in the restaurant after closing. It was at this restaurant that Matthew first listened to an old sailor's tales of the sea.

As a boy, Henson once heard a speech by Frederick Douglass, the most famous African American leader of the time. Douglass's words inspired Matthew to dream of becoming great. Seeking adventure, 13-year-old Matthew noticed a sign one day looking for help on a sea cabin. So he signed on as a cabin boy with the *Katie Hines*. Over the next five years, he sailed to Asia, Africa, and Europe, studying literature, history, and navigation with Captain Childs. He learned everything he could about seamanship. Captain Childs became ill and died when Matthew was around 18 years old. After that, Henson experienced racism and prejudice from many of the white sailors. By this time, he was already an experienced sailor, but he couldn't find another ship whose crew would treat him as an equal. After working odd jobs for two years, he returned to Washington, D.C.

Henson began working as a stock boy in a men's store. A chance meeting in 1887 with a customer forever changed the course of his life. That man was Robert Peary, a lieutenant in the U.S. Navy. Peary offered Henson a job as his personal valet on an expedition to Nicaragua. He was working for the government to chart the Nicaraguan jungle in hopes of building a canal there. The store owner assured Peary that Henson was bright and strong. He was already a world traveler.

During the trip to Nicaragua, Henson demonstrated abilities that Peary felt would prove extremely valuable to further expeditions. He used his mapping skills from his sailing experience to help Peary survey the Nicaraguan jungle. This trip was the changing point in Henson's life. Peary aimed to be the first man to stand on the North Pole—a goal Henson readily shared. Peary was so impressed with Henson that he made him his trusted assistant. Peary asked Henson to be part of an expedition that would ultimately reach the North Pole. Driven by a love of exploration, the two men, along with small teams of explorers, made several trips to the Arctic region from 1891 to 1909.

Each expedition over the next 18 years started from Greenland. Henson's experience proved invaluable at each attempt. He learned everything needed for survival in the Arctic. He embraced the native Inuit people and learned their language. In fact, the Inuit made a legend of Henson, whom they called "Matthew the Kind One." Henson found ways to adapt to the extreme climates of the hostile North Pole. He learned to break trails, make camp, build and fix sleds, drive a dog team, hunt, and even make clothes out of animal skins. Because of his strong preparation for this dangerous journey, Commander Peary remarked, "I couldn't get along without him."

Twice on the polar ice cap, Henson saved Peary's life. But neither danger nor lack of funds deterred them. On their last trip to reach the North Pole, conditions in the Arctic were favorable. However, the men had only enough supplies to make one trip to the area that Peary had calculated to be the North Pole. On April 6, 1909, Peary and Henson along with several Inuit people stood together at the North Pole—making history. Henson is believed to be the first man to actually reach the Pole, some 45 minutes ahead of Peary, who had to be pulled on a sled by the Inuit because his feet were frostbitten. When Peary arrived, he handed Henson the American flag, which he planted in the snow. Henson then posed for a picture with the four Inuit guides who led Peary and Henson to the top of the world.

But back home, controversy greeted the two explorers. Dr. Frederick A. Cook, who had accompanied Peary and Henson on an earlier trip, falsely claimed to have reached the Pole in 1908. Cook's lies gave permanent damage to the honor of the 1909 expedition team. Some authorities dismissed Peary's achievement because a black man had accompanied him. Henson gave lectures to prove that Peary was telling the truth. However, Peary did not want the expedition to be spoken about publicly until it was acknowledged that Peary and his team were indeed the first to reach the North Pole. Peary would not speak to Henson because Henson proceeded to give lectures on their record-breaking feat. At last the National Geographic Society and the U.S. Congress recognized Peary's claim to the North Pole. Admiral Peary died in 1920.

Henson, the first man in the world to reach the North Pole, was reduced to carrying luggage and parking cars to earn a living. In the years that followed, Henson worked as a clerk for the U.S. Customs Service in New York and retired in 1936. He occasionally lectured on his experiences. In 1912, he published his autobiography. Toward the end of his life, he finally received some recognition. Henson was accepted as a member of the Explorers Club in New York. Several other famous explorers such as Stefansson, MacMillan, and Bartlett kept close friendships with him. The club worked to get Henson recognized as the true discoverer of the North Pole. Their efforts paid off. In 1954, President Dwight D. Eisenhower presented him with an award acknowledging

his great accomplishment. He also received honors from Howard University, the Geographic Society of Chicago, the U.S. Congress, and the U.S. Navy. Matthew Henson died on March 9, 1955.

Henson continued to receive his due recognition after his death. In 1959, a memorial plaque honoring the accomplishments of this great explorer was placed in the Maryland State House. There is a school with his namesake in the county where he was born. The U.S. Navy ship USNS *Henson* sails the world's oceans. Henson is also commemorated in a U.S. Postal stamp along with Peary. In 1988, Henson was moved to Arlington National Cemetery to be buried beside Peary. In 2000, Henson was recognized with the National Geographic Society's Hubbard Medal for distinction in exploration, discovery, and research.

Throughout his life Matthew Henson overcame great adversity. Today, Matthew Henson is finally remembered as a truly remarkable man. He was always quick to help others, never spoke unkindly of others, displayed enthusiasm, and possessed skill in many disciplines. When men were starving with no food to be found anywhere, Henson found game, and he returned with fresh meat to keep them alive. When others could not go on, he carried them home. When his fellow explorers looked in his face, they gained courage. Matthew Henson demonstrated the finest qualities of the human spirit.

UNIT 3

Early America

Unit 3: Early America

THEME Question

How was America founded?

Focus Questions

What was life like for Native Americans before new settlers arrived?

What did America mean to the first European settlers?

How were people's ideas changed by historical events in early America?

What changes occurred after America won its independence?

128 Unit 3

Early America 129

A Place Becomes a Country

by Amanda Ramirez

My Words Are Tied in One

My words are tied in one
With the great mountains,
With the great rocks,
With the great trees,
In one with my body
And my heart.

Do you all help me
With supernatural power,
And you, day,
And you, night!
All of you see me
One with this world!

– traditional poem of the Yokuts, a Nation of Native Americans in California

How was America founded?

Focus Questions

What was life like for Native Americans before new settlers arrived?

What did America mean to the first European settlers?

How were people's ideas changed by historical events in early America?

What changes occurred after America won its independence?

A Place Becomes a Country

by Amanda Ramirez

My Words Are Tied in One

My words are tied in one
With the great mountains,
With the great rocks,
With the great trees,
In one with my body
And my heart.

Do you all help me
With supernatural power,
And you, day,
And you, night!
All of you see me
One with this world!

– traditional poem of the Yokuts,
a Nation of Native Americans
in California

Contents

Chapter One

Who Lived Here First?

Long before Europeans came, people lived in hundreds of different groups across North America and South America. These people are called *Native Americans*, but each group had a name for itself. The names often portrayed a group's way of life—"people of the bayou," "forest dwellers," "fire keepers," "strong people," and "peaceful ones."

People living in different parts of North America (see the map on these pages) made and used the **artifacts** shown here. How might learning about these objects help you understand how the people lived?

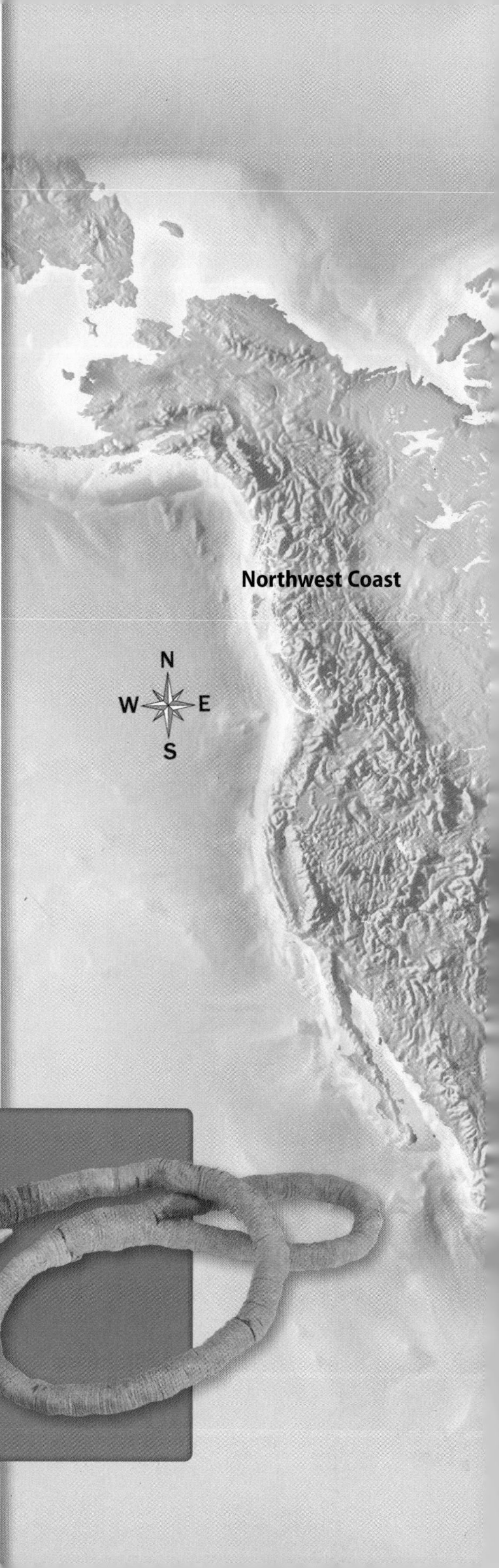

Northwest Coast

N
W
E
S

People from the Northwest Coast used cedar bark holders to help protect the sharp tips of their harpoons.

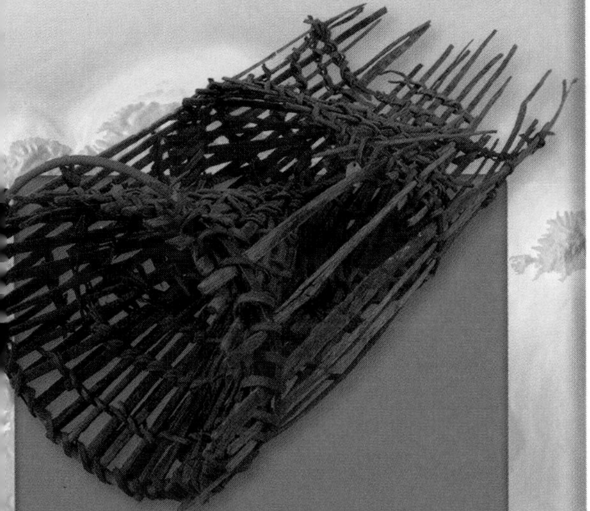

People from the Eastern Woodlands used a basket-like trap to catch eels.

Eastern Woodlands

Great Plains

How the First People Lived

Native Americans share many cultural similarities, but each group lived in communities with their own languages and traditions. Those living along major rivers fished. Groups in forests hunted the animals living there.

Native Americans respected, or valued, all animals. They did not let any part of an animal go to waste. In addition to food, animals gave people other things they needed. Native Americans shaped bones into tools, such as needles that they used for sewing. They used sinew, a strong animal connective tissue, to make thread. Animal skins were used as clothing and as shelter. Native Americans even used animal stomachs as containers for holding liquids. Trading animal parts with other tribes for other goods was important to their economies.

Native American people had different ways of life, but they all shared a respect for nature. Many believed that nature's power lived in certain animals, places, and people. They often sang, chanted, or danced in order to find success in battle or in getting food.

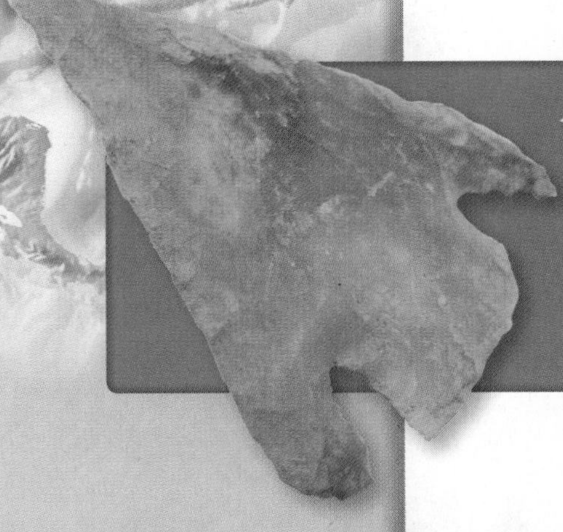

People from the Great Plains fashioned arrowheads from stone.

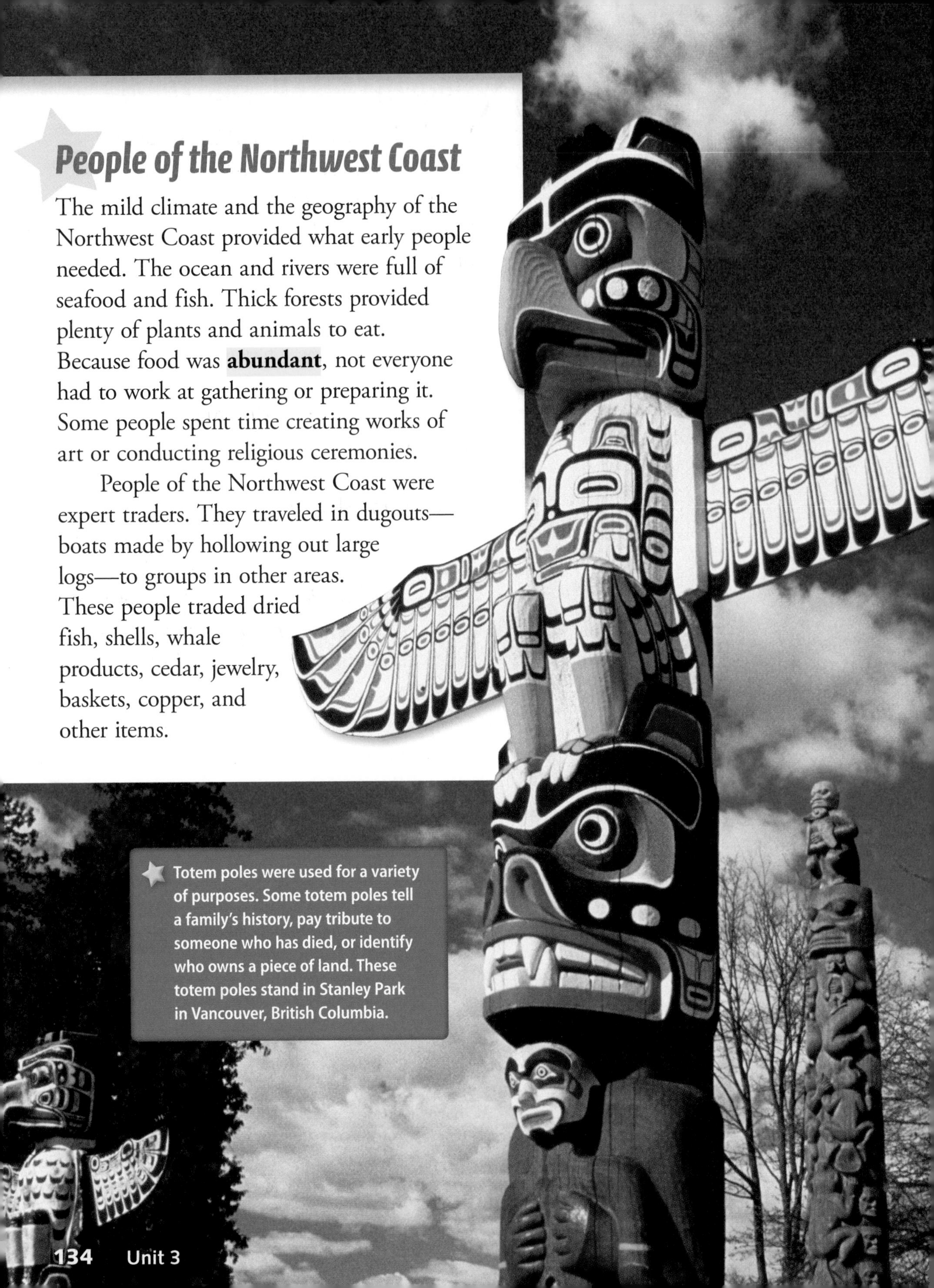

People of the Northwest Coast

The mild climate and the geography of the Northwest Coast provided what early people needed. The ocean and rivers were full of seafood and fish. Thick forests provided plenty of plants and animals to eat. Because food was **abundant**, not everyone had to work at gathering or preparing it. Some people spent time creating works of art or conducting religious ceremonies.

People of the Northwest Coast were expert traders. They traveled in dugouts—boats made by hollowing out large logs—to groups in other areas. These people traded dried fish, shells, whale products, cedar, jewelry, baskets, copper, and other items.

Totem poles were used for a variety of purposes. Some totem poles tell a family's history, pay tribute to someone who has died, or identify who owns a piece of land. These totem poles stand in Stanley Park in Vancouver, British Columbia.

Respect for the Whale

For the Makah (muh KAH) people of the northwest Pacific coast, the whale was an animal of great power. A whale hunt, therefore, was a dangerous job. People often prayed and fasted—gave up eating for a period of time—before a whale hunt.

When they spotted a whale, hunters moved in with their canoes. The head harpooner threw a harpoon. The harpoon was not meant to kill the whale; it was meant to secure sealskin floats, attached to the harpoon line. The floats acted like big balloons and slowed the whale. When the whale tired, the hunters killed it and towed it home.

Native Americans used all parts of the whale. Whales gave the Makah oil, meat, bone, sinew, and other useful things. In return the Makah showed respect for whales by honoring them in their songs, dances, and artwork.

A whale hunt

People of the Plains

The Plains lie between the Mississippi River and the Rocky Mountains. The region stretches up to Canada and down to Texas. Once millions of bison roamed the prairies of the Plains. The American bison, commonly called buffalo, were very important to the people who lived there.

Some Plains people, such as the Cheyenne (shy AN), moved from place to place, following the bison. The Cheyenne made shelters by tying together wooden poles at the top and covering them with buffalo skins. These cone-shaped shelters, called *teepees*, were easy to take apart. They were also easy for the Cheyenne to carry on their frequent moves.

Many Native American groups lived on the Plains. Some, such as the Mandan (MAN duhn), lived in villages along rivers, where the land was lush and good for farming. The Mandan women built domed homes called *lodges* made from clay, mud, sticks, and hay. The women also did most of the farming, growing maize, beans, pumpkins, sunflowers, and tobacco. The men's responsibilities included hunting and fishing.

Before horses arrived with Europeans, Plains peoples hunted buffalo on foot. One method was the buffalo jump. Some hunters waved blankets and shouted, chasing the buffalo over the edge of a cliff. Other hunters waited below and cut up the carcasses, or bodies, of the dead animals.

The Importance of Buffalo

Buffalo were critical to the survival of the Plains people. They ate the meat and used other parts of a buffalo's carcass in many ways. The chart below shows a few examples.

These teepees are at Head Smashed In, the oldest known buffalo jump in Canada, at the base of the Rocky Mountains.

HOW PEOPLE USED THE BUFFALO

Parts of buffalo	Use
meat	eaten fresh or preserved
hide	teepees, clothing, moccasins, blankets, shields
bones	arrow shafts, tools, sewing needles
teeth	jewelry
sinew	laces, thread
hooves	glue, rattles, spoons
horns	arrow points, cups, spoons, fire carriers

People of the Eastern Woodlands

More than 25 different groups lived in villages along the northeast Atlantic coast and in the forests that stretched west toward the Mississippi River. In order to get along, peoples of the Eastern Woodlands formed confederations. A confederation is a government that links different groups. The confederations had formal codes that governed their relations.

The people of the Eastern Woodlands cleared land to grow corn, beans, squash, and other foods. They hunted and fished. The Wampanoag (WAM puh NOH ag), for example, used basket-like traps to catch eels. They baited the trap and put it into the water. When the tide changed, eels swam in and were trapped. The fishers then returned to collect their food.

Some Eastern Woodland Native Americans built and lived in longhouses. Several families lived in each longhouse.

New Settlers

The first European settlers began arriving in North America in the 1500s. In 1565 Spain set up a settlement in St. Augustine, Florida. In 1608 the French set up a settlement in Quebec, Canada.

In 1607 about 100 settlers arrived at what is now Jamestown, Virginia and formed the first permanent English settlement. They had been sent by the Virginia Company, who hoped the settlers would make them huge profits.

In 1620 another group traveled from England to North America. Many people in this group were Pilgrims who traveled to North America in order to find religious freedom. They set up the colony of Plymouth in New England. Unfortunately the group had a difficult beginning. More than half of them died in the first winter. The colony managed to survive, however, in large part because of help they received from the Native Americans in the area.

Squanto, the Interpreter

In the spring a Native American named Squanto came to a Pilgrim village. Squanto lived among the Wampanoag, but he spoke English. As an interpreter, he translated what the English said into a language the Native Americans understood, and the other way around. He helped the Pilgrims learn farming methods from the Wampanoag. He also helped arrange an agreement between the two peoples. The Pilgrims' leader called Squanto "a special instrument sent of God" to help the Pilgrims.

Chapter Two

Growing the Colonies

Over the years small settlements grew. England began establishing, or setting up, colonies in North America. The first was Virginia in 1607. Georgia, the last of the original colonies, received its charter in 1733.

Religious People Many European settlers came to North America to live in a place where they were free to worship as they pleased. They did not want to worry about being persecuted, or treated unfairly, because of their religious beliefs. In some cases they could only do this if they moved to a new area to worship in their own way. The Puritans were one such group.

In the early settlements of North America, religion played an important part in the lives of people. Laws were often based on religious beliefs. For example, in some areas, only male members of the church could vote.

Enslaved men and women worked in tobacco fields in Virginia.

Indentured Servants Sometimes people paid for workers to come to the colonies. By signing a contract, these workers became indentured servants. In return for the trip to North America, they worked for a time without being paid. Some indentured servants were farmers, housekeepers, and builders.

Artisans The colonies needed people who knew how to build, weave, work with metals, make pottery, and so on. Some of these people worked for pay, others started their own businesses.

Enslaved People Many people were shipped from Africa and enslaved against their will. These people usually worked for wealthy colonists and were considered property. Some enslaved Africans worked on farms. Others worked in towns and cities—some as skilled crafts people, others in people's homes as servants. Enslaved people in the South worked mostly on plantations.

A Plan for Success

Regardless of what brought people to America, the successful ones made good use of the local geography and climate.

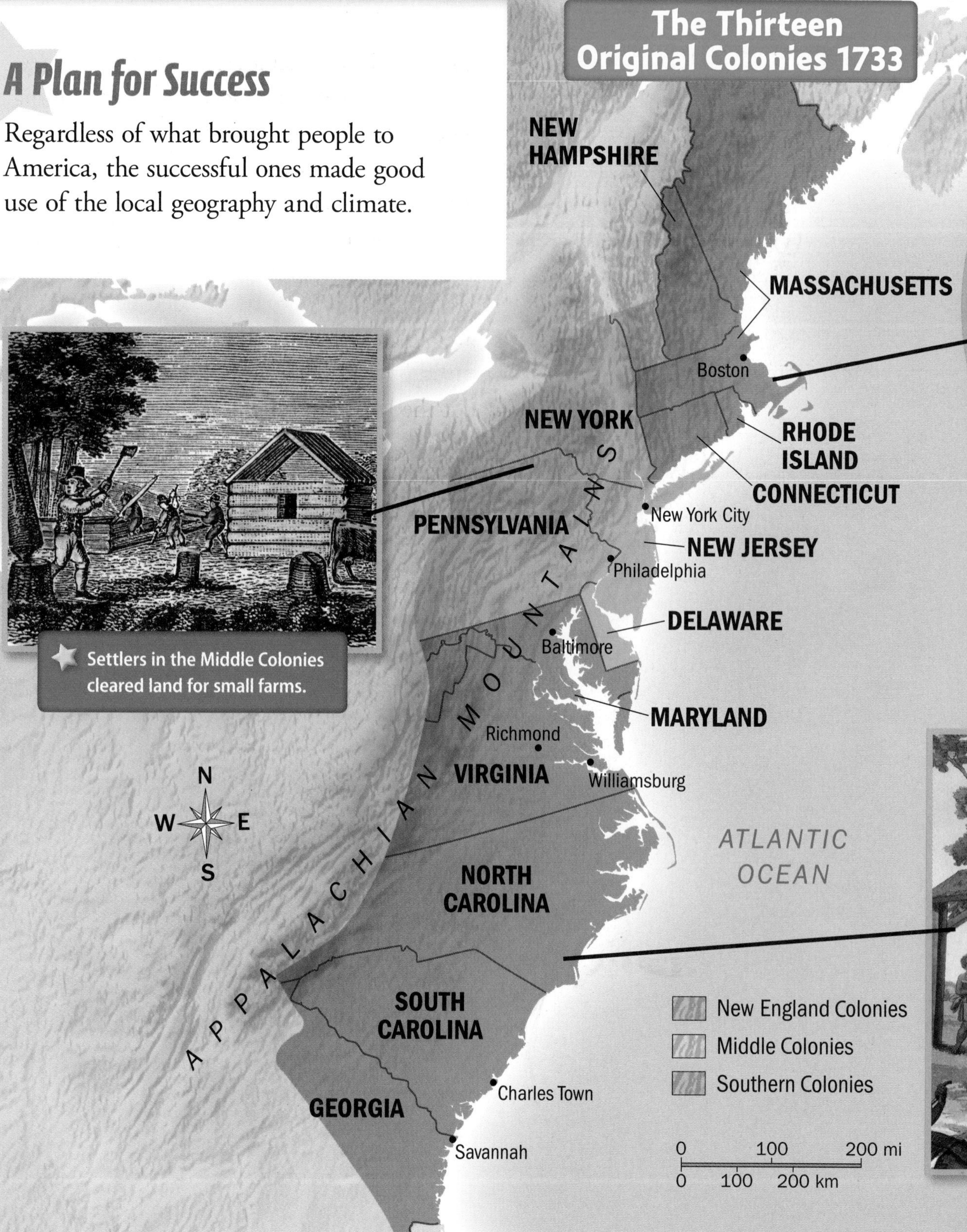

Settlers in the Middle Colonies cleared land for small farms.

Shipbuilding was important in New England.

Shipbuilding

The soil in Massachusetts is thin and rocky, which means it is not very good for farming. The colonists, however, worked with two other natural materials: the **resources** of forests and water.

In the 1600s thick forests covered the East Coast. Colonists started lumber mills near the many rivers. They cut down trees and floated the logs downstream to their mills. The flowing water powered saws that cut the logs into lumber. Woodworkers used the lumber to make furniture and ships. Shipbuilding helped Massachusetts **prosper**, or succeed financially.

Enslaved people worked on large farms in the South.

Farming

Unlike Massachusetts the soil in Pennsylvania is good for farming. The climate is milder than in New England. Farmers here were able to grow many crops, including wheat.

Like Massachusetts, Pennsylvania has many rivers. Farmers set up mills next to the rivers. The flowing water powered stones that ground the wheat into flour. Millers packed the flour into barrels and shipped it to other colonies and even to Europe. Farming helped Pennsylvania prosper.

The Southern Colonies offered rich soil and an even warmer climate. Farmers in Virginia and North Carolina planted tobacco. Rice was another important crop for the people of North Carolina. In South Carolina, farmers grew indigo, a plant used to make a blue dye. These crops were cash crops, meant to be sold rather than used by the people growing them, and they helped the South prosper.

Crops such as tobacco, rice, and indigo were grown on huge farms called plantations. A plantation was like a village. Plantation owners had many people working for them. Some were paid workers. Some were indentured servants, who worked for a time without pay. Others were enslaved people, who worked all their lives for no pay.

Eliza Lucas, Indigo Farmer

At the age of 16, Eliza Lucas, the daughter of a plantation owner, started growing indigo, a tropical plant. She developed a plant that did well in the cooler climate of South Carolina. Indigo dye became an important export when Britain decided that officers in the British Navy should wear blue uniforms—"navy blue!"

By the mid-1700s Boston's harbor had become a busy place.

What Happened Next?

The colonies attracted more and more people, and so small towns grew into large cities. Boston, with its harbor, was one of these cities. Ships came to trade from the other colonies and from Europe. Lively trading made Boston an exciting place. People in Boston could buy books, clothing, tools, all kinds of food, furniture, silver goods—almost anything they wanted!

King George III watched the colonies grow rich. Because the colonies belonged to Britain, he wanted colonists to keep paying taxes to Britain. Some colonists disagreed. They were proud of their success in North America. In time such disagreement led to open conflict with Britain—the Revolutionary War.

Chapter Three

Hear Ye! Hear Ye!

Because they were so far from England, the people of the 13 Colonies were used to making their own laws and governing themselves. However, England still saw the colonies as English land and felt it had the right to tell the colonists what to do.

This engraving of the Boston Massacre was produced by Paul Revere.

In the 1750s Britain and France fought against each other in the French and Indian War. This conflict came about partly because both countries wanted to claim the land between the Appalachian Mountains and the Mississippi River. Britain eventually won the war and gained control of all the land east of the Mississippi. At the end of the war, King George III issued the Royal Proclamation of 1763, which said that the colonists could not settle west of the Appalachian Mountains. By doing this, Britain hoped to ease tensions with the Native Americans, many of whom had been allied with the French during the war.

Cobblestones at the site of the Boston Massacre

Though he may have once been enslaved, Crispus Attucks was buried with honor along with the others killed in the Boston Massacre. You can still see the grave today.

During the French and Indian War, Britain built up a lot of debt. In order to repay this debt, Britain began to place higher taxes on the colonists. The Sugar Act of 1764 placed a tax on goods such as sugar, coffee, silk, and wine. The Currency Act of 1764 prevented people from printing money in the colonies. The Stamp Act of 1765 added a tax, which was paid to Britain, to all legal documents, newspapers, licenses, and leases.

The colonists were angry. They did not feel it was right to be taxed by a government so far away, especially since the colonists could not be part of the decision making.

The Boston Massacre

On March 5, 1770, in Boston, Massachusetts, a fight broke out between a crowd of citizens and British soldiers. The exact cause of the fight is in question. The results are not.

The British soldiers felt that they were in danger from the angry crowd. Several soldiers fired their rifles toward the crowd. Three people in the crowd were killed. Later, two more people died of their injuries.

The event was quickly called the Boston Massacre. The confrontation showed the growing anger of Bostonians toward British rule.

Among the dead was Crispus Attucks, a merchant sailor and possibly a former enslaved African. The funeral of those killed was attended by thousands of people.

Buckman's Tavern was the headquarters of rebel activity in Lexington. It was restored in the 1920s and is open to the public.

Samuel Adams

A Declaration of War

Samuel Adams was one of several people who thought colonists should demand independence from Great Britain. He wrote newspaper articles and gave speeches explaining why the colonists should be allowed to govern themselves. At that time, however, some colonists disagreed.

Then, in 1773, the British government decided that the East India Company should be the only company allowed to export tea to the colonies. Colonial traders would now lose money on tea. They joined people like Samuel Adams in seeking independence. A **rebellion** was started.

The British planned to end the rebellion by capturing **patriot** rebel leaders John Hancock and Samuel Adams. Then the British planned to destroy supplies hidden in Concord, a village just west of Boston. These actions, they thought, would stop the colonial uprisings.

Word got out, and Hancock and Adams escaped. Other patriots rode out to warn that the British were coming. On the march to Concord, the British soldiers reached the village of Lexington. They found Americans waiting for them. Someone—no one knows who—fired a shot. The British fired in force, killing eight people.

In Concord, British soldiers clashed with more colonists, killing two but losing three of their own. Colonists continued to fire as the soldiers returned to Boston.

On April 19, 1775, the American Revolution began!

Declaring Independence

In the midst of the war, the colonists decided to explain in writing their reasons for seeking independence. In 1776 the Continental Congress, the acting government of the colonies, met in Philadelphia. The Continental Congress was made up of delegates, or representatives, from each of the colonies. The members of the Congress debated whether to formally declare independence from Great Britain.

After a long debate, the Congress officially declared that the colonies were free from Britain. On July 4th, 1776, the Congress approved a Declaration of Independence that explained why the leaders of the colonies felt the need to separate from Britain. The Declaration also described the rights colonial leaders believed people should have. The words of the Declaration have guided Americans to this day.

The Declaration of Independence was printed and copies were sent north and south. As crowds gathered to hear the Declaration read aloud, they cheered and even lit fireworks. A new nation was born!

A statue of Sybil Ludington commemorates her historic ride. You can see it today in Carmel, New York.

Ordinary People Contribute

The colonies formed the American Continental Army to fight the British. However, it was not just soldiers who contributed to the war effort. Ordinary citizens played important roles too. On the night of April 26, 1777, a messenger brought news to Colonel Henry Ludington: The British had attacked and were burning the nearby city of Danbury, Connecticut. The messenger begged for help, he was too tired to keep riding. Someone needed to alert the soldiers under Colonel Ludington's command.

Sybil, the colonel's 16-year-old daughter, took the job. Riding her horse some 40 miles through the darkness and the rain, she spread the word to the soldiers in their homes. By the end of her journey, about 400 soldiers had gathered. They bravely fought British forces the next day.

Lydia Darragh, Secret Informer

The British captured Philadelphia in September 1777. Shortly thereafter British officers demanded the use of William and Lydia Darragh's house. Lydia listened secretly to one of the officers' conversations about a surprise attack on General Washington's forces. On December 2, saying she needed to buy flour, Lydia left the house and found someone to take the information to General Washington. The British attack failed.

The 1st Rhode Island Regiment

In 1775 the Continental Congress appointed General George Washington commander-in-chief of the Continental Army. Washington had previously fought in the French and Indian War and was known for his patriotism and military leadership.

General Washington's army depended on the colonies for soldiers. However, getting soldiers from some colonies was difficult. To get more troops, Rhode Island's leaders did something unheard of: they decided to enlist enslaved people. In return for their military service, these soldiers would receive their freedom.

The 1st Rhode Island Regiment fought bravely in many battles. They also played an important part in the Battle of Yorktown. In September 1781 Continental forces and French allies cornered the British at Yorktown, Virginia. The British dug trenches and built redoubts (defensive positions). The 1st Rhode Island Regiment helped attack the redoubts.

Washington led a force of about 17,000 soldiers. They sieged the British, surrounding them and cutting off their outside access. French cannons bombarded the British day and night. Without access to the outside world, the British ran low on supplies.

Overwhelmed the British gave up. Soon after the Battle of Yorktown, on October 19, 1781, the British surrendered.

Jean Baptiste Antoine de Verger fought in the Battle of Yorktown. His painting shows the uniforms for the 1st Rhode Island Regiment, the New England Militia, fighters from frontier areas, and the French officers.

You can see this reconstructed redoubt at Yorktown Battlefield in Virginia.

Chapter Four

What Happened Next?

After years of fighting, the war was over. What did the colonists gain, and what did they lose?

Independence from Britain On September 3, 1783, the United States and British Representatives signed the Treaty of Paris. This treaty, or agreement, ended the American Revolution.

Land The treaty pushed the borders of the United States north and west. The United States now stretched from the Atlantic Ocean to the Mississippi River and into what is now Canada. However, much of this land was not part of any of the colonies.

Hardships More than 25,000 Americans died in the American Revolution. The war destroyed property, such as farms and ships. The war cost a lot of money too. Congress later collected taxes to pay for the war.

without Difficulty and without requiring
any Compensation.

Article 10th.

The solemn Ratifications of the present Treaty expedited in good & due Form shall be exchanged between the contracting Parties in the Space of Six Months or sooner if possible to be computed from the Day of the Signature of the present Treaty. In Witness whereof we the undersigned their Ministers Plenipotentiary have in their Name and in Virtue of our Full Powers signed with our Hands the present Definitive Treaty, and caused the Seals of our Arms to be affix'd thereto.

Done at Paris,

D Hartley John Adams. B Franklin John Jay

The Treaty of Paris

Money During the war, Britain upset the colonies' **economy**—their ways of producing and using goods. The British occupied major ports, such as Boston, and they stopped goods from being exported. Colonial artisans and farmers lost money when they couldn't sell their goods. After the war Americans had to find new places to sell their goods. Britain used its power with other nations to block these efforts. It took time to rebuild the American economy.

Moving West Some Americans who were losing money decided to move west. People began clearing land and building homes all the way to the Mississippi River.

A Constitution for the Nation

After the war the nation was briefly governed by a plan called the Articles of Confederation. Under this plan the states had more power than the national government. This made national laws hard to enforce. In 1787 representatives from the states met in Philadelphia to improve the laws.

A big concern at the meetings was which should be stronger: separate state governments or the national government. People argued for each side, and in the end, they replaced the Articles of Confederation with a new document. It was a **constitution**—a document that explained the organization and basic rules of the government. This constitution set up a system of shared powers, called a federal system, that gave more power to citizens—including the power to change the system when necessary.

The Constitution of the United States of America still guides our country today. It is one of America's most important documents, and over the years it has become a model that other countries have used to form their governments.

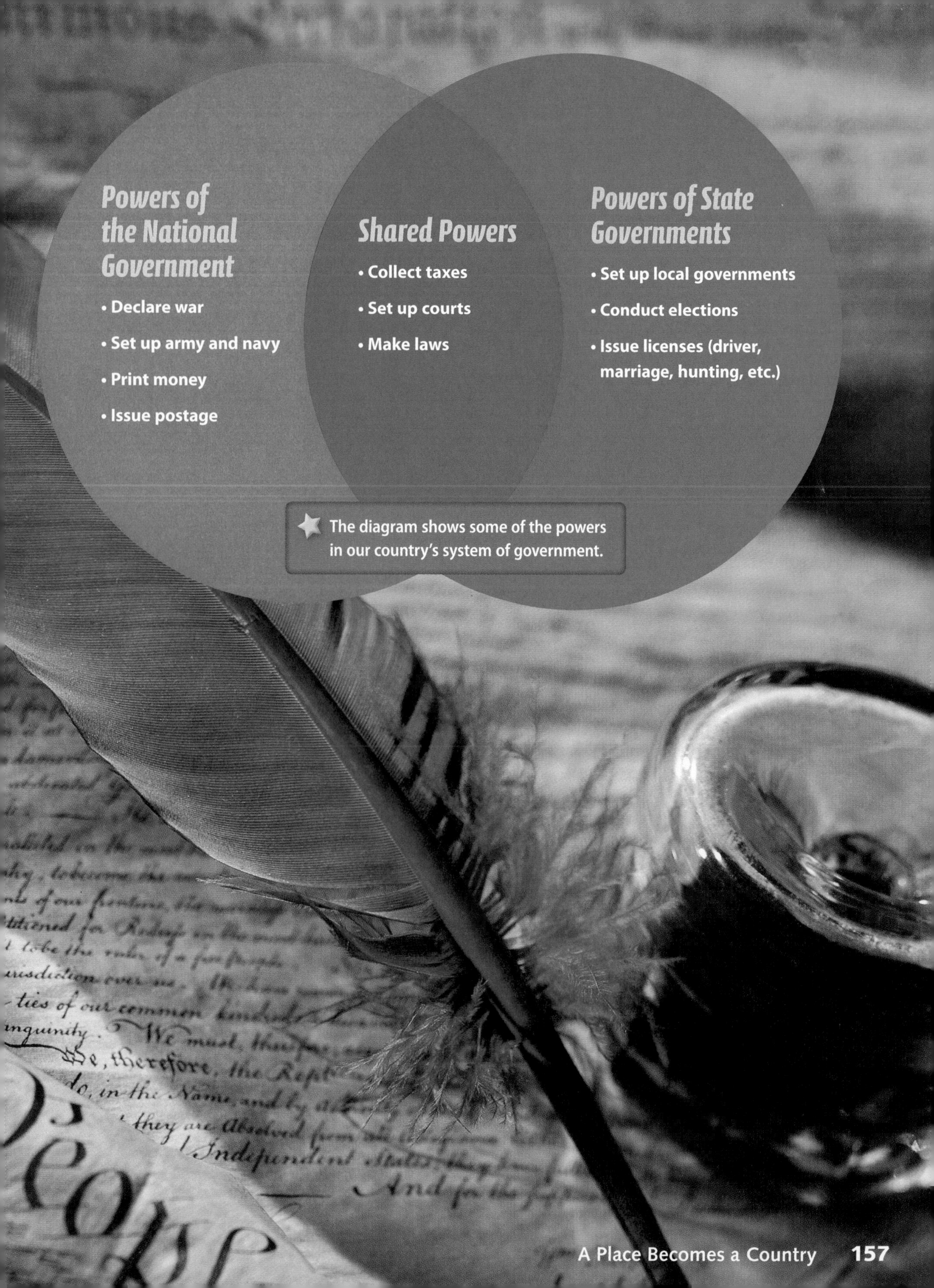

Powers of the National Government

- Declare war
- Set up army and navy
- Print money
- Issue postage

Shared Powers

- Collect taxes
- Set up courts
- Make laws

Powers of State Governments

- Set up local governments
- Conduct elections
- Issue licenses (driver, marriage, hunting, etc.)

The diagram shows some of the powers in our country's system of government.

Sum It Up

North America was—and still is—rich with resources. Its lands and waters supported Native Americans and European colonists alike. Both groups built communities that depended on the natural resources of those places. Eventually American colonists wanted to rule their communities themselves. To gain independence they fought and won a war with Britain. After the war they worked to create a new government for their new nation.

What part of America's early history interests you most? Why?

What part would you have liked to play in the early history of our country?

THE Buffalo Jump

written by PETER ROOP

illustrated by BILL FARNSWORTH

Little Blaze threw back the buffalo robe covering the lodge entrance. He picked up his bow and arrows from where he had thrown them. He knew a man must always treat his weapons with respect, but now he didn't care. An angry fire flared inside him.

He notched an arrow and aimed at a raven. Little Blaze remembered that *Omuk-may-sto*, the Raven, was good medicine for his people. He would bring bad luck upon his family if he harmed the bird. Still, Little Blaze wanted to strike out against something, anything, to make him feel better.

Little Blaze ducked behind a lodge when he saw Morning Eagle. His friend had seen him disappear and easily discovered Little Blaze.

"Why are you hiding from me?" asked Morning Eagle.

"I don't want to see anyone," growled Little Blaze.

"Even me? Aren't we friends?"

"Yes, you're my friend. But even a friend can do nothing for me."

"Tell me what angers you," said Morning Eagle.

"It is my father!"

"Your father?" asked Morning Eagle. "What has he done that his son storms around camp?"

"He has chosen Curly Bear to be the *ahwa waki,* the buffalo runner. He will stampede the buffalo over the jump tomorrow," Little Blaze said.

"Curly Bear is your brother. He will bring glory to your family."

"But I can run faster than he can," Little Blaze cried, angrily yanking a handful of grass from the earth.

"Doesn't your father know this?"

"He does. He still says that Curly Bear will lead the buffalo over the jump because he is the eldest son. As second son I must stay behind the stacked stones and only help frighten the buffalo."

"Your father has spoken. You must obey him," Morning Eagle said.

"My father is wrong. Curly Bear may be as fast as the antelope, but I am as fast as the wind," Little Blaze said, tossing the grass into the air and watching the wind carry it away. "I should lead the buffalo over the jump. Besides, I am tired of my name. I want to change it like you did. I hate the child's name, Little Blaze."

Morning Eagle looked at his friend. He saw the **disappointment** in his face. He saw the anger in his heart.

"There is nothing to be done," said Morning Eagle. "You can't change your name until you do something brave. You must forget your anger. Come, let's hunt along the river bottoms for deer. *Omuk-may-sto* brings us his good luck."

"No!" Little Blaze said. "You go."

Little Blaze watched Morning Eagle until he was out of sight. Then he turned and walked in the other direction.

Little Blaze walked fast. Then he began to run, and threw away all thoughts of his brother and the jump

and let his feet carry him where they would. As he ran, Little Blaze felt his anger fading away just as a crackling fire dies out at night.

Little Blaze found himself at the *piskun*, the buffalo jump cliff. He stopped at the edge and looked down. Far below he could see the smoke-white buffalo bones from his tribe's earlier jumps. He kicked a rock over the edge and watched it bounce down the steep slope.

Many times before Little Blaze had seen his people drive a buffalo herd over the cliff. Each jump meant food for his people and new buffalo skins for robes and lodges. A jump was also a chance for the *ahwa waki* to earn a new name. If only his father would let him lead the herd to the cliff!

Little Blaze turned away from the cliff. He walked between the stacks of stones marking the entrance to the jump. The twin rows of stone stacks opened wide like the jaws of a hungry wolf. He knew tomorrow he would be standing behind one of the stone piles, waiting to leap up and frighten the charging buffalo.

Suddenly Little Blaze turned around and began running with all of his might to the edge of the cliff. Little Blaze ran faster and faster. In front of him was the empty air beyond the cliff's edge. In the distance he could see where the earth and sky met once again.

Without stopping Little Blaze ran over the edge of the cliff. The air whizzed by. Then, as he knew he would, Little Blaze landed in a small cup of rock jutting out from the cliff. Many men had landed on this thin ledge as hundreds of buffalo flashed by.

Little Blaze lay in the cup catching his breath and dreaming he was leading the herd tomorrow. If only he could be the *ahwa waki*. He already knew what new name he would choose.

But it was only a dream. His father had spoken.

As the sun sank behind the Backbone-of-the-World Mountains, Little Blaze returned to camp. He hastily ate his dinner and lay down on his buffalo-robe bed.

In the morning Little Blaze joined the other men for their daily swim. Then, after a quick breakfast, he followed the men and boys as they walked the trail to the buffalo jump.

Long before the sun rolled into the sky, Curly Bear had gone in search of buffalo. No one knew when he would find a herd to drive back. But they must be prepared when he returned with the thundering herd.

Each man positioned himself behind one of the stacks of stones. Little Blaze hid with Morning Eagle.

The sun burned down. Little Blaze and Morning Eagle gave up battling the biting flies. The heat made the land dance in the distance. Both boys strained their eyes for the dust of the approaching herd.

Morning Eagle saw the cloud of dust first.

"There, beyond the last pile of rocks," he cried.

Little Blaze squinted until he saw it too. Then, he ran to his father. "They come! We saw the dust," he said.

"Hyi! You're right, my son. Your brother leads a good herd. Now quickly go back to your place."

Little Blaze sprinted back. Now he could see Curly Bear running swiftly in front of a small herd of buffalo.

"Ah, we will eat well tonight, Little Blaze," whispered Morning Eagle.

"Yes, it's a good herd," Little Blaze said with only a hint of sadness in his voice. "I only wish it was me out in front."

"Maybe next year your father will choose you," suggested Morning Eagle.

Little Blaze grunted and kept looking at the herd. He could see Curly Bear very well now. Suddenly he grabbed Morning Eagle.

"Curly Bear is not very far in front of the herd!"

"*Hyi!* You're right! The buffalo will run him down!"

The stampeding herd was an arrow's shot behind Curly Bear as he reached the first stack of stones. The men leapt into the air, waving skins and shouting. The frightened buffalo entered the funnel of rocks.

The hard hooves of the buffalo beat the earth like thunder. Curly Bear slowed down just when he needed to be running his very fastest.

Curly Bear passed the third, the fourth, the fifth stone stack. At each one, men shouted and waved. The buffalo gained on Curly Bear until they were less than a spear's throw behind his tiring feet.

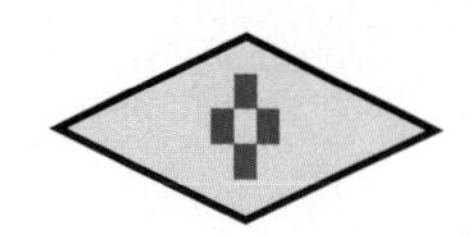

As Curly Bear neared Little Blaze's stack he turned and looked back. He never saw the sharp stone sticking up in front of him. Curly Bear hit the rock running and tumbled into a heap.

Little Blaze dashed to his brother. He grabbed Curly Bear under his arms and yanked him to his feet. The ground rocked with the crash of the buffalo.

Little Blaze ran with Curly Bear to the cliff's edge. The buffalo got closer and closer. Then, like stones dropped into a pond, the two boys disappeared. The stampeding buffalo followed. One by one the herd plunged over the cliff.

In the narrow cup, Little Blaze hugged his older brother. The earth shook as the buffalo crashed far below the huddled boys.

Then a strange silence filled the air. Little Blaze looked up. No more buffalo hurtled past them. He lifted Curly Bear to his feet. The boys watched the tribe gather below to butcher the dead buffalo.

Little Blaze heard a voice call from above them.

"Come, my sons. The sun has shone on our tribe. Let us **celebrate** this good jump. And let us celebrate the brave deeds of both my sons."

That night, after a huge meal of boiled buffalo ribs, Little Blaze was called before his father.

"Little Blaze, today without thinking of your own safety, you ran in front of the buffalo and saved your brother. When any man does a deed of **courage** he is given a new name to honor his act. I give you the name Charging Bull."

Hyi! Charging Bull! Little Blaze could scarcely believe his father's words. Just the name he had wanted for himself. He felt a warm glow spreading through his body like sunshine after a storm.

Charging Bull, a good name. It was a name that would be spoken with pride around Blackfeet campfires for many moons to come.

A Note on the Story

Millions of bison, commonly called buffalo, once roamed America's plains and prairies. Long before horses galloped over the land, Native Americans armed with arrows and spears hunted buffalo on foot. A successful hunt was the key to survival. The great shaggy beasts provided food, shelter, and clothing. A poor hunt meant starvation and death.

Different methods were used to hunt buffalo. Sometimes a lone hunter stalked a small herd on foot, hoping to get close enough to make a kill. Other times large groups, even whole villages, joined together to make a kill big enough to feed the tribe for the winter. *The Buffalo Jump* is based on the prehistoric hunting method of driving a buffalo herd over a cliff.

To decoy a herd the buffalo runner, wearing a wolf or buffalo skin as a disguise, cautiously approached the grazing buffalo. Each herd had a lead animal, usually a cow, which the other buffalo would follow. The buffalo runner attracted the attention of the lead cow. The cow, curious about the "new animal," would come closer to see just what it was. The buffalo runner would then move farther away. If his luck held, the cow would follow, bringing the herd with her. The buffalo runner would then begin to move away more quickly. If the herd continued to follow, the buffalo runner would throw off his robe and break into a run. If his deception worked, the whole herd would stampede behind the sprinting buffalo runner.

Buffalo jumps were best in the fall when a herd was easier to decoy. Disguised under a buffalo or wolf skin, a fast runner stampeded a herd to a cliff where other hunters were waiting. This decoy, the Blackfeet *ahwa waki*, then jumped over the cliff, landed on a ledge, and watched as the buffalo crashed to the ground. Any buffalo not killed in the fall would be shot with arrows or speared by hunters waiting below.

After the buffalo jump, the tribe gathered to skin the animals, cut up the meat, and tend the cooking fires. Every part of the buffalo was used. The meat was eaten immediately or dried for future use. Skins were tanned and made into sturdy tipis and soft shirts, skirts, and moccasins. Thick wooly buffalo robes kept out winter's chill. Bones were shaped into needles, scrapers, and other tools. Horns became drinking cups and ladles. Rib bones made wonderful sleds. Pouches from bladders were waterproof. Intestines became war charms. Buffalo hair and strips of hide were woven into ropes. Skulls were used in religious ceremonies.

A successful buffalo jump was indeed a joyous occasion.

Buffalo jump sites are scattered throughout the western United States and Canada. The site that inspired this story is the Madison Buffalo Jump in Montana. Standing on the cliff, looking down at the ledge where the *ahwa waki* landed as a thundering herd of buffalo plunged over the cliff, made me wonder what would happen if . . . ?

The answer is *The Buffalo Jump.*

A portion of the profits from this book will be donated toward the protection and expansion of the bison habitat.

The author would like to thank the Society of Children's Book Writers and Illustrators for its generous Work-In-Progress grant, which supported research for The Buffalo Jump. *The Council for Indian Education and the Blackfeet Nation are thanked, too, for first publishing* Little Blaze and the Buffalo Jump *so that Native American children could learn about their ancestors. Thanks to* Cobblestone Magazine *for also publishing the story.*

The illustrator offers special thanks to Steve DiPietro and Marlin Spoonhunter.

UNIT 4

Forces of Nature

What forces work to change Earth's surface?

Focus Questions

How do destructive forces lead to the creation of something new?

How does the power of water change Earth's surface?

How does climate change affect Earth?

How does the changing Earth affect living things?

Earth Is Always

by Theo Tucker

Changing

Contents

Chapter 1

Building the Hawaiian Islands

How did the Grand Canyon or the Great Lakes form? Many old stories explain why Earth looks the way it does today. Here's one such story, a myth, about how the Hawaiian Islands were formed.

Pele, Goddess of Volcanoes

Long ago there was a goddess named Pele who had such a bad temper that her father sent her away. She paddled her canoe out to sea and landed on the island of Kauai (KOW eye).

Pele made her home in a volcano on the island. However, a huge wave came and filled the volcano. Some say that Pele's sister, the goddess of the sea, did this.

Pele moved south to other islands. Each time the sea ruined her volcano home and Pele moved again. Finally Pele reached the Big Island of Hawaii. There she found Kilauea (kee low AY uh), a volcano too high for the sea to fill. Some say Pele still resides there today.

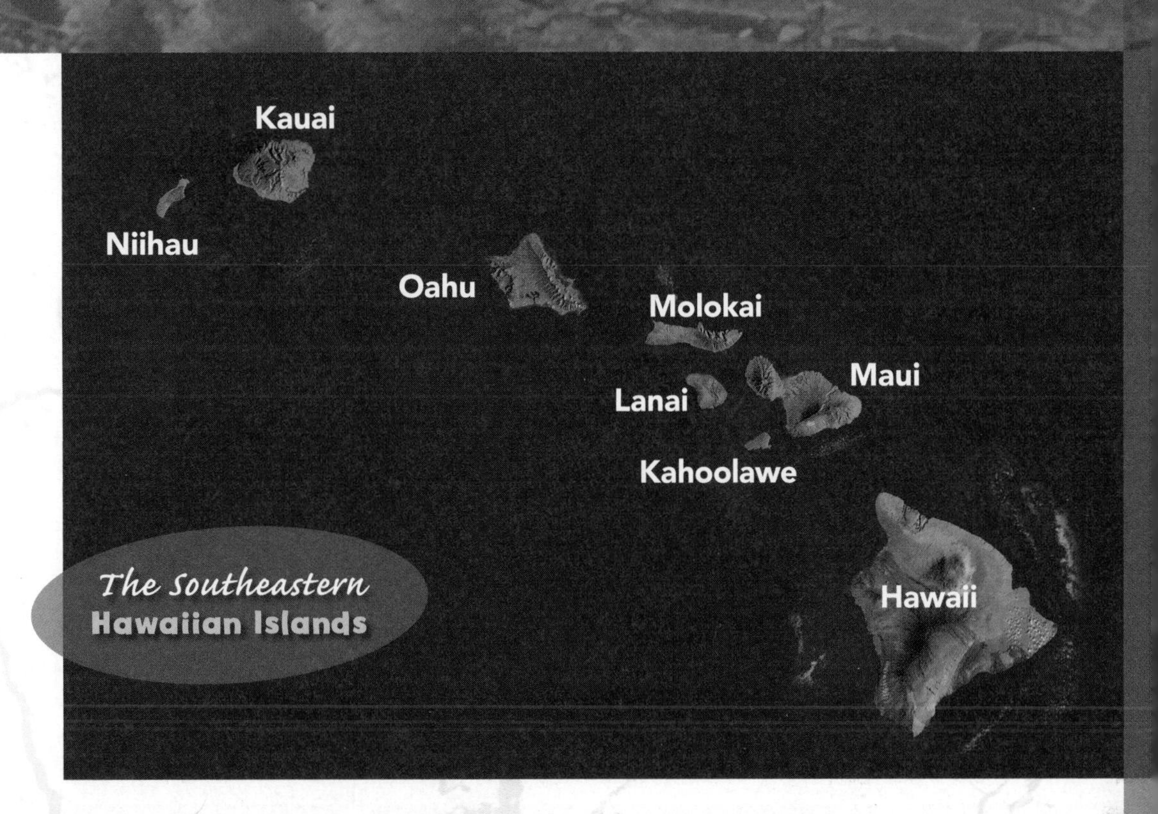

What Is Hawaii?

Hawaii is the largest island in an archipelago, or chain of islands, known as the Hawaiian Islands. The islands were formed when volcanoes erupted on the seafloor long ago. Powerful forces inside Earth pushed the land up and out of the ocean. Each of the eight main islands is actually the top of one or more volcanoes.

The Big Island of Hawaii has active volcanoes. Those volcanoes erupt, but volcanoes on the other islands are inactive, or **dormant**. Hawaii has the world's largest volcano, Mauna Loa (MOW nuh LOH uh), and one of the world's most active volcanoes, Kilauea.

According to legend, it is bad luck to take lava rocks away from Kilauea Volcano. Park rangers say that they receive rocks in the mail, sent by people who have had bad things happen to them after taking the rocks.

Sitting on a Hot Spot

A volcano is an opening in Earth's surface. Powerful forces underground send hot, melted rock—magma—up through the opening. When magma reaches Earth's surface, it is called lava. The lava cools into hard rock (also called lava) around the opening. It builds up and forms a cone-shaped mound or mountain—a volcano.

Scientists believe that Hawaii lies over a very active place called a *hot spot*. Long ago magma was forced up through Earth's crust at this place. The lava on the surface then cooled and hardened, creating a volcano. In time the lava built up and rose above the ocean's surface as an island.

Force *and* Pressure

In many ways, geysers are similar to volcanoes. A geyser is a hot spring that erupts from below Earth's surface. Many people visit Yellowstone National Park to see Old Faithful, a famous geyser. Old Faithful sends steam and boiling water—as many as 8,000 gallons (30,000 liters) in less than five minutes—up out of the ground. The same forces of temperature and pressure deep within Earth cause volcanoes!

Old Faithful erupts every 50–90 minutes.

The Hawaiian Islands have many volcanoes. Why aren't all of them active today?

At one time each island sat over the hot spot. Magma erupted through an opening. Lava flowed out, cooled, and built up. In time an island was formed. Over many years, however, parts of Earth's surface, or crust, moved away from the hot spot. The Hawaiian Islands have moved with the crust. When the Big Island of Hawaii eventually moves away from the hot spot, its volcanoes will stop erupting too. Then a new island will start to form at the hot spot.

Magma is forced up to the surface and flows out as lava.

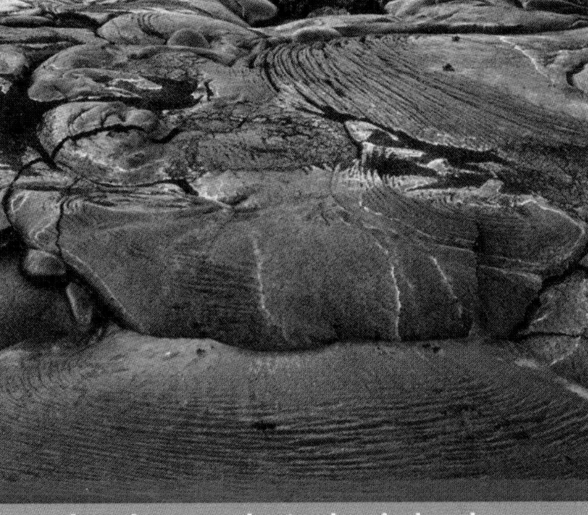

When lava cools, it slowly hardens into rock.

Over time a new island forms.

Is the Ground Moving?

Earth's crust is a layer of rock that covers the planet. It makes up the continents and the ocean basins—the surface at the bottom of the oceans. The crust is thicker under the continents than under the oceans. Beneath the crust is a thick layer of semi-solid rock called the *mantle*. The temperature of the mantle increases closer to Earth's center, or core. In some places the rock melts and becomes magma. The magma, which is lighter than solid rock, rises and cools a bit. It then falls back down. Magma constantly **circulates** like this under the crust.

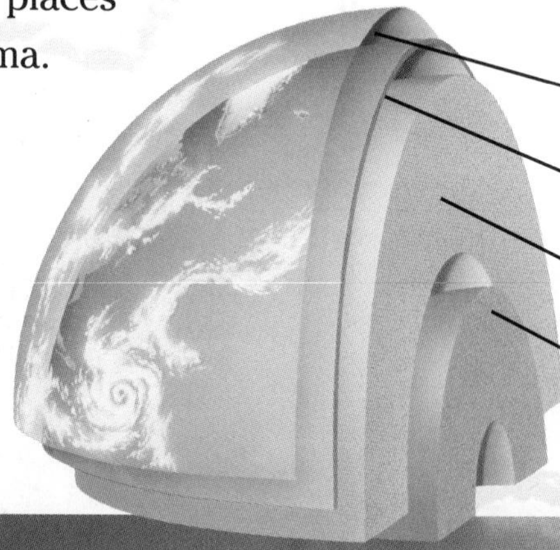

The rocky shore at Cligga Point, near Perranporth, Cornwall, England shows one landform found on Earth's crust.

Giant Moving Plates

The crust doesn't encircle our planet in one piece, like the shell of an egg. It is broken into plates, which rest on the mantle. The plates look like a gigantic jigsaw puzzle. The map below shows the boundaries, or outer edges, of the plates. Most of these boundaries are located beneath the oceans, so they cannot be seen. We can use measurements from satellites to track where the boundaries are.

These plates move! They travel only a few centimeters each year, but their movement causes changes in Earth's surface. The Pacific and Antarctic plates are two of the largest. The Pacific Plate is moving northwest, carrying the Hawaiian Islands in that direction. *Think back:* What happens to the islands as they move over the hot spot?

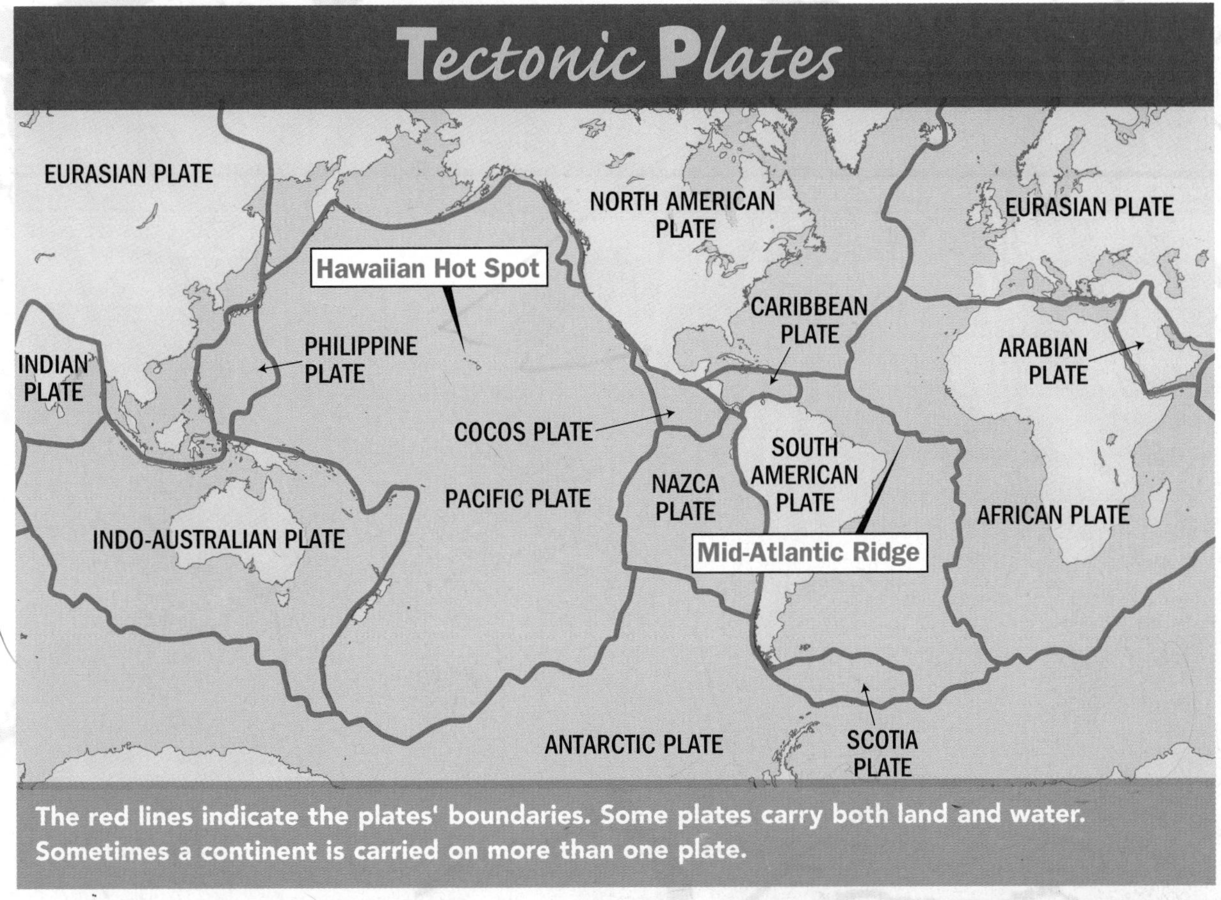

The red lines indicate the plates' boundaries. Some plates carry both land and water. Sometimes a continent is carried on more than one plate.

Plates Around the World

Forces deep inside Earth keep plates moving on the mantle. When one plate moves, the plates next to it are also affected. But how?

Sometime plates gradually "crash" into one another and over time create new landforms, such as mountains. The Andes Mountains of South America resulted from the crash between an ocean plate and a continental plate.

Hacienda Yanahurco is a large mountain ranch and private wildlife refuge located in the Andes Mountains. The Andes is the longest exposed mountain range in the world and stretches nearly the entire length of South America.

Plates sometimes rub against one another along their boundaries. Have you heard of the San Andreas Fault? This is a very long crack in Earth's crust caused by the boundaries of two plates that meet in California. Since the mid-1800s several strong earthquakes have occurred in California, at or near the San Andreas Fault.

Plates may pull away from each other, too, causing land to physically split apart. In Africa's Great Rift Valley, two continental plates are slowly pulling away from each other.

This section of the Great Rift Valley is in Eritrea.

This aerial view of the San Andreas Fault shows that valleys, mountain fronts, and lines of lakes have formed along it.

The light-blue area shown snaking through the center of the Atlantic Ocean is an example of a mid-ocean ridge.

mid-ocean ridge

New Crust

If you could drain the oceans, you would discover an amazing landscape. The movements of the plates have created mountains, trenches, and other features under the oceans.

Ocean ridges are places where the mantle pushes up between two plates. A crack forms at the top of the ridge. Magma flows up through the crack. Lava pours out onto the seafloor and cools into new rock—new crust. The undersea network of ridges totals more than 37,000 miles (60,000 kilometers) in length!

How to Make a Model Volcano

What you need:

safety goggles
small plastic bottle
¼ cup (60 ml) water
few drops of detergent
¼ cup (60 ml) vinegar
few drops of food coloring
1 tablespoon (15 ml) baking soda
small square of tissue

What to do:

1. Put on the goggles.
2. Put the water, detergent, vinegar, and food coloring into the bottle.
3. Wrap the baking soda in the tissue and drop it into the bottle.
4. Step back and watch what happens!

Where Is Pele Now?

In the story about Pele, the goddess moved through the Hawaiian Islands, making volcanoes and getting washed out of them. In reality the older islands in this archipelago are being worn down. Waves, wind, and rain easily erode the rock formed by volcanic lava. Over time these forces will wear away the older islands.

Right now another island is forming south of Hawaii. At the moment it is just a volcano erupting in the ocean. Check back in about 100,000 years to see how it's growing!

Chapter 2

The Arch Falls!

In Arches National Park near Moab, Utah, rocks seem to balance atop one another, spires reach up to the sky, and arches curve across the landscape. This unusual scenery is the result of forces of nature.

Long ago there was an ocean beneath the park. The sea evaporated, or changed from a liquid to a vapor, but it left behind a bed of salt. This salt bed is very thick—thousands of feet deep in some places. Over the years thick layers of rock buried the salt bed. The weight of the rock put a lot of pressure on the salt, and salt under pressure moves. Eventually the salt pushed itself up through the rock, forming domes.

Wall Arch *before it fell in August 2008*

More changes happened. Water **seeped** into cracks in the rock, and then ice formed. Enough ice formed that it put pressure on the rock, eventually causing pieces to break off. Wind also eroded the rock, blowing away even more small pieces. Little by little, as water and ice and wind continued to affect the rock, larger chunks fell. Sometimes parts of the rock were strong enough or balanced enough to remain even when other parts fell. The result was an arch.

There are more than 2,000 arches in Arches National Park. The smallest ones have a three-foot (one meter) opening. The longest, Landscape Arch, has an opening about 300-feet (91 meters) wide! Because forces continue to affect the rock, some arches fall and others reshape. In recent years large slabs of rock have fallen from the underside of Landscape Arch, leaving the arch thinner. But still it stands. Other arches collapse completely. In August 2008 nature's forces took its toll on Wall Arch, destroying what was the 12th largest arch in the park.

Wall Arch
after it fell

A ranger at the park tells more about **Arches National Park.**

Reporter: What are your responsibilities as ranger at the park?

Ranger: I supervise the team of interpretive rangers; they do the "real" work. Interpretive rangers teach people. They share the stories about what makes Arches National Park special. They give visitors an awareness of their role of protecting this beautiful place.

Reporter: Will other arches fall down like Wall Arch did?

Ranger: Yes, all arches will eventually fall. Gravity happens!

Reporter: Do you have a favorite arch?

Ranger: Wow, a favorite? Each arch has its own special character. One of the best things about arches is that they can look like so many things—an elephant parade (Parade of Elephants), eye glasses (North and South Windows). I like to imagine all sorts of shapes in the rocks, and not just the arches!

Reporter: What surprises visitors to Arches National Park?

Ranger: The park is in a desert, but there are many plants and animals here. That surprises people. People are also surprised that the arches fall down!

South Window **Arch**

Parade of
Elephants

Chapter 3
A Big Desert Gets Bigger

The Kalahari is a desert in southern Africa. It covers about 100,000 square miles (about 260,000 square kilometers), and scientists think it may still be increasing in size. Why is this happening?

Droughts are periods of very dry weather and little rain. They are often linked to **climate** change and are part of the reason why the Kalahari seems to be growing. Without rain, soil dries out. Plants die. Soon plant roots no longer hold down the dusty soil and sand, and winds carry it away. When the winds stop, the dust and sand fall, often covering green, growing areas. In this way fertile land—land rich in nutrients and water to make healthy plants grow—becomes desert. Growing deserts hurt the survival of living things in these places. Animals and humans are forced to move to places where it is possible for them to survive or they risk death.

By moving sand and dust, sandstorms sometimes cause deserts to grow.

A farmer in Niger, Africa, inspects his crop.

Over many thousands of years, deserts have both grown and become smaller. This is a natural cycle of the land and may help explain the spread of the Kalahari.

Other changes, however, have proven to be direct results of human activity. For example, in some places people raise cattle at the edge of a desert area. Cattle graze there eating the plants. Normally these plants enrich the soil and hold it in place. Without the plants the soil loses nutrients and dries out even more. Soon the soil is so poor that plants cannot grow and the cattle can no longer graze. In this way humans cause desertification. The once fertile land dries out and slowly turns into a desert.

Chapter 4

Climate Change

Climate is the average condition of the weather at a place over time. Climate change affects all living things. That is why scientists study it so closely.

What Is Global Warming?

One sign of climate change is global warming. Global warming is the rise in the average temperatures of Earth's atmosphere. The atmosphere is the blanket of air that surrounds our planet. Global warming can make some places on Earth hotter and drier. The Kalahari is one example of this. Global warming also melts ice at the North Pole and may cause places in the tropics to become dry.

Earth's atmosphere contains dust, water, and gases, such as carbon dioxide. Sunlight passes through the atmosphere and warms Earth's surface. Water vapor and other gases in the atmosphere retain some of this heat and control Earth's climate. This is known as the greenhouse effect. Gases that trap the sun's heat are called greenhouse gases.

A greenhouse traps heat from the sun. Its glass or plastic panels let in light but keep heat from escaping. This causes the greenhouse to heat up. It keeps plants in it warm enough to live in wintertime.

There is a balance between carbon dioxide and oxygen, which living things need. Greenhouse gases serve a good purpose, up to a point. They keep Earth's temperatures **stable**.

Global warming happens when there is too much of the greenhouse gases. The atmosphere then traps more heat. As a result, the temperature of Earth's atmosphere rises.

Over the last several decades, many more greenhouse gases have gone into the atmosphere. These gases are produced by the burning of coal and gas for fuel, among other things. These added gases are likely one major reason average temperatures have risen. For example, the average global temperature in 1920 was about 56.4°F; in 1960, about 57.2°F; in 2000, about 57.9°F. Rises like these may seem small. However, some scientists believe rising temperatures have caused some important changes.

Coal-fired power plants send significant amounts of greenhouse gases into the atmosphere.

Melting Ice

Global warming can cause climate change, but climates have changed before. So why is global warming a serious concern today?

Have you ever seen a glacier? About 20,000 years ago, these huge sheets of ice covered about 30 percent of Earth. Scientists believe that Earth has had several ice ages, separated by periods of warming. During ice ages Earth's climate zones, or regions, are colder and glaciers cover large areas of Earth's surface. In warmer times the glaciers retreat, or melt. In some places during some of these warmer times, temperatures on Earth may have been even higher than they are now. But at those times Earth's human population was far smaller than it is now, so the effect was not as noticeable.

These two images show glacial change to Chaney Glacier from 1911 to 2005 at Glacier National Park in Montana.

Today huge glaciers of melting ice from Earth's polar regions are more of a danger. The gradual rise in sea levels caused by the melting ice can lead to disaster for people living in coastal areas. People living inland are also affected because the people once living on the coast now move into their areas, often causing overpopulation.

El Niño

El Niño is a warming climate change that lasts for a relatively short time. Changing currents in the Pacific Ocean create changes in the weather. El Niño brings heavy rains to some places. It causes flooding in South America and mudslides along the coast of California, as shown in this photograph. On the other hand, places in Southeast Asia that usually get lots of rain become dry during El Niño years.

Hurricanes

On September 8, 1900, a hurricane hit Galveston, Texas. More than 8,000 people died when eight- to fifteen-foot tides caused by the hurricane's high winds covered the entire island city. More than half of all the homes and buildings were destroyed. To date, that hurricane has killed more people in the United States than any other weather disaster.

Hurricanes continue to cause **devastation**. In 2005 Hurricane Katrina and Hurricane Rita caused severe damage in the Gulf Coast and along the Atlantic coast. In 2008 Hurricane Ike damaged much of the Texas coast. Then it traveled north through the Midwest and into Canada. This hurricane was one of the most destructive storms on record.

Hurricanes form over warm ocean water. Global warming raises ocean temperatures. As a result more water vapor evaporates into the air over the oceans. Some scientists have shown that with a warmer, wetter atmosphere, hurricanes become stronger. When they come ashore, hurricanes can destroy more property and can kill more people than any other kind of extreme weather.

This photograph shows destruction caused by Hurricane Ike along the beach of Galveston, Texas.

Droughts

An increase in the atmosphere's temperature can lead to a change in Earth's water cycle. When temperatures become warmer, there is more evaporation from water sources such as oceans, lakes, rivers, and the groundwater beneath Earth's surface. Higher temperatures also increase the rate at which plants transpire, or release water into the atmosphere.

In areas not located near a water source, an increase in evaporation and the rate at which plants release water vapor into the air can dry out plants and soil. There are fewer clouds and less rain. Less water will seep into the ground. An area like this could face more droughts. Too little water in an area affects humans, plants, and animals that live in this environment.

Scientists are unsure how drier climates will affect wildfires. Lightning from storms can ignite wildfires in dry areas. Drier conditions produce fewer storms, but any fires that do occur in dry areas may be more intense.

Droughts can lead to damaged crops.

This 50,000 acre wildfire occurred at Henry Coe State Park in California.

Floods

Too *much* water can affect human beings, plants, and animals, as well. In areas located near a water source, an increase in the temperature of Earth's atmosphere can lead to more clouds, evaporation, and transpiration. With more water vapor stored in the atmosphere, there will be more rain. A steady increase in the amount of rain an area receives will lead to more water seeping into the ground and flowing into an area's surface and ground water.

This could lead to more flooding and the formation of new lakes and rivers on ground that was once dry. If there is more water underground and more surface water covering an area, everything will be wetter. This affects the types of plants that are able to grow in an area as well as the humans and animals that live there.

Floods affect many parts of the world, including this community in Portland, Oregon.

Seasonal Changes

Warmer temperatures affect the seasons. These changes also affect living things. If spring comes earlier, farmers may plant crops earlier. In some places this means a longer growing season and more crops. However, some crops may mature before insects are available to pollinate them. In addition, the longer season means crops may need more water to keep from drying out.

Because of seasonal changes, some plant and animal species are moving. For example, to escape hot summers red foxes are moving north, where they have to compete for food with Arctic foxes. Butterflies, many kinds of birds, some mammals, and some plants are moving up mountain sides and adapting to conditions at higher altitudes. Therefore, the effects these animals had on their previous environments no longer exist. This forces the living things remaining there to make their own adaptations or struggle to survive.

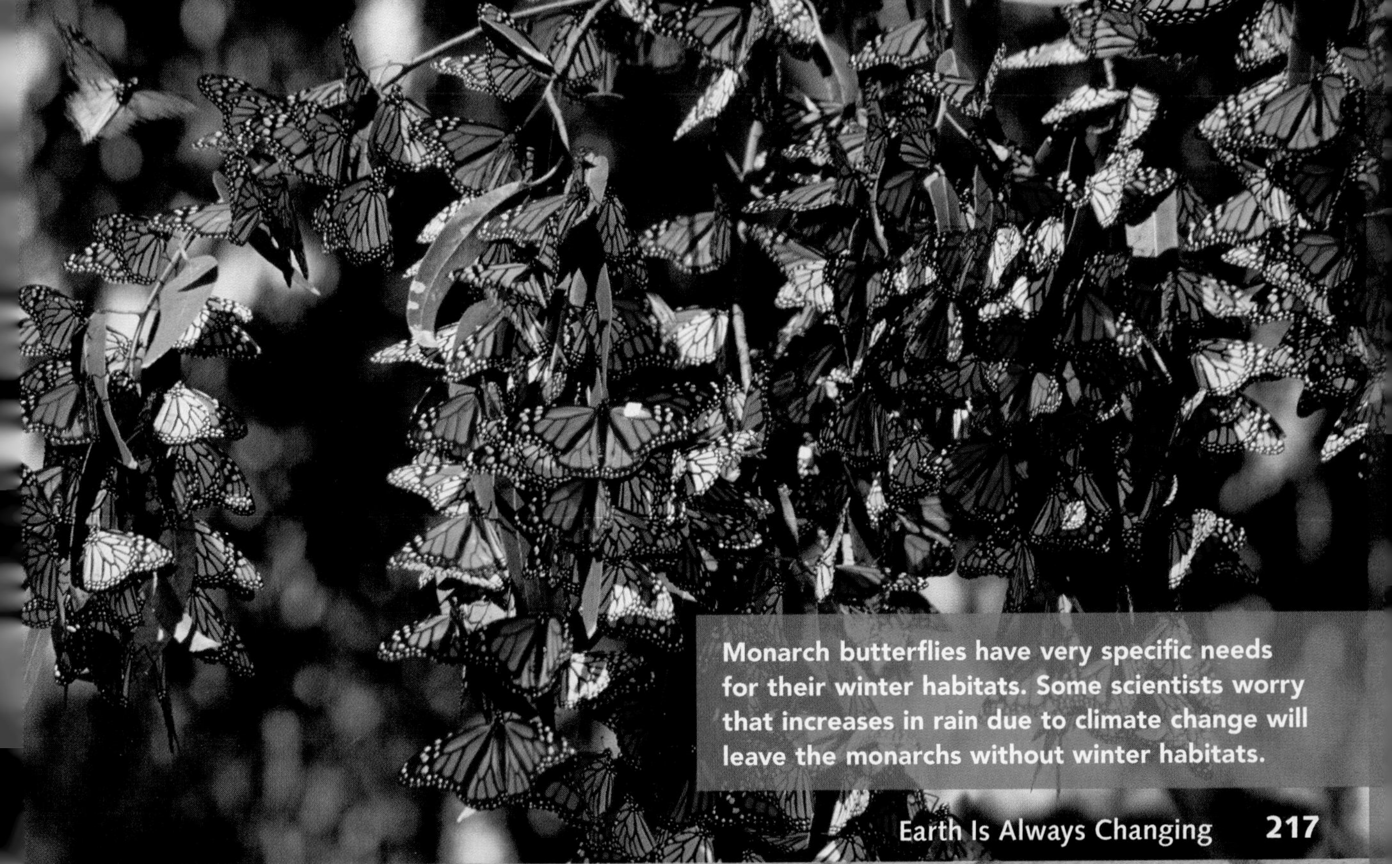

Monarch butterflies have very specific needs for their winter habitats. Some scientists worry that increases in rain due to climate change will leave the monarchs without winter habitats.

Living Things

Warmer temperatures have been linked to melting of Arctic ice. Polar bears need this ice to survive. They can die if the ice floes from which they hunt are too small or too far away from each other.

Other living things are affected by climate change in unique ways. In 1997, near Alaska in the Bering Sea, there was an early, massive "bloom" of microscopic plants. The huge numbers of plants so discolored the water that the sea turned turquoise! Scientists suspect that part of the reason the plants bloomed early is because the temperature of the water rose.

Polar bears will be threatened if global warming melts polar ice.

Responding to Climate Change

Climate change can create serious problems. Climate change affects everyone on Earth. Scientists continue to study the problem. Governments are working together to find solutions. What can you do to help? Here are some ideas:

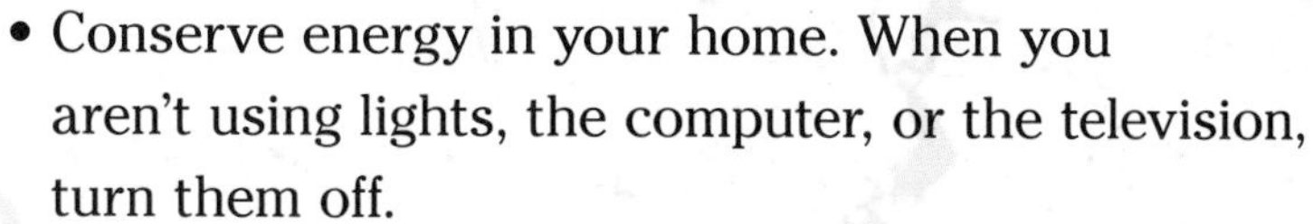

- Conserve energy in your home. When you aren't using lights, the computer, or the television, turn them off.
- Take shorter showers with warm, instead of hot, water.
- Don't depend on a car so much. Can you walk to places? Can you ride a bike? Can you combine errands? Can you carpool?
- Recycle paper, plastic, glass, and cans.
- Plant a tree!
- Keep learning about global warming and ways to solve it. Tell other people what you're learning—and what they can do to help too!

Earth is always changing! Mountains form. Islands disappear. The ground cracks. Deserts grow. Polar ice melts. All these changes—and more—are caused by forces at work on Earth.

- Some forces that change Earth's surface work quickly. Others do their work over long periods of time.
- A destructive force like a volcano can create a new landform.
- Water and wind are powerful enough to break apart rock.
- Earth's climate changes. In the past there have been ice ages as well as periods of warming.
- Global warming is one example of climate change. It can affect many living things.

PLANET PATROL

A Kid's Action Guide to Earth Care

by MARYBETH LORBIECKI
illustrated by NANCY MEYERS

The More Kinds, the Better

Have you ever taken apart a radio or computer and tried to put it back together? There are hundreds of pieces, and it's hard to tell what they all do. But if one part is missing, a job won't get done. Other parts won't be able to do their jobs either.

The Earth works the same way. Different places, such as small areas of woods, ocean, desert, or rain forest, are called habitats. Each habitat has its own kind of soil, landscape, weather patterns, and mix of plants and animals. All these parts work together.

Scientists often judge how healthy a place is by how many different species, or kinds, of creatures and plants live in an area. For example, in a healthy stream you may find stone flies and dragonflies, skinks and frogs, snails, clams, and many kinds of fish. The more different species there are in one place, the more jobs get done, the more food is made and eaten, and the more healthy a place is. That's **diversity**.

How to Heal a Habitat

In Kenya, a cement company had stripped the top layers of soil and stone from 900 acres of land. This left a dusty, rocky place without trees, grass, or flowers. But a scientist named Dr. René Haller had a plan to heal this habitat. In the early 1970s, he dug into the crumbly limestone and planted hardy, fast-growing trees and grasses. After a layer of dead leaves piled up, he added millipedes. These bugs ate the leaves and left droppings that helped improve the soil. Then Dr. Haller made fishponds and brought in larger wild animals, such as antelope and oryx.

The animals drank at the ponds and ate the leaves, bark, and grasses. The animals' manure made the soil richer, and more plant and animal species appeared. Then lions moved in to hunt. Because of Dr. Haller's efforts, local people can now fish and hunt there. Others have jobs working to restore the land. "It's surprising what nature can do when you lend a helping hand," said Dr. Haller.

ACTION TIP - SPECIES COUNT

List all the species you can find in your backyard, schoolyard, or park. Sort the species into plants, insects, birds, reptiles, amphibians, fish, and mammals. You can look them up in field guides. See how many different species live right alongside you!

We Are All Related

Doctors study how a body works, and **ecologists** study how the earth and its habitats work. They want to discover the relationships between species, and how each species relates to the land, water, and air.

Like a spiderweb, everything in nature is connected in many different ways. Some species share homes. Others eat the same food—or each other. Some animals live in the fur or hair of other animals or clean their hosts' teeth. All species depend on others for survival. Scientists call these webs of life interdependency. And if just one species in a web is removed, the whole web is harmed.

"I'll have what he's having."

Otters and Urchins

Sea otters love to eat crabs. So do people. Crab fishermen used to kill otters so there would be more crabs for them to catch. But when the otters disappeared, so did the seals and bald eagles. Why? Because seals and eagles depend on otters. Besides crabs, otters also eat sea urchins, and the urchins eat sea plants. Without otters, the sea urchins multiplied. The urchins ate up most of the kelp and sea grasses in the area. The fish that lived among these sea plants swam away. The seals and eagles that ate the fish had to look for new homes, too.

Eventually, crab fishermen got the point. They stopped hunting otters, and the sea plants grew back. Soon the fish, seals, and eagles returned. Nature was back in balance.

ACTION TIP - BE A SPECIES SPY!

Pick a species that lives near you—it could be in a garden, pond park, or yard. Visit the place it lives every day at the same time and watch the species quietly for 15 to 30 minutes. Keep a journal with notes and/or sketches. Does your species act differently when the weather changes or when other animals are near? Pretty soon you'll get to know that animal—how it acts and how it is connected to other species.

Saving Species

Endangered: Panda

Endangered: Green Sea Turtle

Did you know that pandas, snow leopards, mountain gorillas, Atlantic salmon, green sea turtles, and blue whales may soon become extinct? They could disappear from the earth forever. Right now, thousands of mammals, birds, insects, fish, reptiles, amphibians, and plants you've never even heard of are struggling to stay alive. Other species have already been wiped out.

Scientists and governments label struggling species as endangered (at serious risk of dying out) or threatened (almost endangered). The main reasons that species become endangered are:

- ☹ Loss of their habitat
- ☹ Invasion by a new species that takes away their homes or food, or brings deadly diseases
- ☹ Too much hunting, trapping, or poisoning
- ☹ Pollution
- ☹ Major changes in weather patterns

Schoolyard Scientists

Why are burrowing owls becoming rarer? To find out, students in Fort Myers, Florida, built owl perches on their playground so they could watch the owls and take notes. Their observations became part of the University of Florida's study on burrowing owls and their habitat needs. Kids at other schools have joined in wildlife research projects. Fifth-graders in Baltimore used Eye of the Falcon software to track young bald eagles around Chesapeake Bay. Perhaps researchers at a university or nature center near you could use your help.

A Howling Good Time

The woods of Wisconsin were once home to many wolves. But by 1960, every wolf in the state had been shot, poisoned, trapped, or driven into Canada. Without these predators, deer herds grew too large. The herds stripped forests of bark and leaves. By the end of each winter, many deer had starved.

To help the state bring back the wolves, children in northern Wisconsin joined the Adopt-a-Wolf program. They taught adults not to be afraid of wolves and helped pay for adding new wolves to the wild. Slowly, the wolves returned, and the forests and deer herds grew healthier.

How to Save a Mint

In California, school-children discovered that a rare desert plant called the San Diego mesa mint lived in only two places on the earth. One site was nearby—and a home builder was about to bulldoze it! The school's ecology club alerted the state's Department of Fish and Game. They wrote letters to the local newspaper, made door-to-door visits, and held neighborhood meetings. They let everyone know what was happening, and they saved a mint!

ACTION TIP - NATURE'S CALL

Call a local nature center or your state's office of the U.S. Fish and Wildlife Service to find out about the endangered species near you. (You can also visit the website of the National Wildlife Federation.) Pick a species and research its habits and habitat. Find out what can be done, and start your own club to help save your species.

ECO CHALLENGES

Breathing Hard

Thinking about air can be a breath-taking experience. Feel it as you breathe. Does it flow easily, or make your chest tight? Sniff it. Can you smell cut grass and flowering trees or something not so nice?

Air is made mostly of two gases: oxygen and carbon dioxide. Animals (that includes us!) use the oxygen (O^2) and breathe out the carbon dioxide (CO^2). In contrast, plants take in CO^2 and give back 0^2. Nature is in balance, right?

The trouble is, we humans also have vehicles and other machines that produce CO^2, so the plants can't keep up. Plus, there are other forms of air pollution. Anything that gives off smoke, fumes, and gas may cause problems: cars, trucks, and motorboats; lawn mowers and leaf blowers; barbecue grills and fires; factories and power plants; fertilizers and crop dust.

In the 1970s, laws were passed to make North American air cleaner, and they worked. That's something to cheer about! But big challenges remain.

Asthma Attacks!

Guess who can be hurt most by air pollution—kids! That's because their lungs are still developing. Many health professionals think more children are getting asthma (an illness causing coughing, wheezing, and difficulty breathing) because of indoor and outdoor air pollution. The EPA—the United States Environmental Protection Agency—now has a web site for kids with an air quality index (AQI). Using colors, it shows daily how safe the air is in major cities. So check it out!

"Motor vehicles are a major source of air pollution in the world."

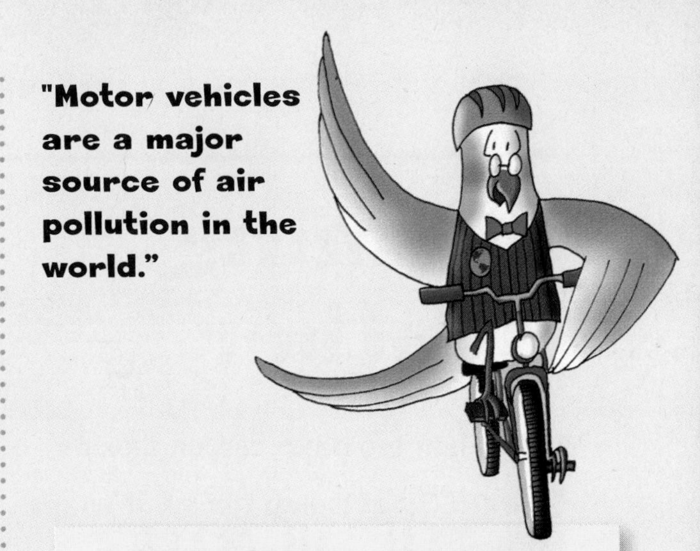

ACTION TIP - AIR TEST

Spread petroleum jelly inside four wide-mouth glass jars. Place one jar in your home and place one in a safe place outside. Put another in your classroom and one in a safe place outside your school. Keep a chart. After one week, compare the jars. Which jar is darkest? Look around. What things nearby could be causing pollution? What solutions can you suggest?

Pollution can mix with rain to make acid rain. This toxic mixture can burn holes in leaves, making plants and trees more open to disease. Acid rain can also ruin lakes and harm the fish (and anyone who eats them!).

Warming Weather

When too much carbon dioxide (CO^2) gets into the air, it wraps around the earth like a heavy blanket, warming up the planet. This dangerous change is known as global warming. It can make icy places such as Greenland, the Arctic, and Antarctica melt around the edges. This cold meltwater raises sea levels, cools sea temperatures, drops salt levels, and shifts the currents. These changes can kill ocean life. Sea levels are now rising at three times their usual rate. The seas may begin to flood low, coastal areas, such as Venice, Italy, and much of Florida.

Global warming can also change weather patterns, spread hot-weather diseases to new areas, and change plant and animal life in many ways. No one really knows what chain reactions these changes could cause in our lifetimes. Or our children's lifetimes. But some of the planet's most respected scientists are worried. While scientists and world leaders are talking and acting, so can we!

ACTION TIP - LOW-CAR DIET PLAN

For each mile you ride in a car (even a small car), one pound of CO2 is put into the air. For a day, jot down every mile you ride in a car. Add these miles up. How many pounds did you put into the air in one day? Try it for a week. Can you think of ways to reduce these pounds for the next week?

Nature Knows

Scientists studying wild plants and animals are seeing patterns in the changes to climate. Migrating birds are consistently coming to Wisconsin at least 10 days earlier in the spring and leaving 10 days later in the fall than they did in the 1930s. Flowers are blooming 10 days earlier, and growing seasons are ending 10 days later. In many places, the summer seasons are getting longer and hotter, and winters in northern and southern regions have less snow and ice.

A Hole in the Sky

Our planet has a protective shade around it called the **ozone** layer, which shields us from the sun's burning rays. However, the ozone layer is being thinned out by certain chemicals, such as chlorofluorocarbons, or CFCs. CFCs are used in aerosol spray cans, cleaners, foam, refrigerators, and freezers. In one area over the South Pole, the ozone layer has thinned so much it is referred to as the "ozone hole." So wear sunscreen and sunglasses, and buy hair spray, paint, and cleaners in pump spray bottles or cans instead of aerosols. And write your government officials, asking them to stop companies from using dangerous ozone-thinning chemicals.

Catching CO^2

A new machine can suck some carbon dioxide out of the air and pump it into deep holes in the earth. But CO^2 can only be buried in very hard rock, because it mixes with water and makes an acid that eats away soft rock. This tricky but promising new technology may prove helpful in getting rid of a little of the CO^2 already out there.

Shrinking Forests

One cure for too much CO^2 is more trees. For every pound of new tree wood grown, two pounds of CO^2 are absorbed from the air. Unfortunately, around the world, forests are being cut faster than they can grow back or be replanted. Some are being cleared permanently to make farm fields or cattle ranges. This can harm not just the places where the trees are cut, but the whole planet!

And trees are good for more than just cleaning the air. They give shade, so each tree makes a place cleaner and cooler. Their branches break the wind, stopping topsoil from blowing away. Their roots hold the soil in place. Animals use them for food and shelter. Can you think of anything more useful than a tree?

Rain-Forest Facts

☺ 40% of the world's oxygen comes from the Amazon rain forest.

☺ Many cancer-fighting drugs come from rain-forest plants. One of these, the rosy periwinkle, grows in only one place —the rain forest of Madagascar.

☺ Many things can be harvested from rain forests without cutting them down, including fruits such as bananas and oranges; spices such as cinnamon, paprika, and cloves; shade-grown coffee; rubber; nuts; cocoa beans; and wood oils.

☺ North America has rain forests, too. They are found in the Pacific Northwest: Oregon, Washington, and British Columbia. The bark of the yew trees there are used for cancer medicines.

ACTION TIP - HOW MANY TREES DO YOU OWE?

It's estimated that by the time we reach 80 years old, we each owe the earth 2,000 trees—to balance out the CO^2 we've breathed out plus the CO^2 we've added through the use of cars and electricity from power plants. This total doesn't even count the trees we use up in wood and paper products. If you start this year, how many trees do you need to plant each year to reach 2,000 by the time you are 80 years old? Better join with friends and family and start planting!

Beat the Stock Market—Plant a Tree!

In the early 1990s, you could buy a tree seedling for $5. A scientist estimated that in 50 years, that tree would provide goods and services worth about $191,000: $31,000 for making oxygen; $61,000 for cleaning the air of dusts, CO^2, and other gases; $37,000 for absorbing water and breathing the moisture into the air for rain clouds; $31,000 for adding nutrients to the soil; and $31,000 for providing wildlife homes and food. In 50 years, it would be worth 38,200 times its original $5 price tag. This doesn't even count the benefits that are harder to measure: it increased the value of the land, cut noise levels, shaded and cooled nearby homes (without air conditioning!), held the soil in place, and made its surroundings more beautiful.

Wow, money really does grow on trees!

Species Storehouses

Did you know that more species of ants live in one tree in a Peruvian rain forest than in all of England? Certain habitats, like rain forests and old-growth forests (wetlands and coral reefs, too!) are jammed with species. This diversity makes them super important, for they are the earth's living storehouses.

Stumped?

If trees are worth so much alive, should we stop cutting them completely? No! Then we couldn't ever build things of wood. But some ways of cutting trees are better than others.

Clear cutting, or cutting all the trees in a large area at once, can be disastrous. It leaves the ground bare, so that wind and rain can tear the topsoil away. Nearby rivers and lakes may become sludged with it. Shade plants and important soil organisms may die.

Selective cutting is healthier. Loggers carefully cut some trees and leave the rest to grow. The remaining trees hold down the topsoil and make seeds. Then it's easier for the forest to grow back naturally. There are healthier ways to replant trees, too. Scattering a mix of different ages and kinds of native trees is better than planting only one kind of tree in rows. Selective cutting and mixed plantings cost more money at first. But they also create more jobs and save the diverse life of our forests.

Tree Treasures

Tree products are almost endless. Besides things like fruits, nuts, and sap, trees give us lumber and furniture, paints and glues, fabrics and carpets, paper and some plastics . . . even Ping-Pong balls and insulation! Thankfully, some of these products can now be made out of other materials to save trees.

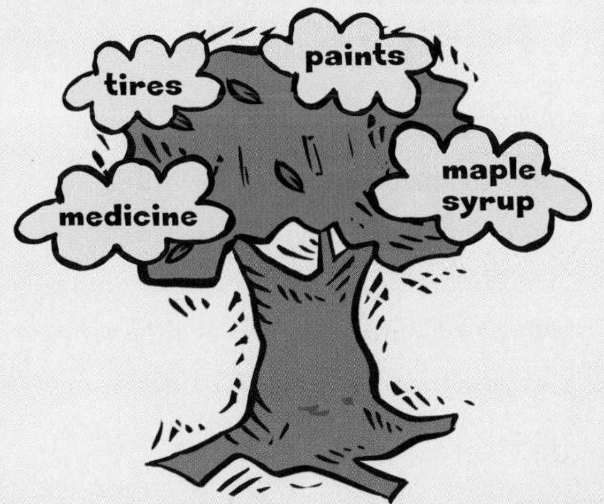

Planters for the Planet

After a forest fire in Indonesia, local Scouts planted 240 acres of trees. In Kenya, women's groups, schoolchildren, and communities have planted over 25 million trees. In El Segundo, California, third graders started the Tree Musketeers Club. (Kids in the club help other kids plant trees.) They also started an educational TV show, a water conservation program, and the Partners for the Planet Youth Summit. Think what you and your friends can do!

Falling Giants

Some of the largest and oldest living things on earth live right here in North America. California's giant redwood trees grow taller than the Statue of Liberty, weigh as much as 800 school buses, and live to be 3,500 years old. Yet it takes just two hours to cut down one of these giants.

Paper Possibilities

To save trees, paper can be made out of other materials, such as old clothes, algae, sugarcane, and kenaf (a fast-growing, woody-stemmed plant).

ACTION TIP - ADDRESSING THE PAPER PROBLEM

In North America, most of the trees we cut are used to make paper. And over half the garbage we throw out is paper. That means we are turning our trees into trash! So what can we do? Cut down on paper use! And RECYCLE. Every time we recycle a ton of paper, we save 17 trees, conserve energy, and prevent pollution.

"I made this paper from a pair of old blue jeans."

Sea Sickness

Oceans cover over three-fourths of the planet. Like forests, they give off moisture and oxygen and provide habitats for thousands of animals and plants. Unfortunately our oceans and marine wildlife are facing large troubles. Humans are polluting, poisoning, and changing the oceans in many ways:

- ☹ Oil spills from drilling and ships
- ☹ Soil, fertilizers, pesticides, and mining wastes that wash into the water
- ☹ Mercury and acid rain from polluted air
- ☹ Chemicals, sewage, and garbage dumped from ships and factories
- ☹ Invasive species carried in and on ships

Commercial fishing is adding to the problem. Populations of some fish, turtles, and other ocean animals are being harmed. Other animals are caught accidentally and die before they are thrown back. Still others get tangled in nets or lines and drown.

How can you help? Get to know your oceans and the amazing life in them. The more you know, the more you will be able to help protect them.

Where Has All the Color Gone?

Coral reefs and kelp beds are the ocean's rain forests. Coral reefs may contain over one-fourth of the ocean's species and may live to be 2.5 million years old. (They grow slowly!) But now these brightly colored reefs are turning white and dying. Pollution and temperature changes may be weakening them. So some scientists are helping them by zapping the live coral with electricity. This improves their ability to use calcium from the water to build their reefs. But more than anything, the coral need protection from pollution.

ACTION TIP - VISIT AN AQUARIUM

Take the time to read books about ocean life and visit aquariums. Beware of buying real seashells or sea animals such as sea horses or starfish. The people who sell these items often collect them while the animals are still alive. And if you find shells on the beach, be sure they are not occupied before bringing them home.

Kids to the Rescue!

In 1989, a group of kids in Alaska helped clean up after the tanker Exxon Valdez leaked oil. Sixth- and seventh-graders mucked around to count the injured and dead animals and plants. Their data has helped scientists understand oil spill effects. In 2002, Canadian high schoolers at a British Columbia leadership camp unveiled a technology they'd invented for faster oil-spill cleanup. To learn more about oil-spill cleanup efforts, visit the website of the Australian Maritime Safety Authority.

"Some of the most beautiful and amazing animals on earth live under the sea."

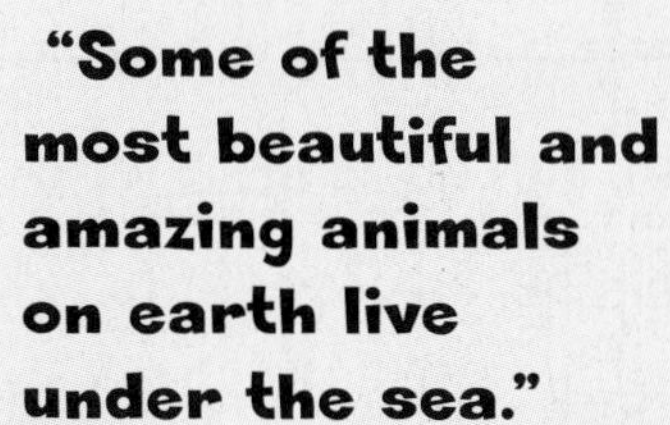

Wasting Away

Doesn't it seem like almost everything we do makes garbage? Food scraps, cans, bottles, packages, and wrappings are left after we eat. Paper and used envelopes pile up after we get the mail or do homework. There are broken games and toys, clothes we've outgrown, and books we no longer read. North Americans each throw away between 1,300 and 1,600 pounds (600–725 kg) of solid waste a year. How much do you weigh? Can you figure out how many times your own weight you create in garbage each year?

From sea to shining sea—and even under the sea—this garbage is piling up. Trash is dumped into landfills, down drains, into the ocean, into compost bins, and tossed around as litter. Some of these choices are better than others. But if we want to keep our planet from turning into one big garbage heap, we need to start rethinking what we buy and what we throw away.

ACTION TIP - DOWN WITH TRASH CONTEST

For one weekend, put all your personal trash in your own bag or basket. (Weigh the bag or wastebasket first.) At the end of the weekend, weigh the filled container. Subtract the weight of the bag or basket to find your total. How much trash did you make? How did your friends compare? The person who made the least trash wins. Share strategies for keeping trash totals down.

Trash around the World

Americans win first prize . . . for the amount of garbage they produce! The trash cans below show how much garbage the average person makes in different countries. Citizens of countries with less money usually make less garbage than citizens of countries with more money, because they buy fewer things and reuse more of them. Also, some countries encourage more reuse and less packaging.

United States 4 1/2 pounds

Canada 4 pounds

Sweden 2 pounds

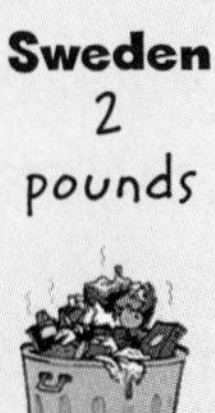

Japan 1 3/4 pounds

Philippines 1 pound

Egypt 3/4 pound

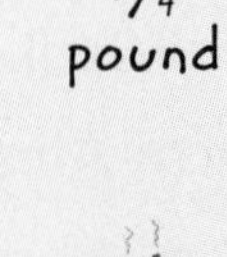

Sri Lanka 3/4 pound

Guana 1/2 pound

Garbage Archeology

What will archeologists dig up centuries from now to learn about us? Probably trash in our landfills! There, garbage gets smashed so tightly that even things that are biodegradable, or able to rot and break down, don't have enough oxygen to do so. Sometimes poisonous gases develop. Here's how long some pieces of trash take to biodegrade even if they do have oxygen:

Garbage, the Great Resource

Did you know that much of the garbage we throw away can be reused? Some leftover food and lawn waste can be turned into compost for the soil. You can clean and pass on old clothes, or turn them into scarves, rugs, or rags. Empty bottles and jars can be cleaned and refilled. Worn tires can be made into shoes or purses, or ground into roadway material. Decorate a cake, gift bow, or mosaic with old toy figures. Plastic containers can be used for planting or for sorting and storing things.

If an item can't be fixed or reused, it can probably be recycled or transformed into a brand new object. Factories melt glass bottles and jars into new glass containers, marbles, decorative tiles, and even surfboards! Metal objects are melted down and molded into car and bike parts, cookware, and yes, new cans! Plastic bottles go into everything from park benches and playground equipment to ski jackets. Used paper and cardboard can be remixed into new paper and cardboard. As you can see, garbage is a great resource!

Borrow It!

You don't always have to buy something new. Try borrowing what you need instead. Just remember the borrower's motto: Always return something in better shape than you received it!

Trash to Cash

To earn money, kids around North America collect bottles, cans, ink cartridges, and cell phones. They sell these items to recycling companies. This helps the environment AND makes money for the kids' groups and schools. Everybody wins!

"Americans recycle more than half of all their aluminum beverage cans and large appliances."

ACTION TIP - MAKE A SOIL FACTORY

Landfills get filled quickly with fall leaves, grass clippings and food scraps. Why not turn this waste into soil? All you need is space for a pile or bin behind your home or school. Try this experiment to see how composting works. Take an old plastic container and fill it with veggie scraps, dry leaves, and grass clippings. Punch holes in the container and put it outside in the sun. Stir it up every few days. To speed up the process, add some worms! You can even ask your school to start a worm composting program to clean up school lunch scraps.

Trashy Trivia

☺ North Americans are now recycling 28% of all their garbage. That is almost double what they did in 1993. But countries such as Austria, Belgium, Switzerland, and the Netherlands recycle at a rate of 70%.

☺ The United States recycles 42% of all paper and 40% of all plastic soft drink bottles. Even athletic shoes are being recycled!

☺ Some computer manufacturers take back used equipment and recycle the parts. Businesses and homeowners can donate their older computers to schools and nonprofit organizations.

☺ Recycling is good for the economy—it saves energy and materials PLUS creates jobs. The recycling industry employs more people than the mining industry and about the same number as the auto industry.

Transforming Transportation

It's a good thing our planet has as much creative energy as it has CO2. Inventors and scientists are working hard to develop new fuels so that we can reduce the number of vehicles that use gasoline. Some of these new fuels are alcohols (methanol and ethanol), hydrogen gas, natural gas, liquid natural gas, battery-stored electricity, liquids made from coal, and biodiesel fuels made from plant oils or animal fat. Some cars can even run on sunshine! Their special engines are solar powered, soaking up energy from the sun's heat and using that to run their engines. They don't pollute at all.

Unfortunately, most of these new cars are still very expensive and hard to find. In the meantime, we need to change our habits more than our cars. So walk, skateboard, bike, or skate to get where you need to go. Share rides and do all your errands in one big trip. Take buses, subways, and trains.

Catch a Ride on the Future

All-electric or hybrid vehicles—those that run on a combination of electricity and gas—are showing up all over. These vehicles include cars, buses, trolleys, and light-rail trains. Some of the new trains are powered by magnets, while electric buses have special rechargeable batteries. Over thirty U.S. cities, such as New York City; Santa Clara, California; Anderson, Indiana; Cedar Rapids, Iowa; and Honolulu, Hawaii are running electric or hybrid buses. Universities and school districts are changing over, too.

Take the Veggie Van!

When you're in Yellowstone National Park, you may smell French fries when a bus goes by. That's because some Yellowstone buses run on 20% recycled cooking oil (such as mustard seed or soybean oil) and 80% regular diesel fuel. Other Yellowstone buses run on pure biodiesel fuels. These fuels, made from animal or veggie fats, are biodegradable, or able to rot away, and the exhaust is not harmful. There are already some vehicles that run on old cooking grease. Perhaps someday you will pull up your car to a fast-food restaurant and say, "Fill 'er up!"

Race for Clear Skies

Every spring, student teams and car manufacturers enter their new, earth-friendly vehicles in the Swiss Tour de Sol or the American Tour de Sol. Cars are judged on how easy they are on the environment and how well they perform. Some cars reach 127 miles per gallon (54 km per liter) with 1/7 of the exhaust of a regular car. The U.S. Department of Energy sponsors the Junior Solar Sprint for solar powered cars created by sixth-, seventh-, and eighth-grade students. So start inventing!

ACTION TIP - MAP YOUR WAY TO CLEANER AIR

Find or make a map of your neighborhood. Mark the locations of your school, your friends' homes, parks, gyms, place of worship, places you shop or hang out. Now map the safest routes for biking or walking to these places. If there aren't sidewalks, bike paths, or bike lanes, talk to your neighborhood group or the city or town council.

"The average piece of food eaten in America has traveled 1,300 miles. That's a lot of gas for one tomato!"

Powerful Choices

What makes your lights go on, your computer work, and your TV run? Electricity. But what makes electricity? Most electricity is made in only a few ways—by burning coal, oil, gas, or garbage; through nuclear processes; or by capturing the power of river water with a dam.

All of these processes can be harmful. Burning materials puts smoke into the air. Coal mining usually strips the land of trees and topsoil, and leaves behind wastes that wash into rivers, lakes, and oceans. Drilling and shipping oil can lead to large oil spills. Nuclear energy doesn't give off air pollution, but it leaves behind potentially dangerous wastes that last for hundreds of thousands of years. Dams cause the fewest problems, because they are naturally powered by the water, but they change a river's habitat, which hurts fish and other wildlife. So what can we do?

We can make electricity with other natural energies, such as wind power, solar energy, ocean waves and tides, and geothermal heaters (powered by the earth's heat). Methods that take advantage of the earth's own powers are called renewable energies.

Pleasant Valley Is Pleasanter

This New York town provides power for its 10,000 citizens with wind power. Its changeover from a coal-burning power plant has saved the town from putting 356,000 pounds of CO^2 per year into the skies. The governor has pledged to make the wind the source of one-fourth of the state's power by 2013.

Garbage Power

Garbage may soon provide electricity in a whole new way, with an invention called the Plasma Converter. It uses a stream of heat three times hotter than the sun to vaporize garbage. Vaporizing the garbage breaks it down into its atomic elements, or its smallest mineral ingredients. The process not only gets rid of the garbage but produces clean-burning gases that can be used to create electricity.

ACTION TIPS - CONSERVING EVERY DAY

☺ Turn off the lights, radio, TV, CD or DVD player, and computer when you leave a room.

☺ During the winter, open your shades to let the sun in. Wear the "layered" look—a sweater or sweatshirt worn over another shirt—and turn down your furnace to 65 to 68 degrees Fahrenheit (18 to 20°C). Before snuggling into bed, turn it lower.

☺ During the summer, shut shades during the day to keep out the sun's heat. At night, open your windows to let in evening breezes. Save air conditioning only for the hottest of days!

☺ Wash dishes by hand, or, when using the dishwasher, fill it up completely, then stop it before the drying cycle. Let the air dry your dishes instead.

☺ Ask your parents to use energy-efficient light bulbs and appliances.

Coal Countdown

How much CO^2 is given off at a coal-burning plant to power your appliances?

Television	1 hour	.64 pounds
100-watt light bulb	10 hours	1.3 pounds
Clothes dryer	1 load	10 pounds
Refrigerator	1 day	12.8 pounds

That's why turning off anything you're not using is SO important!

"The average American uses enough energy a year to put 20.5 tons of carbon dioxide into the air."

Kid Power for the Planet

When kids pay attention and care for the environment, they inspire adults to do it! That's why you have so much power.

You have seen stories of kids who have worked together with their parents, teachers, or group leaders to make their place on the planet cleaner or better for wildlife. There are so many more, they can't fit in this book! Kids in the U.S. have saved acres of woodlands and rain forests, and they have convinced restaurants to use more earth-friendly packaging. Canadian kids have transformed yards and vacant lots into wildlife habitats. But the good work doesn't stop there. Around the world, the list of children's accomplishments is as endless as their imagination and commitment.

We know YOU too can help make the world a better place. Think about your favorite Planet Patrol ideas and get started. **The Planet Needs You!**

In Kenya, children taught conservation classes for adults.

Egyptian kids cleaned up streets and parks.

Kids in the U.S. shared blankets with homeless people.

Earth Day Is Every Day

In North America, people celebrate our planet on Earth Day, April 22. That leaves the rest of the year to do the work of taking care of it well!

Planet Care=Peace

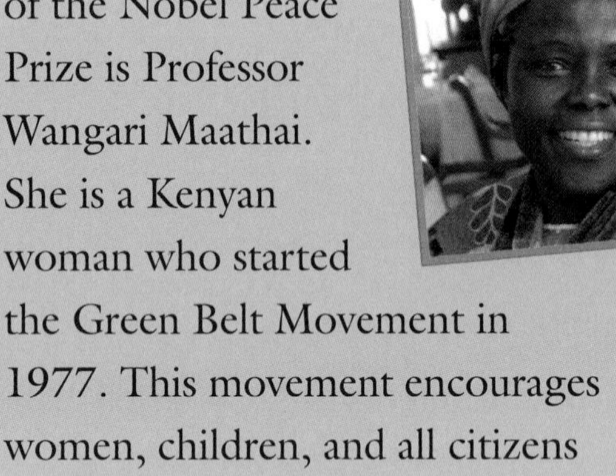

One of the most recent winners of the Nobel Peace Prize is Professor Wangari Maathai. She is a Kenyan woman who started the Green Belt Movement in 1977. This movement encourages women, children, and all citizens to plant trees and care for the environment.

ACTION TIP - PUTTING PAPER TO GOOD USE

To let local or national leaders know about a planet patrol problem, find out all the information you can on the subject from many sides first. (Don't forget the scientific information—you can even call experts at universities.) Then you're ready to write. Begin with a few sentences that ask your questions or state your concerns. Then explain your ideas for a solution. Finally, thank the person for reading your letter, and ask for a reply. Give your name and address, and perhaps your age. Consider sending a similar letter to your local newspaper. And don't forget to have your friends and others write, too!

UNIT 5

New People, New Places

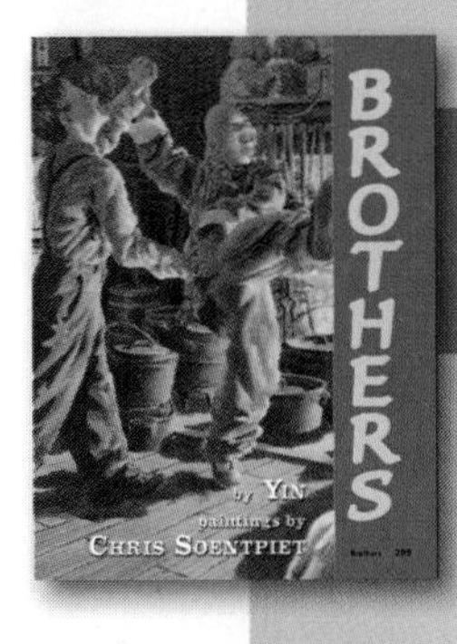

What events have shaped America?

Focus Questions

Why did America grow geographically?

Why do people move to new places?

What did America represent to immigrants?

How do people shape a nation?

A Nation

by Gordon West

Grows

This land is your land, this land is my land
From California, to the New York island;
From the redwood forest, to the Gulf Stream waters;
This land was made for you and me.

As I was walking that ribbon of highway,
I saw above me that endless skyway;
I saw below me that golden valley;
This land was made for you and me.

from *"This Land Is Your Land"* by Woody Guthrie

Contents

Chapter

Chapter 1

"Seeing the Elephant"

Have you ever seen an elephant? In the early years of the United States, elephants were rare, so a circus with an elephant drew large crowds. An elephant looked big and **intimidating**, but Americans wanted to see one!

Later, Americans who moved west sometimes spoke about "seeing the elephant." They meant that making the move was dangerous—but that it was exciting too.

Looking West

In 1803 President Thomas Jefferson acquired a large area of land, called the Louisiana Purchase, for an expanding United States. Jefferson hoped that it had a water route across North America to the Pacific Ocean. Such a water route would be good for transportation and trade. To explore this land Jefferson sent Meriwether Lewis and William Clark.

Meriwether Lewis

William Clark

Lewis and Clark kept detailed journals. They also sent a live lizard to President Jefferson.

The Corps of Discovery

In the early 1800s people wondered what would be found in the land beyond the Mississippi River. No one had made accurate maps of this land. Lewis and Clark led a team of explorers called the Corps of Discovery. Clark carefully mapped trails for later travelers to follow.

People living on the East Coast did not know for certain what would be found there. What unknown animals or plants might live there? Jefferson speculated, or thought, that Lewis and Clark might actually see live woolly mammoths and erupting volcanoes during their expedition, or journey. Jefferson was mistaken about the woolly mammoth. However, the Corps described 122 animals and identified 178 new plants. The animals and plants had never been seen or described by scientists, although they were probably known by the native people living in the area.

The Corps also learned about the lives of the different Native-American groups they met on their trip.

Although the Corps didn't find a water route across North America, they brought back a great deal of important information about the land that made up the Louisiana Purchase.

An Amazing Adventure

Lewis and Clark and the Corps of Discovery began their historic trip in May 1804. They traveled in a keelboat—55 feet long and able to carry ten tons of supplies—and two smaller boats called pirogues (pi ROHG). In the Great Plains the expedition saw animals that were unknown to people living in the Eastern part of the United States: coyotes, antelope, mule deer, and others. On the trip the Corps navigated the Missouri River and crossed the Bitterroot Mountains in what is now the state of Montana. Finally, in November, they reached the Pacific Ocean. They returned to St. Louis in September 1806 after a trip of over 7,000 miles.

Along the way the explorers faced cold, hunger, and other dangers. They often got help from the Native Americans they met. When Lewis and Clark returned, people called them heroes. Today we know them as great adventurers. Although they were not trained as scientists, they made many contributions to the scientific knowledge of the areas they explored.

OREGON COUNTRY

Lewis and Clark's trail west

Lewis's trail east

Clark's alternate trail east

SPANISH TERRITORY

Pacific Ocean

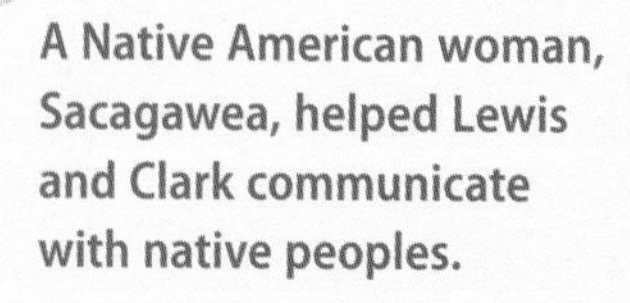

A Native American woman, Sacagawea, helped Lewis and Clark communicate with native peoples.

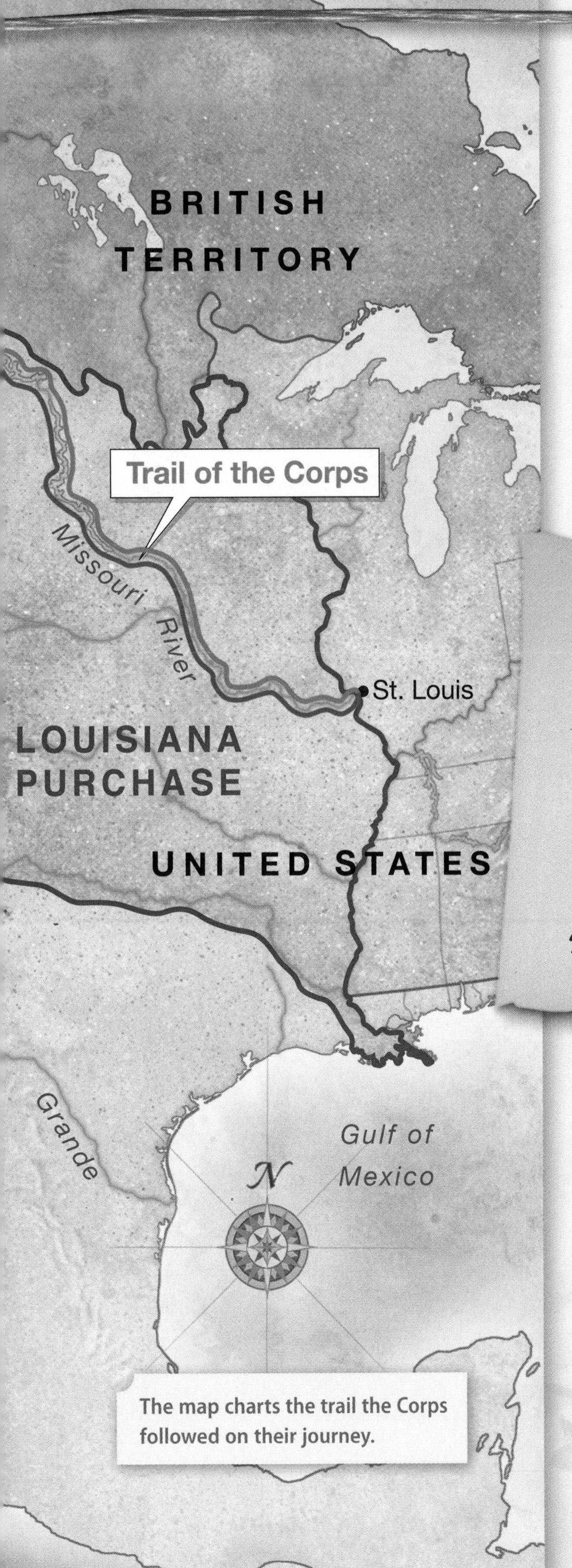

The map charts the trail the Corps followed on their journey.

The Journals Both Lewis and Clark kept journals. These journals included detailed observations of what they saw and experienced on their travels. The explorers wrote about huge herds of buffalo—scientifically known as bison—rock towers, snowy mountain peaks, and encounters with Native Americans. Here is an entry from Clark's journal. Does the old-fashioned spelling look strange? Try reading the entry aloud.

From the Journal of William Clark

Sunday, May 5, 1805

"In the evening we saw a Brown or Grisley beare on a sand beech, I went out with one man Geo Drewyer & Killed the bear, which was verry large and a turrible looking animal. . . . I think his weight may be stated at 500 pounds [227 kilograms]."

Grizzly bears were honored and respected by Native Americans for their intelligence and strength.

Going West for Land and Gold

In the nineteenth century a trip to the western United States was long and difficult. You may ask: "Why would people go?" There are several important reasons. Many people wanted something new. They wanted better opportunities for making money and a better life. Other people wanted their own land for farming.

So in the 1800s people who lived in the East began moving westward. These people became known as "settlers." Some of the settlers followed the Santa Fe Trail. This trail led from Independence, Missouri, to Santa Fe, New Mexico. Other people traveled northwest from Independence. This journey along the Oregon Trail was more than 2,000 miles long. It crossed the Rocky Mountains and could take five to six months to complete.

The United States government provided help for these settlers. It gave land to people who were willing to clear it—cut down trees and brush—and farm it. After five years of living on the land, the people then owned it.

This cartoon from 1849 poked fun at how desperate many easterners were to get to California.

This pioneer family paused in Nebraska to mark their journey.

In 1848 a major discovery encouraged more people to travel to the West. Gold was discovered in California!

John A. Sutter was born in Baden, Germany, in 1803. He was an admirer of the United States, and friends persuaded him to settle here. Sutter became a businessman in California. He owned a sawmill near Coloma, California. One day a worker found a piece of gold. Sutter tried to keep the find a secret, but the news spread quickly. Thousands of prospectors, or gold-seekers, raced to California. Some came overland by wagon train, others by ocean-going ships, with a single goal—to find gold and get rich.

Most prospectors didn't find gold. Some of them left, but many of them stayed in the area. Some who stayed became farmers; others became storekeepers and business owners. Many of these people grew rich without finding a single speck of gold.

Miners in California using a pan to sift for gold.

What the Journey Was Like

In the nineteenth century any journey west was a challenge. One historian called it "exhausting, boring, dangerous, frightening, and exciting—probably in about that order."

The Oregon Trail was more than 2,000 miles long. Still, many people walked it because their wagons were full of supplies, especially food. The **pioneers** also took tools, rope, pots and pans, dishes, and firearms. Sometimes they took a cow or a few chickens. They took personal items, too, such as the family Bible.

Pioneer families outfitted, or equipped, themselves in towns such as St. Louis. There they bought supplies. They bought wagons and oxen to pull the wagons. They joined other pioneers so that they could travel together to form a wagon train.

Coffee Saved Lives

Pioneers carried hundreds of pounds of food, including coffee. To make a cup of coffee, people boiled water. Boiling water for coffee also killed cholera germs in the water. Cholera is a serious disease spread in water. Cholera killed some pioneers. However, drinking hot coffee probably kept other pioneers from dying, especially from cholera.

To celebrate their arrival, travelers carved their names into Independence Rock. Although many names have eroded, some are still visible.

Pioneers buying supplies in Helena, Montana in the 1860s.

Kids on the Trail Children traveling west faced the same hardships and dangers as the adults they traveled with. Being part of a wagon train was hard work; but along the way children had some time to have fun. They played games and sang songs. Some even adopted wild animals as pets, including prairie dogs and antelopes.

On the journey pioneers looked for landmarks, such as Independence Rock in Wyoming. If a wagon train left Missouri in the spring, travelers hoped to reach Independence Rock by July 4. That would mean that they were on schedule. Pioneers usually celebrated when they reached Independence Rock.

Chores

Kids on a wagon train had lots of jobs to do.

- **Carry water from a stream.**
- **Help pack and unpack supplies for cooking and sleeping.**
- **Gather firewood or buffalo chips to burn as fuel.**
- **Milk the cow.**
- **Help cook and do laundry.**
- **Walk ahead of the wagon and throw stones out of the way.**
- **Put branches over muddy spots on the trail so that wagon wheels wouldn't get stuck.**

Chapter 2

Connecting East and West

At the same time that tens of thousands of people were moving west, thousands of other people were **emigrating** from other countries. They wanted to live in the United States. **Immigrants** helped the nation grow and prosper.

Chinese Immigrants

In the mid-1800s many people from China made the difficult journey to the United States. Packed into tiny spaces on ships, they made their way to California. They had heard of the Gold Rush, so they came to the United States to make their fortune.

For example, there is the story of "John John." He worked in a laundry in Weaverville, California. Other citizens made fun of him because he washed the miners' clothes for free.

The miners thought he was foolish. A year later one of the miners came across "John John" wearing expensive clothes. The "foolish" laundry man had washed enough gold dust out of pant cuffs and shirttails to become rich!

Most Chinese landed in San Francisco. They called California the "Golden Mountain."

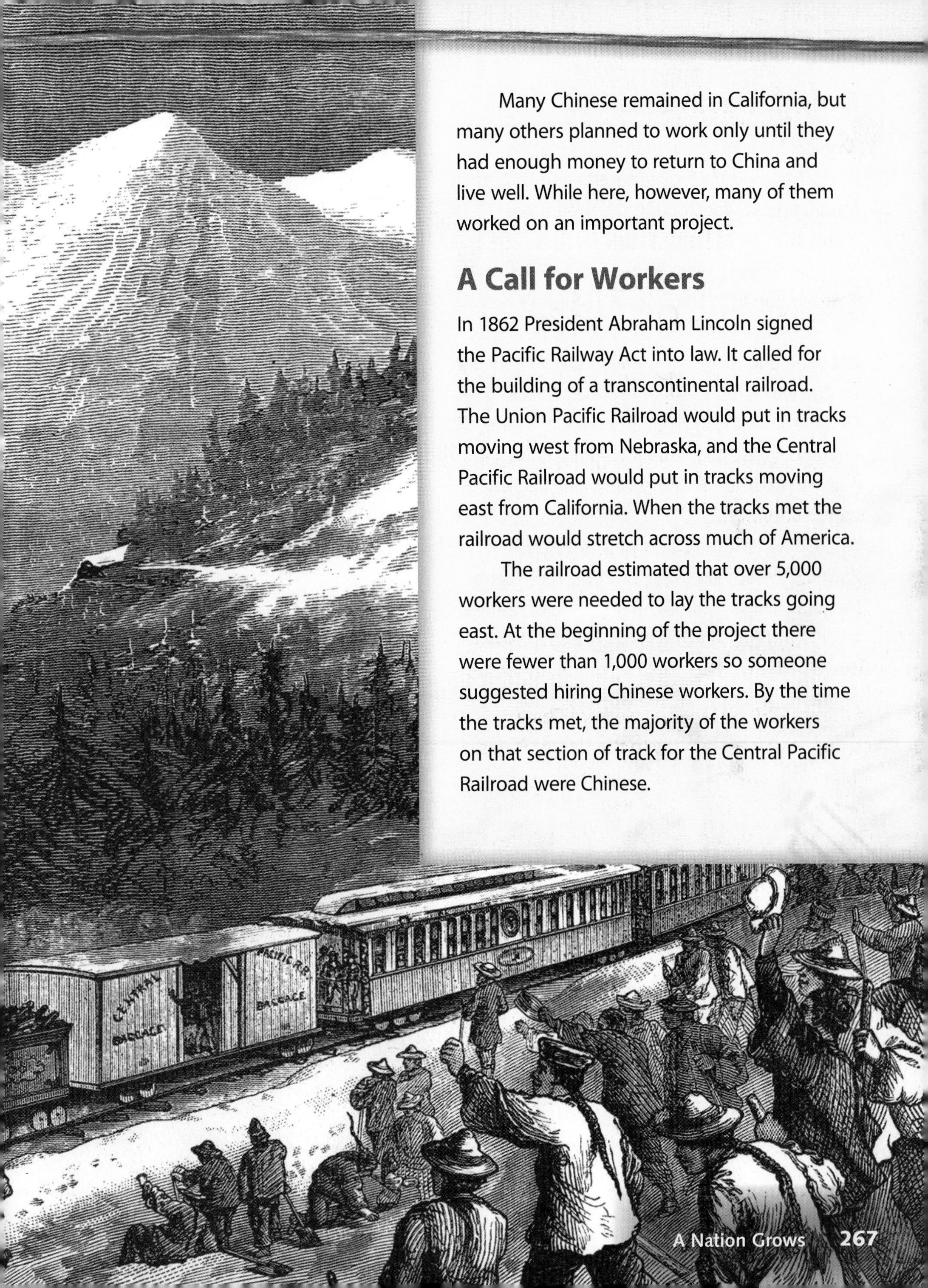

Many Chinese remained in California, but many others planned to work only until they had enough money to return to China and live well. While here, however, many of them worked on an important project.

A Call for Workers

In 1862 President Abraham Lincoln signed the Pacific Railway Act into law. It called for the building of a transcontinental railroad. The Union Pacific Railroad would put in tracks moving west from Nebraska, and the Central Pacific Railroad would put in tracks moving east from California. When the tracks met the railroad would stretch across much of America.

The railroad estimated that over 5,000 workers were needed to lay the tracks going east. At the beginning of the project there were fewer than 1,000 workers so someone suggested hiring Chinese workers. By the time the tracks met, the majority of the workers on that section of track for the Central Pacific Railroad were Chinese.

Doing the Impossible

Workers building the railroad did amazing work. They laid track over deserts and through mountains. To get through the mountains teams worked 24 hours a day.

Going west, work on the Union Pacific Railroad began in 1863. At first, progress was very slow. Only 40 miles of track had been put in by the end of 1865. In 1866 General Grenville Dodge was hired to supervise the project. General Dodge had been an engineer in the Civil War. He supervised his workers using military methods of discipline, loyalty, and competition.

Going east the tracks of the Central Pacific Railroad had to pass through the Sierra Nevadas. These mountains are made of granite, a very hard rock. Even with picks and blasting powder, the workers could remove only inches of granite in a day. Still the workers made 12 tunnels through the mountains.

Much of the work in the mountains was done in winter. During one winter more than 40 feet of snow fell. In addition to making tunnels through the mountains, the workers made tunnels through the snow, just so they could get to the work site.

Constructing the railroad was difficult. In some places, trestles were built so tracks could run over streams and rivers.

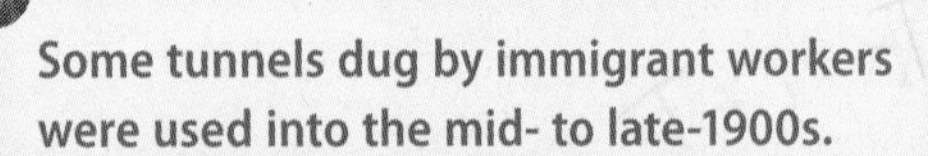

Some tunnels dug by immigrant workers were used into the mid- to late-1900s.

Another problem was creating ledges to work from along the cliffs. Chinese workers were lowered down the cliff on ropes. They drilled holes into the cliff, filled the holes with blasting powder, and attached a fuse. They lit the fuse—and were quickly lifted up and out of danger. In this way they made ledges that allowed them to work hundreds of feet above the valley floor.

A Great Accomplishment

On May 10, 1869, the track from the East met the track from the West at Promontory Summit in the Utah Territory. A trip across the country that had once taken months now took as little as one week. Goods could move quickly from one coast of the country to the other. Hard workers—especially Chinese workers—had helped connect East and West with a transcontinental railroad.

Tea Saved Lives Too

Some people made fun of the Chinese for drinking tea. The tea, however, kept many of them alive in a similar way that coffee did for the pioneers. By boiling water to make tea, Chinese workers killed disease-causing bacteria.

Chapter 3

"I Have to Go to America"

Many people came to America to live better lives. Some came to join family members who already were here. Others came to escape persecution. Here is what one young immigrant from Poland said:

"When I was about 10 years old, I said, 'I have to go to America.' Because my uncles were here already, and it kind of got me that I want to go to America, too . . . I was dreaming to come to America . . . and my dream came true. When I came here, I was in a different world. It was so peaceful. It was quiet. You were not afraid . . . I'm free . . . ."

Helen Cohen, interviewed in 1985

A statue of Annie Moore stands at Ellis Island.

Much of Ellis Island has been restored. The center is a popular destination for tourists and school groups.

America's Doorway

Before 1890 most immigrants arriving from **abroad** entered the United States at Castle Garden in New York City. Between 1855 and 1890 about 8 million people passed through Castle Garden. Most of the immigrants were from England, Ireland, Germany, and the Scandinavian countries.

In the late 1800s, because of **poverty** and political instability in Europe, more people wanted to move to the United States. This ever-increasing number of immigrants could not all be processed at Castle Garden. The United States government built Ellis Island in New York Harbor as the new immigration station. The first person to enter the United States through Ellis Island was fifteen-year-old Annie Moore. On December 20, 1891, Annie left Ireland with her two younger brothers. They spent 12 days in steerage before arriving in New York on December 31. Steerage provided few comforts. It was an inexpensive, but very uncomfortable way to travel. The next day Ellis Island opened. Annie was the first person to enter the United States through the new immigration center. Between 1892 and 1954 more than 12 million people came into the United States through Ellis Island.

A Difficult Journey

People traveled across the Atlantic Ocean on crowded ships. The cheapest tickets were for steerage class. A steerage ticket provided the traveler a bunk on the lowest level of the ship. Dinner was served out of huge pots. The air stank. There were few toilets—and no privacy. There could be hundreds of other people crowded into steerage. Still the travelers managed.

Paul Sturman arrived in 1920 from Czechoslovakia. He was twenty years old. He wrote this about his ocean journey:

"[The] time between meals was spent on deck if the weather was good. In the evening there was usually dancing and music. Some immigrant would always come out with a harmonica or some musical instrument and the dance would follow."

At Ellis Island, immigrants gathered in the Great Hall. Processing began here. The restored hall is seen in the photo at the left.

Ships delivered their passengers to a pier where a large boat could dock with safety. Smaller ferries or barges then took the newly arrived immigrants to Ellis Island. At Ellis Island most of the new arrivals spent three to five hours being processed. They stood in long lines and were inspected by doctors for signs of disease. They could also be kept for a longer time at Ellis Island for observation. Some unlucky people were denied entry and were sent back to their country of origin.

When they entered the United States, immigrants quickly discovered how difficult life in their new homeland could be. New immigrants to large cities often lived in small, crowded tenements where disease was a constant threat. Many immigrants worked hard in sweatshops, a shop or factory where people worked many hours for little pay.

When they first arrived, most immigrants spoke little English. Without a knowledge of English, few jobs were available to them. The immigrants had to learn a new language and adjust to new customs while trying to keep their own traditions. For example, Jewish immigrants adopted many aspects of American culture, but they also established theaters and newspapers in their native language of Yiddish. New Americans learned how to make their new homes more comfortable and make better lives for themselves.

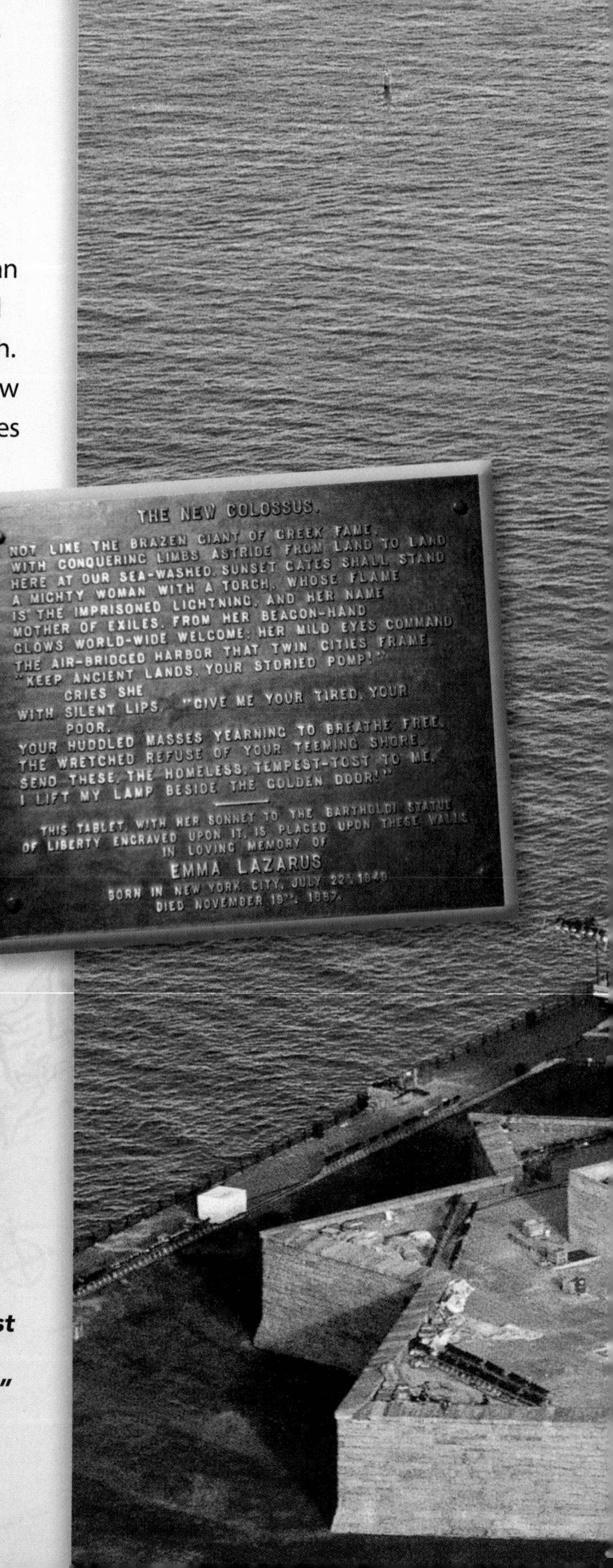

Statue of Liberty

After entering New York Harbor, one of the first things the immigrants saw was the Statue of Liberty. The statue stands tall and proud not far from Ellis Island. A poem called "The New Colossus" is engraved on a plaque there. These words are an invitation to people who are searching for a better life.

The New Colossus

"Give me your tired, your poor,
Your huddled masses yearning to breathe free,
The wretched refuse of your teeming shore.
Send these, the homeless, tempest-tost to me,
I lift my lamp beside the golden door!"

by Emma Lazarus

Immigration Today

The United States is still a place where many people want to live. People come here for many of the same reasons as they did in the 1800s. They come for opportunities and for freedom.

The line graph below shows information about America's immigrant population from 1840 through 2000. Today most immigrants enter the United States through California. They are processed at borders and at airports. In 2007 over one million people immigrated to the United States.

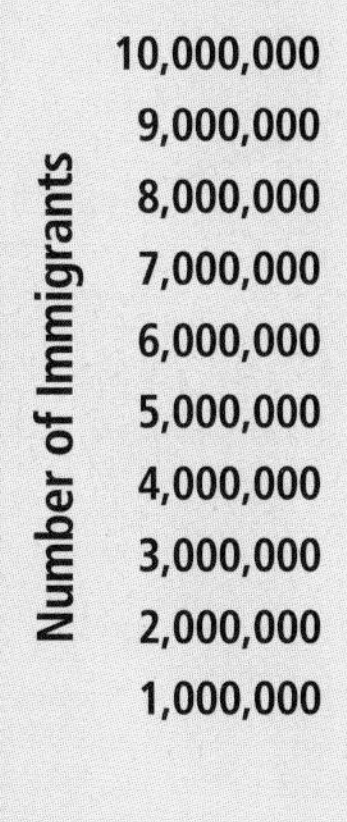

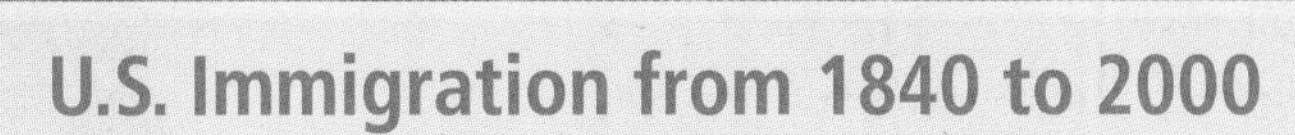

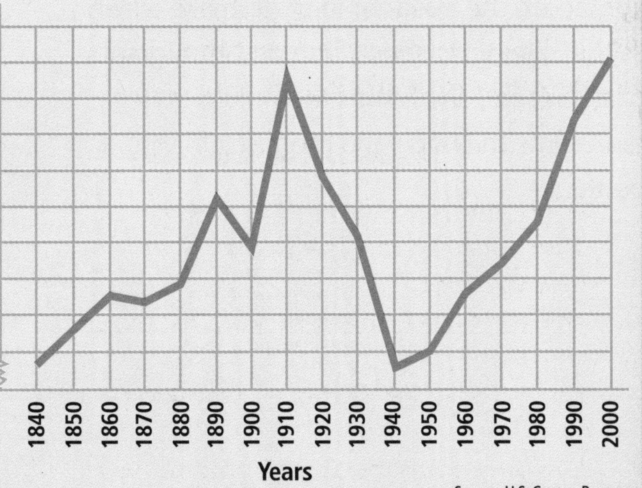

Crossing Borders

The United States is bordered on the East Coast by the Atlantic Ocean. On the West Coast, the Pacific Ocean acts like a wide barrier between the United States and the islands of the Pacific and mainland Asia. In the past, immigrants coming to the United States from Europe and Asia had to face long and difficult ocean voyages. Today a trip by airplane takes only a matter of hours to reach the United States from the farthest places on Earth. Whether the trip was long or short, easy or difficult, immigrants have come here since the country was first settled by Europeans in the seventeenth century.

For many immigrants the United States represents freedom. Some immigrants come from countries with repressive governments, and so they treasure the freedom here to vote and participate in democracy. Other immigrants appreciate the freedom to try to make a living as they please. In short, for many immigrants past, present, and future, the United States represents the hope and promise of living a better life.

The citizenship ceremony is very important for many immigrants. Sometimes it is held on a special day, such as July 4.

Chapter 4

An Enriched America

Immigrants **triumphed** in their new home. They settled here with hopes and dreams for a better life. They have enriched this country with their talents, traditions, languages, music, food, and stories. Immigrants help to make America a diverse and exciting place for all people who live here. Immigrants in every profession have made contributions to life in this country. A few outstanding examples follow.

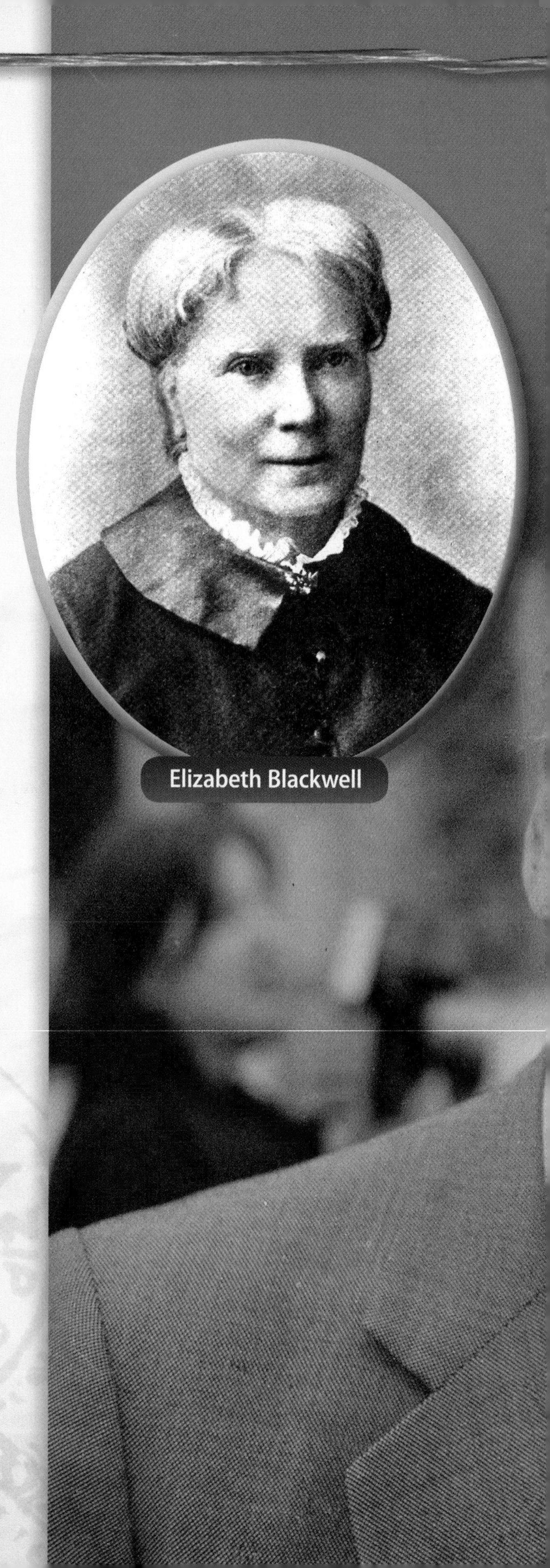

Elizabeth Blackwell

Elizabeth Blackwell

Elizabeth Blackwell was born in England in 1821. She emigrated with her family to the United States in 1832. After her father died, she, her mother, and her sisters made a living by running a private school.

From an early age Blackwell dreamed of becoming a doctor. However, women at this time were not accepted into medical schools. After being rejected by dozens of schools,

I. M. Pei

Blackwell was finally accepted by a college in western New York. Overcoming skepticism and hostility, Blackwell worked hard and became the first woman in the United States to be awarded a degree as a Doctor of Medicine. Blackwell went on to found a hospital in New York City and to help train nurses for work in the Civil War.

I. M. Pei

One of America's most famous architects, I. M. Pei was born in Canton, China, in 1917. Pei came to the United States to study architecture at the age of eighteen. He became a naturalized citizen of the United States in 1954. Within a few years Pei started his own architectural office. His designs are famous for their geometric patterns and their use of glass. Among the buildings Pei designed are the East Wing of the National Gallery of Art in Washington, D.C.; the John F. Kennedy Memorial Library in Boston, Massachusetts; and the Rock and Roll Hall of Fame in Cleveland, Ohio. In the buildings he designed, Pei made important contributions in defining the faces and culture of many American cities.

Madeleine Albright

Madeleine Albright was born in Czechoslovakia in 1937. Fleeing the communist takeover of her country, Albright moved with her family to the United States in 1948. She became a U.S. citizen in 1957. Among other jobs, Albright served as a staff member on the National Security Council, a professor at Georgetown University, and as the U.S. representative to the United Nations. In January 1997 she was unanimously confirmed by the U.S. Senate as Secretary of State under President Bill Clinton. Madeleine Albright is the first woman to have been Secretary of State. In office Albright worked to foster continued U.S. leadership in foreign affairs.

Madeleine Albright

Felix Frankfurter

Felix Frankfurter is one of the few immigrant citizens of the United States to have served on the U.S. Supreme Court. Justice Frankfurter was born in Vienna, Austria, in 1882. Frankfurter moved with his family to the United States in 1894. In 1914 he became a teacher at Harvard Law School, where he earned a reputation as a leading constitutional scholar. He advised President Roosevelt on many important issues, such as which people to select to lead government agencies established during the New Deal. In 1939 Frankfurter was nominated by Roosevelt to be an associate justice of the Supreme Court. He served until 1962 when he retired due to illness. He died in 1965.

Felix Frankfurter

Maria Hinojosa

Maria Hinojosa was born in Mexico City in 1961. She moved to the United States with her family when she was very young. Hinojosa grew up mostly in Chicago, Illinois, and attended college in New York City, after which she embarked on a career as a journalist.

Working both in radio and television, Hinojosa became a keen observer of the immigrant experience in general and of Latin American issues in particular. Hinojosa was the host of one of the first nation-wide radio programs to focus on the experiences of Latin American immigrants in the United States. A frequent award winner for her journalism, Hinojosa has reported on topics ranging from the lives of young people in big cities to the importance of the arts. Hinojosa is frequently named as one of the most influential people of Latin descent in the United States.

Maria Hinojosa

John Muir

John Muir

John Muir was born in Dunbar, Scotland, in 1838. When he was eleven, Muir moved with his family to Portage, Wisconsin. He enjoyed exploring the beautiful countryside there. In 1867 he began his travels around America. Muir's writings about the Sierra Nevada became popular. He wrote a series of articles explaining the destruction of open spaces by ranch animals. His writings led Congress to create Yosemite National Park. Muir also helped establish Grand Canyon, Sequoia, Petrified Forest, and Mount Rainier National Parks. Muir founded the Sierra Club to protect and preserve natural areas in the United States. Muir became a United States citizen at the age of sixty-five.

Sum It Up

Starting in the 1800s Americans moved west. The United States grew and prospered as people made this move. Some people wanted to own their own land, others wanted to find good jobs, and some hoped to find wealth in our country's natural resources, such as gold.

People from other parts of the world also come to this country for many reasons. They come for opportunities to find meaningful and rewarding work. They also come to this country for the freedoms that may not have been available in their home country. Immigrants have enriched the United States with their talent, work, and their cultures.

What do you think would be the hardest part of moving to a new place? Explain.

Suppose that you could make a movie about something in this unit. What would it be? Why?

BROTHERS

by YIN

paintings by
CHRIS SOENTPIET

It is warm when I finally arrive in San Francisco. I have been at sea for over a month. I can't wait to see my older brothers. I wonder if they will recognize me. It has been years since they left home. I especially miss Brother Wong as we were neither the oldest nor the youngest. I wonder if I will make new friends in America.

I stagger toward the crowd of people waiting. My knees wobble from the long voyage. Onshore, a voice calls, "Over here, Ming!"

"Hello," I say. "Are you my older brother?"

"Yes," the young man tells me in Chinese. "Do you remember me? I am Shek."

I bow to him, but I am disappointed to learn that Brother Wong has gone back to work on the dangerous railroads. I worry that I will never see him again.

"Come . . . climb up, before you fall." Shek kneels on one knee. "We are still brothers."

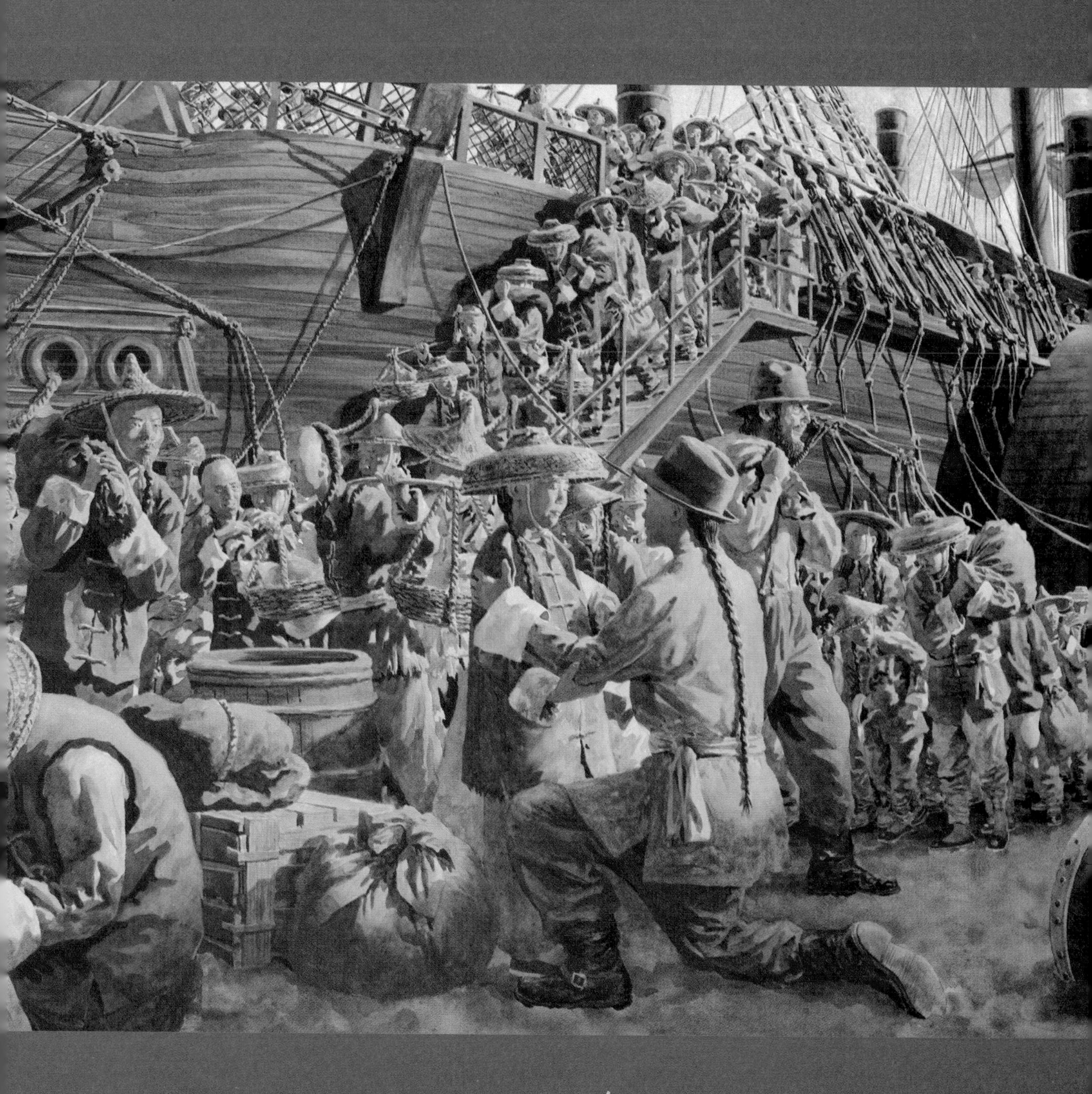

I can walk more steadily once we arrive in Chinatown. I whistle with amazement at my brothers' wood-framed store. Inside, the sun beams through the window where the dried sausages and ducks hang. This is proof of my brothers' hard work laying railroad tracks years earlier. Still, I am sad Brother Wong is not here.

"A year ago, there was a big fire in Chinatown," Shek tells me. "But with hard work, we opened this new store."

I look into a barrel at some rotten apples. "Do you sell these?" I ask.

"Unfortunately, most of the Chinese left Chinatown to work on the railroad up north. I am fearful there will be fewer and fewer customers coming around here." Shek sighs.

At the back of the store, Shek hoists buckets of hot water on a long wooden pole over his shoulder and pours them into a tub.

"A hot bath for a tired body," Shek says, signaling for me to get in. As I soak in my bath, Shek hands me a bowl.

I take a sip. "Yuck!"

Shek laughs. "Herbal medicine is always bitter," he says.

That evening over dried fish, duck eggs, and hot steamy noodles, Shek tells me, "We must work hard and send money home to our family in China. I found extra work farming vegetables and fruits some miles from here. I'll come back for a few days each week. Ming, you will mind the store while I am gone."

"Me?" I ask, alarmed.

I do not want to disappoint my older brother. The next morning, I get up before dawn. After breakfast of leftover porridge, Shek hands me a broom. "Sweep the front . . . stack the barrels . . . unload the baskets . . . wipe the windows . . . ." He has a long list. "And do not go past Stockton Street. Chinese should not go outside Chinatown."

I wonder why.

I watch Shek ride off to work in the darkness. It is real quiet. I have a lonely feeling.

I start my work moving heavy crates and barrels. I unravel the stitching across the top of a rice sack and use it to wipe the store clean. I help a Chinese customer load his basket with rice, tea leaves, and some white radishes. As I watch him carry his goods on the long pole, I hope for another customer.

My brother is right—only a few customers come in, and they're always Chinese. They have little money to pay for the goods and they are too few. There is nothing I can do but sit and wait.

I long for a friend.

劉記蔬菜肉食店

The days pass with almost no customers.

One day, I grow curious. I look down the road and wonder what is beyond Chinatown. I dart past Stockton Street. I am met by stares and grumbles. I cannot understand the people who speak, but the look on their faces is not pleasant. I run back to the store. As I try to catch my breath, I get an idea! In my brother's closet, I find a jacket and hat. I hide my long braid under the hat and turn the brim down so no one will recognize me. I run past the road where Shek tells me not to go. I walk carefully. No one stares. My disguise is working!

I run faster as my braid falls from my big hat. Quickly I hide behind a tree. I peek and see kids playing. The sounds are unlike the silence of Chinatown. I follow the children with my eyes. Some are holding books and heading toward a big house. A school, I think. I have heard about schools in America. I would like to go. Someday.

Suddenly, I feel a tap on my shoulder. This boy with brown hair and eyes the color of the bright sky surprises me.

He points his finger to his chest and says, "PAAA-TRICK."

"Ah-PA-TOO-LICK," I mutter. I try again but have to cover my mouth and bite my cheeks to keep from laughing.

He repeats, "PAAA-TRICK."

"Ah-PA-TWO-RIC," I repeat and struggle, "PAA-TRICK." My Chinese tongue is not used to the sounds.

We both laugh.

Then I remember—I must go back to the store! I wish I knew English. But I can only wave good-bye. For now I must go back to Chinatown. I run.

The next day, I sit and wait. It is three o'clock, no customers. I think of Patrick. I want to go back! I wear my disguise and quickly run past the road and wait by that same tree. This time, a group of children swarm out of the schoolhouse. From behind, I feel a hand on my shoulder. It's Patrick!

With a sneaky grin, I push the book out of Patrick's arm and he chases me. He passes me a few times. I run after him. He runs fast, but I can run faster. We run past a busy street all the way to Chinatown. At the store, I dip my bowl into the barrel of water and offer it to my new friend.

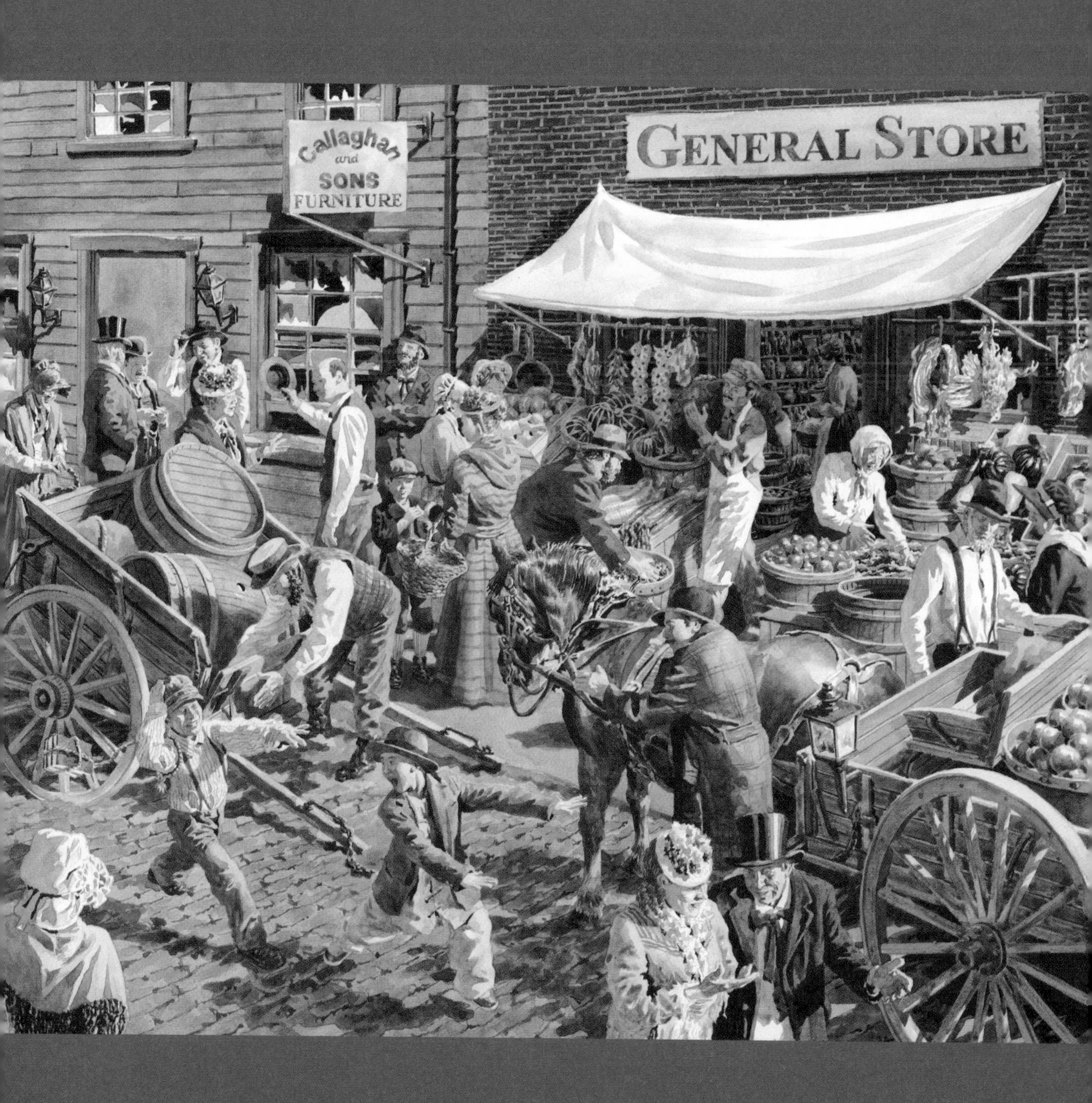
Callaghan and SONS FURNITURE
GENERAL STORE

While we rest in the store, Patrick digs in his pocket and pulls out a piece of chalk. He writes his name: P-A-T-R-I-C-K. He points to the letters and then points to himself and slowly says, "Paaaaa-trick!"

Then he points to me as if wondering what my name is. I say, "Ming!"

"Ming," he repeats. He writes the letters of my sound. I beam with delight.

I place my hand on Patrick's shoulder. I shake his hand and say, "Pun yao." This is how you say "friend" in my language.

Mr. Patrick

That night, Shek comes back to town. As I help him unload the wagon, I long to go to school with Patrick. I ask, "Uhhhh, I . . . ummm . . . a school . . . I saw some kids—"

Shek interrupts in an angry voice, "I told you not to go past Stockton Street."

"But why?" I ask, my voice not so strong.

"People out there are not Chinese. Chinese are not allowed in those schools. We are safer right here in Chinatown," Shek scolds. "Just do as you are told!"

I bow my head in silence. Feeling awful for disobeying my brother, I prepare the water for his bath.

Tonight I must tell Shek about my new friend. Shek dips his hand into the water, and I say, "Ahh . . . Brother Shek, I have a new—"

"I saw you with . . . a boy," he interrupts.

I am afraid Shek will be angry. There is a long silence.

"Your new friend is nice?" he asks.

I nod. "Yes, very. He teaches me English."

Again there is a long silence. With a deep breath, he says, "Just be careful, Ming."

"I will, Older Brother. Please do not worry."

Now that Shek knows of my new friend, I look forward to seeing Patrick when he comes by the store. I don't know why he chose me as a friend. He has a caring heart. When Patrick teaches me English, I say, "More."

He shows me how to write my own name and the English alphabet—all twenty-six letters. In China, we have to remember characters to make a word. Chinese and English are very different. But every month, my English gets better and better, thanks to Patrick.

Some days he helps me at the store, and when there are no customers, we like to play marbles and toss them into the holes we dug for our game. Some days Patrick helps me clean the store.

One rainy day, Patrick invites me to his home. I am afraid of what his family will think. My English is not so good, but with Shek's blessing, I go with Patrick to his home. He shouts, "Ming is here!"

"Ahhhhhh . . . hel-lo," I stutter. I nervously take off my hat and my long braid falls down.

From the corner of my eye, I see Mr. O'Farrell—Patrick's father—wiping his face with a wet rag. He slaps me on the back. "Hello, Ming." He **pronounces** my name almost right.

After checking the pot in the fireplace, Mrs. O'Farrell hugs Patrick and strokes my head. She gives us some bread. I follow Patrick's lead by dunking the bread in the soup. "You boys slow down before you choke." Her voice is soft. I do not understand everything she says, but I feel a tickle in my heart.

With his hands, Mr. O'Farrell tells me a story. In his homeland, their family had nothing to eat. So his father crossed the ocean and saved enough money to bring his family from Ireland to live in America. Mr. O'Farrell has also worked on the railroads—just like my older brothers.

After supper Mr. O'Farrell plays his flute in the air. Mrs. O'Farrell hums and claps while we boys dance out of step.

Before I leave, Mrs. O'Farrell says, "Ming, you are welcome here anytime." I smile back at her as I quickly dart down the dark road back to Chinatown.

The days Shek does not come home, I go with Patrick and have supper with his family. My English is getting better. I look forward to Mrs. O'Farrell's beef stew.

Months pass and still, only a few customers. The fruits have dried and the stalks from vegetables have turned brown with black spots. I toss out the bad ones.

One night, Shek reads a letter outloud:

"My Brothers, I may have to stay here a while longer. Since business is not good at the store, I will move east with the other railroad workers. Take care, ah-Wong."

There is a long silence. "Ming, if we don't get more customers, we will have to close the store," Shek says, clutching the letter.

I bow my head to hide my tears.

As my older brother leaves for work, Patrick asks, "What's the matter?"

"You cannot understand." My shoulders **slump**. "We might move. No people come to our store. We cannot pay rent."

Patrick interrupts, "But why don't you have customers? It's a great store."

I try to explain. "In Chinatown, only Chinese buy things. And Chinese . . . have no money."

There is a silence. Then Patrick leans close. "Maybe you need customers who aren't Chinese. Ming, you can speak with them in English!"

We say nothing for a long time, but then Patrick's words spark a bright idea. Before he leaves, I tell Patrick my idea. I watch as a smile spreads across his face.

Early the next morning, Patrick brings a long cloth and lays it across the ground. I give him my ink and brush. He writes: GENERAL STORE—WE SPEAK ENGLISH!

Then Patrick helps me up the ladder. Thump . . . thump . . . thump . . . thump . . . thump. I nail the sign to the store. When it is finished, Patrick says, "The sign is beautiful!"

All day we wait. No one comes except an old Chinese man who stops to **admire** our new sign. He buys some dried mushroom ears. We wait for another customer. We kick some empty cans around and we wait. We play hide-and-seek in the store and we wait. We play some marbles and we wait.

Darkness falls. Shek should be back soon. Maybe we failed. Finally, a couple riding in a wagon points to our sign. Patrick and I jump up and guide them into the store.

"Let us help you find something," Patrick says. They walk past some almost-rotten fruits. The man buys nails by the keg. The woman buys a small bag of sugar.

I say, "Thank you," in English.

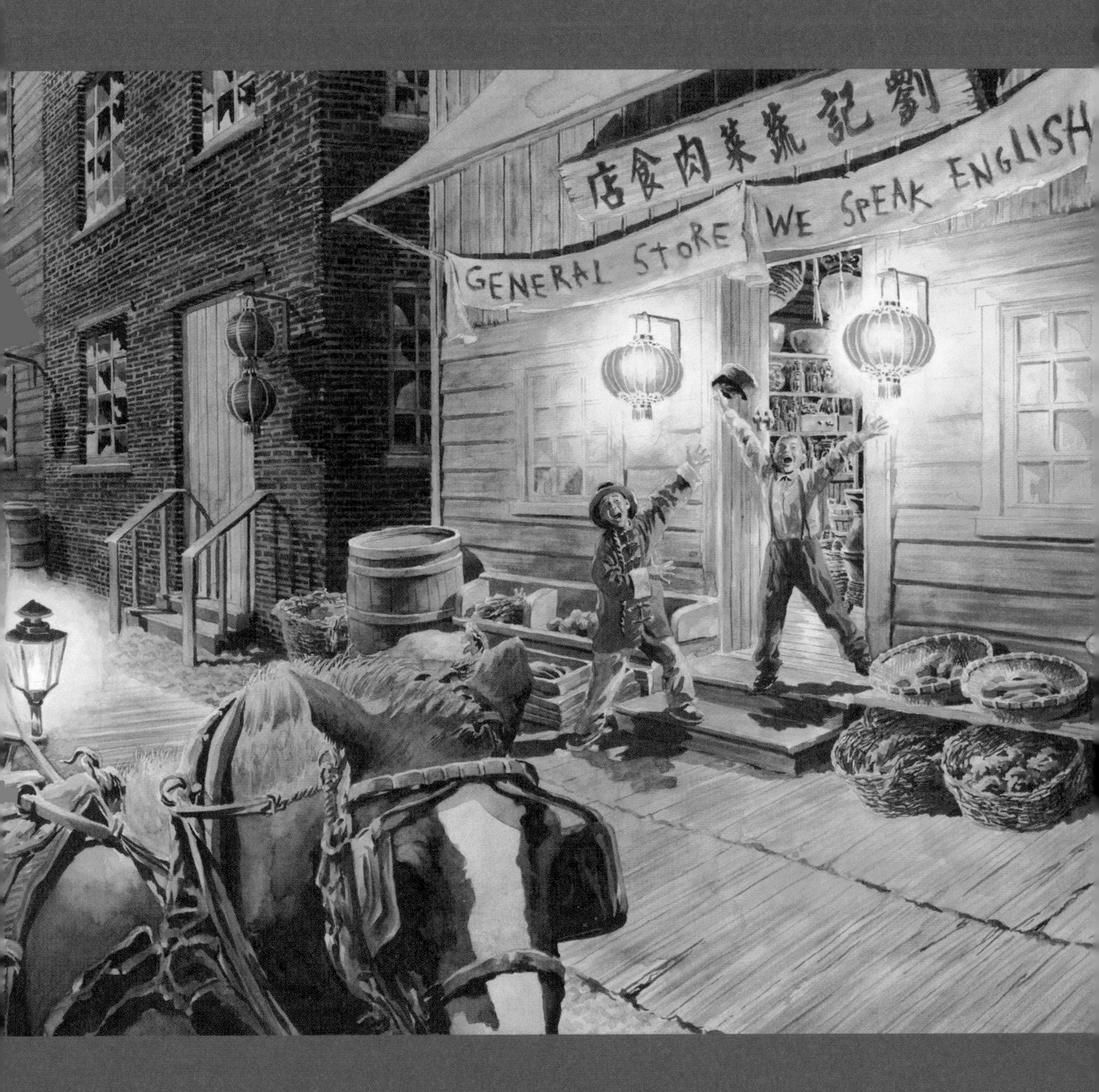
劉記蔬菜肉食店
WE SPEAK ENGLISH
GENERAL STORE

The next morning, Mr. O'Farrell and his coworkers arrive at the store. I am surprised. "Top of the morning to you!" Mr. O'Farrell shouts as he admires the lanterns. He sorts through some baskets and picks up some dried oysters. "Maybe Mrs. O'Farrell can make soup out of these!"

"Two cents," I say. Mr. O'Farrell winks at me.

Days pass, and business gets better, thanks to our new English sign. Sometimes we get four customers, sometimes ten. Today we have thirteen! Shek hauls in his wagon full of fresh greens and glowing fruits from Sacramento. He looks up at the new sign and grins. "Maybe we don't have to leave after all."

Mrs. O'Farrell tells us to stock honey, wheat, oats, and flour for our new customers. And we cannot forget the bamboo shoots, pickled vegetables, and rice for the Chinese customers too.

Wong is back now to help at the store. We are all together.

One day, I teach Patrick Chinese. I write "hing-dai," BROTHERS. We are more than friends—we are brothers.

UNIT 6

A Kingdom of Green

What place do plants have in the world?

Focus Questions

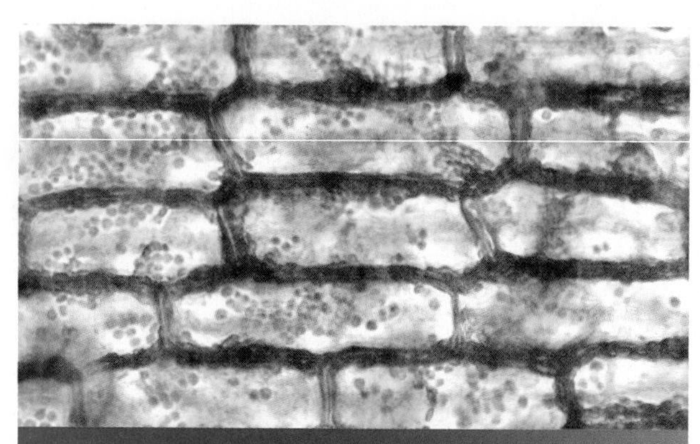

What can we learn by taking a closer look at plants?

How do plants respond to the world around them?

What are the stages of a plant's life cycle?

How do people use plants?

Green Is

by Madisen Lee

Read this riddle. What is it about?

There was a green house.
Inside the green house, there was a white house.
Inside the white house, there was a red house.
Inside the red house, there were lots of babies.

(Find the answer on page 346.)

Golden

Contents

Chapter

Chapter One

Looking at Plants

Are all plants alike? Scientists have **examined** hundreds of thousands of kinds of plants in the world. They have observed many similarities and differences in plants.

Classifying Plants

Every plant is placed into one of two groups: vascular or nonvascular. Vascular plants have tubes inside them. In some tubes, water and **nutrients** are moved throughout a plant. In other tubes, food made by the plant is moved. Vascular plants include strawberries, dandelions, and all other plants and trees that make flowers. Trees that make cones, like pine trees, are vascular plants too.

A nonvascular plant does not have tubes to move water, nutrients, and food. Instead, water and nutrients soak into the plant, passing from cell to cell. Nonvascular plants include mosses and small plants called liverworts.

Comparing Plant and Animal Cells

Plants and animals are made of different kinds of cells. Each kind of cell does a certain job. For example, an animal's skin cells cover the outside of the body. Muscle cells cause movement when they contract or relax. In plants, cells within flowers make seeds. Cells within a plant's roots take in water and hold the plant in the soil.

Plant cells have two structures that animal cells do not have. For one thing, plant cells have a rigid cell wall which supports and protects the cell. Plant cells in leaves and in some stems also have chloroplasts, which are cell structures that make food.

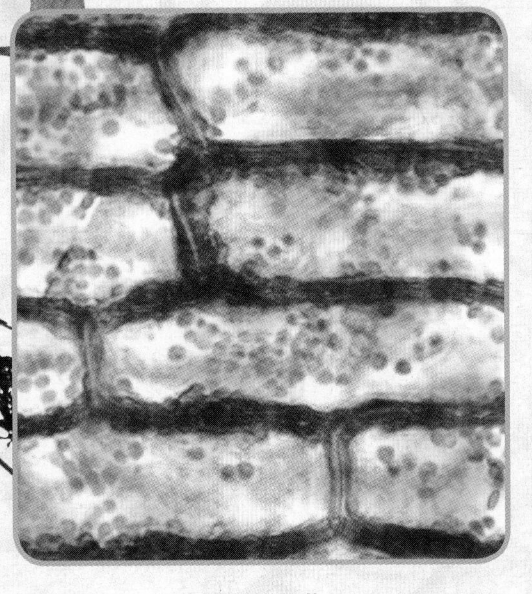

plant cell

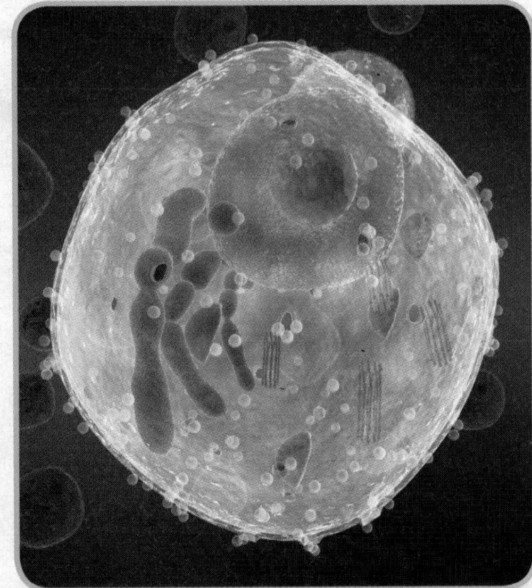

animal cell

Roots, Stems, and Leaves

You are already familiar with some different kinds of vascular plants. You know spinach and broccoli—we eat parts of these plants for food. Maple, pine, mahogany, and fir trees are used to make lumber. Fibers made by cotton plants are used to weave cloth that can be made into clothes that are comfortable to wear. Even though these plants look different, they are similar in many ways because they are all vascular plants.

Roots The roots of a plant usually are underground and act as an anchor for the plant in the soil. You can imagine the roots that are needed to hold up a 100-foot tree. Roots also take in water and nutrients from the soil through tiny root hairs. Some roots also store food for the plant.

Mangrove trees grow in muddy places. A mangrove's roots use oxygen from the air for the tree.

A redwood tree has a thick, woody stem that grows year after year. Redwood trees can live for many hundreds of years.

Stems Above ground a stem supports a plant. The stem holds up the plant so that its leaves will be in the sunlight. The stem also carries water and nutrients to parts of the plant.

Remember: Vascular plants have tubes. Tubes called xylem carry water and nutrients up the stem from the roots. Tubes called phloem carry food that the plant makes to other parts of the plant.

In a woody plant, such as a tree, the xylem is arranged in rings. You can see the rings when a tree is cut down. Lumber for building comes from a tree's woody stem.

The part of a carrot plant that we eat is the taproot. This is where the plant stores food.

The Age of a Tree

Each year a tree adds a ring of vascular tissue. The rings are not always the same width. In times when the climate is good and rain is plentiful, the ring added is wide. In times when rain is scarce and the climate is not good, a thin ring is added. You can tell the age of a tree by counting its rings.

Leaves Unless a plant has large, beautiful flowers or a strong, tall stem, you may notice a plant's leaves first. Leaves vary in size and shape. They may be small, soft, needlelike, or pleated like a fan. Some, like the leaves of a *Gunnera* species, are large enough to cover a doorway! In the fall, some leaves lose their green color and turn red, yellow, orange, or brown before they fall from a plant. Other plants that have leaves like needles also lose their leaves. But most of these do not lose their leaves at one time. They lose some needles all the time.

A leaf has different layers of cells. Cells in a middle layer contain chloroplasts. Chloroplasts contain chlorophyll. Chlorophyll is the substance that makes leaves appear green. Something amazing happens inside the chloroplasts. A plant makes food—food for all of its cells. The stored food can be eaten and used by animals that eat plants.

Are the spines of a cactus plant leaves? Keep reading to find out!

leaves of a *Gunnera*

Photosynthesis

Plants make their own food through an incredible chemical reaction—a process called photosynthesis. The reactions of photosynthesis get energy from light. In nature the sun is the light source. But plants can use the light energy from electric bulbs as well! The chloroplasts use this light energy to combine hydrogen from water and carbon dioxide from the air to make sugar. The sugars are used to make more leaves, stems, roots, and fruits.

How Plants Make Food

Plants give off oxygen when they make their own food. We use this oxygen to live and to make energy. In turn, we breathe out carbon dioxide. Plants use carbon dioxide to make food. This cycle is another way in which plants and people are interdependent.

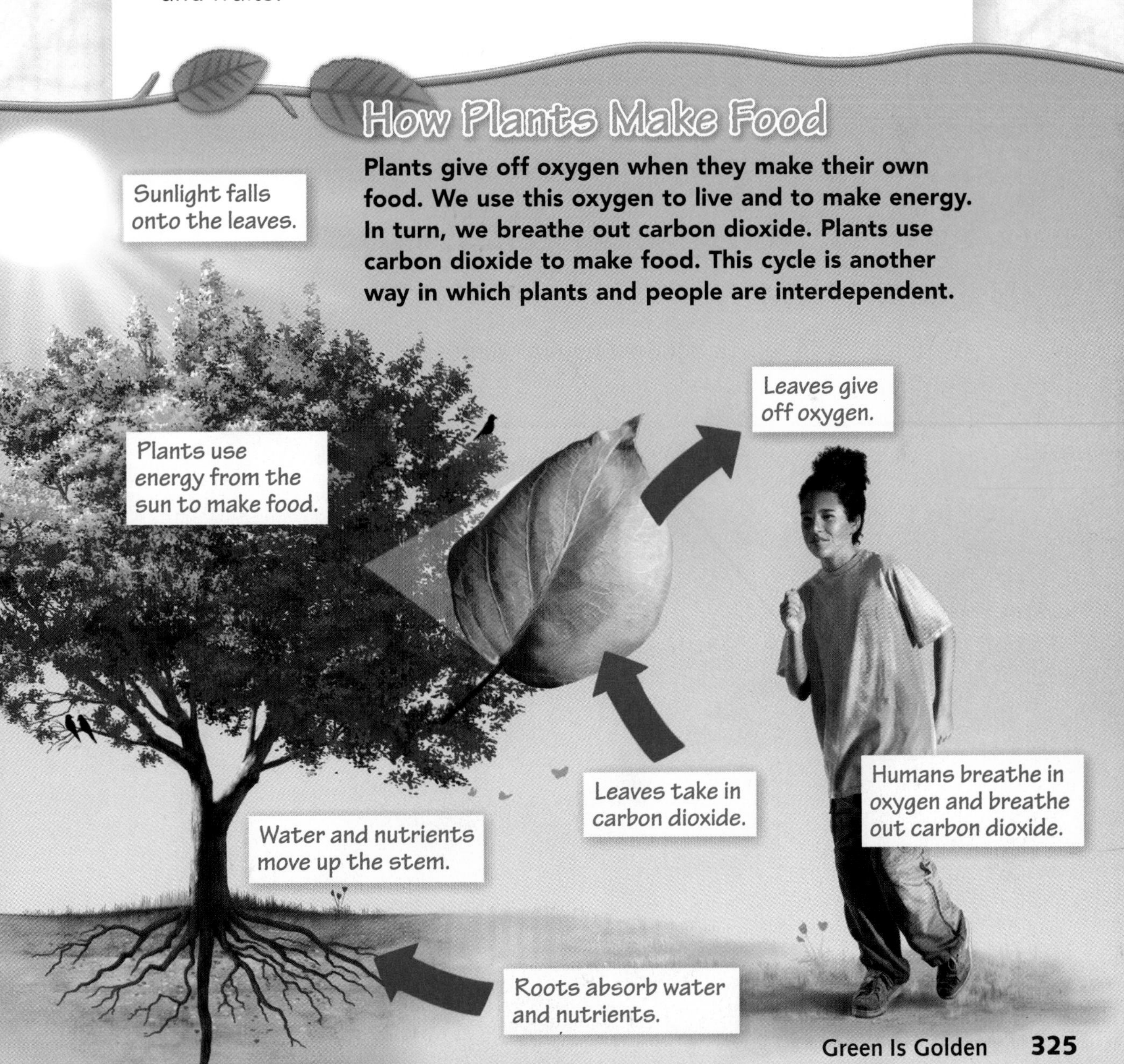

The Edible Schoolyard

Some people do not connect plants to the food they eat. Often they think that food comes from a store or market. The Edible Schoolyard project at a school in California helps students make connections between growing green plants and their food. In this project, learning about plants occurs not only in science class but also in a plot of earth outdoors.

In the Edible Schoolyard project, students grow plants, harvest them, and then eat them! On their first visit, students take a self-guided hike around the garden. For example, they may be guided to do the following:

Pick a yellow cherry tomato and eat it.

Check out all the seeds on a strawberry!

Feel the leaf of a plant.

By doing these things, students get a "hands-on" feel for plants.

On their next visit to the garden, the kids may harvest and roast ears of corn. Then they eat them. Soon the kids are learning how to plant seeds; how to take care of growing plants; and how to prepare, cook, and eat the plants.

In the kitchen everyone helps cook and serve the foods made with the harvested produce. They may grind wheat and corn to make flour. They may make a one-of-a-kind salad or soup.

After the meal, kitchen scraps go into a special pile in the garden. In this pile microscopic organisms break down the scraps. Useful materials in the food scraps are released. This material is called compost. It is then added to the garden's soil to help the next crop of plants grow.

"Yesterday we made pasta with vegetables. I made lots of noodles, Belle cut the broccoli, Isabel cut the carrots, and Jason peeled the garlic." — Kent

Chapter Two

How Plants Get What They Need

Because plants need water to survive, most plants live in **temperate** and tropical climates. Pine trees, petunias, potatoes, and palms are just a few examples. Because you also probably live in a similar climate, you might be able to name many more kinds of plants.

Living in Water

Many different kinds of plants grow near ponds, lakes, and swamps—places that are wet most of the time. Some plants even float on the water's surface. The leaves of some of these floating plants differ from the leaves of many plants that grow on land. Most plants growing on land have small openings called stomata on the undersides of their leaves. Plants whose leaves float on water have stomata on the tops of their leaves. These openings allow carbon dioxide to enter the leaves.

This is a white water lily. Its leaves have a tough, waxy surface that prevents water from settling.

Living in Deserts

Desert climates are dry areas. In most deserts, rain falls only at certain times of the year. Because the rain sometimes falls in heavy downpours, much of the water runs off instead of soaking into the soil.

Desert plants have ways to conserve water. Some desert plants called succulents store water in fleshy leaves or stems. By doing this the plant has water to use during very dry times. Some desert plants can close their stomata during the day. That way they avoid losing water through evaporation. The spines on a cactus are modified leaves. Spines do not lose water and they help protect the plant.

Other plants that live in deserts grow quickly after a rain. These plants are able to grow, flower, and make seeds all within a few weeks of a rare desert rainfall. The creosote bush has a waxy covering on its leaves that helps prevent water loss. This helps the plant conserve water.

This fishhook barrel cactus grows in the American Southwest. Its stem can expand to store water when it rains.

The creosote bush is a common plant in parts of the American Southwest.

Living in Cold

Some plants live high up on mountain slopes. These are called alpine plants. Others live in colder climates closer to the North Pole. Both places have climate conditions with cold temperatures below or close to freezing for much of the year. Plants need water to make food, but often there is no water available for plants—only ice and snow.

Plants have special adaptations to survive high up mountains or in cold polar regions. Plants in both areas are often small and live close to the ground. Many grow in low, dense mats. Even trees remain small. Plants that grow close to the ground dry out less when cold winds blow over them.

Some flowering plants, like the Arctic poppy, are also able to grow under cold conditions. Arctic poppies produce pretty yellow or orange flowers that move to follow the daily movement of the sun, thus using its energy.

The alpine phlox lives in very cold places.

Meat-Eating Plants

Many animals get lots of the nutrients they need by eating meat. Did you know that some plants also get some of the nutrients they need from meat? The Venus flytrap is a good example. This plant lives in damp areas and cannot get all of the nutrients it needs from the soil it grows in. So it does what its name says: it traps insects and other small creatures.

This plant has a leaf that looks like two green half circles with bristles along its edges. When an insect lands on a leaf, it touches several of the small hairs on the inside of the leaf. When this happens, the two halves of the leaf quickly close. The bristles on the edge keep the insect trapped inside the leaf. Then the plants make liquids that digest the insect. It takes some time to completely digest the insect. The nutrients from the insect can be used by the plant. In time, the leaf opens again. The insect, now only a dry shell, falls out of the leaf. Each leaf can trap insects several times before losing this ability. Then other leaves take up the work.

The Venus flytrap is almost *too* interesting. So many people have collected these plants that the plants have become endangered in the wild.

Fire!!

Forest fires are common in some parts of the United States. Although it destroys many plants, fire is an important factor in the life cycle of some plants. Fire can actually help some plants complete their life cycle.

- For some kinds of pine trees, heat is the only way seeds can be released from the cones. A sticky substance in the cones protects the seeds. Heat from a fire melts the substance. The seeds escape from the cones, fall to the ground, and begin to grow.
- Fire releases nutrients from burned plants. The ashes of the dead plants are full of nutrients that can enrich the soil. New plants that begin to grow after a fire can use these nutrients as they grow.
- In some areas large trees no longer shade the area after a fire. The sun can then warm the soil more. This warmed soil helps young plants grow faster. Since fire darkens soil, the soil then absorbs more heat from sunlight.
- More sunlight can reach the ground in an area where the trees have been burned by fire. The plants that begin to grow in an area that has been burned get more light and can grow much better.

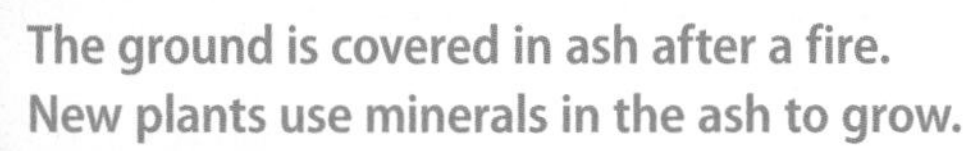

The ground is covered in ash after a fire. New plants use minerals in the ash to grow.

A forest often looks emptier after a fire. In time, plants return.

Plants die when fires happen. But new plants grow after the flames die out.

Chapter Three

From Just a Seed!

In a cold corner of the world, people are collecting seeds. They're doing this in case a disaster someday wipes out food crops.

The Svalbard Global Seed Vault opened in Norway in 2008. Its goal is to store seeds of food plants from around the world. Seeds need to be kept cold so that they don't start to grow. This is why the vault is located on an island in the Arctic Ocean. The seeds will stay cold there even if electricity fails in the vault.

On its first day of operation, a shipment of 100 million seeds was received from more than 100 countries. Here are some examples of things you will find in the vault:

- 70,000 different varieties of rice from 120 countries
- thousands of potato seeds from a seed bank in Peru
- 47,000 seed samples of wheat and 10,000 types of maize from a seed bank in Mexico

Svalbard Global Seed Vault

Diagram of the Svalbard Global Seed Vault

Why Save Seeds?

Seeds can grow into new plants. Blueberries, barley, and beets all start as seeds.

Different plants make different kinds and numbers of seeds. A mature oak tree can produce thousands of small seeds (acorns) in one year. A coconut palm produces a few really big seeds in the same amount of time.

Under the right conditions, seeds sprout, or **germinate**. When a seed can get enough water, warmth, and oxygen, it will grow into a new plant.

As the seed takes in moisture, it begins to swell. The first part to grow from the seed is the root.

The root gets thicker and longer. Then the stem begins to grow up to the light. It is now a seedling.

The first true leaves have emerged. They now make food for the plant.

Fruits and Cones

Most vascular plants produce seeds in very familiar "containers": cones, fruits, and nuts. It all begins with pollination. Pollen from the male part of one plant lands on the female part of the same or another plant. When that happens, fertilization can take place and new seeds can develop.

Many cone-bearing plants have needlelike leaves. Seeds for new pine trees develop between the scales of the pinecone.

A pine tree makes two types of cones. Female pinecones hold the seeds for new pine trees. Pollen made in male cones is carried by the wind to female cones. This makes it possible for seeds to develop inside the female cones.

Seeds in flowering plants are protected inside fruits as they develop. Apples, pears, oranges, tomatoes, and cucumbers are all examples of fruits with seeds inside them.

Most plants that people eat are flowering plants. Most flowers have both male and female parts. A flower makes pollen. It needs pollen to produce seeds.

Wind isn't the only way that pollen is transferred. Insects, such as bees, and other animals carry pollen from one flower to another. Moving pollen from the male part of one flower to the female part of a flower on another plant is called cross-pollination.

Many plants protect their seeds inside fleshy fruits.

Bees often bring pollen from one flower to another. This is an important step in the formation of fruit.

Spreading Seeds Around the World

When fruits become ripe, the plant is ready to release the seeds. In every kind of habitat, insects, birds, small animals, and people release a fruit's seeds. Wind and water also help in seed **dispersal**.

How do seeds travel to places where they might germinate and grow? Here are a few examples.

Dandelion seeds are at the bottom of tiny parachutes. The wind carries these tiny seeds to new homes.

A bird eats berries. Later the seeds in the berries will fall to the ground in another place, along with the bird's droppings.

Some seeds that travel by water have air in them. Air inside the hollow coconut helps it float to a new place and wash up on shore.

A dog or other animal might give some seeds a ride.

A squirrel buries an acorn—a seed in a hard case. The acorn may germinate if the squirrel doesn't come back and dig it up.

Chapter Four

People Need Plants! Plants Need People!

Many cultures tell stories about plants and people. Here is a creation myth about the rainforest.

The Sun, the Old Man, and the Rainforest

Before the world had many of the plants and animals that we know today, there was a village. In the village lived an old, old man.

At that time the Sun lived among the people. No one was wiser than him. The elders of the village talked to Sun about the old man. "How old will he become?" they asked. "Will he ever die?"

Sun said, "It is time for the old man to bring forth his gifts." Sun told the elders to bring the old man to him. When all was ready, Sun told the elders to cut off the old man's hair.

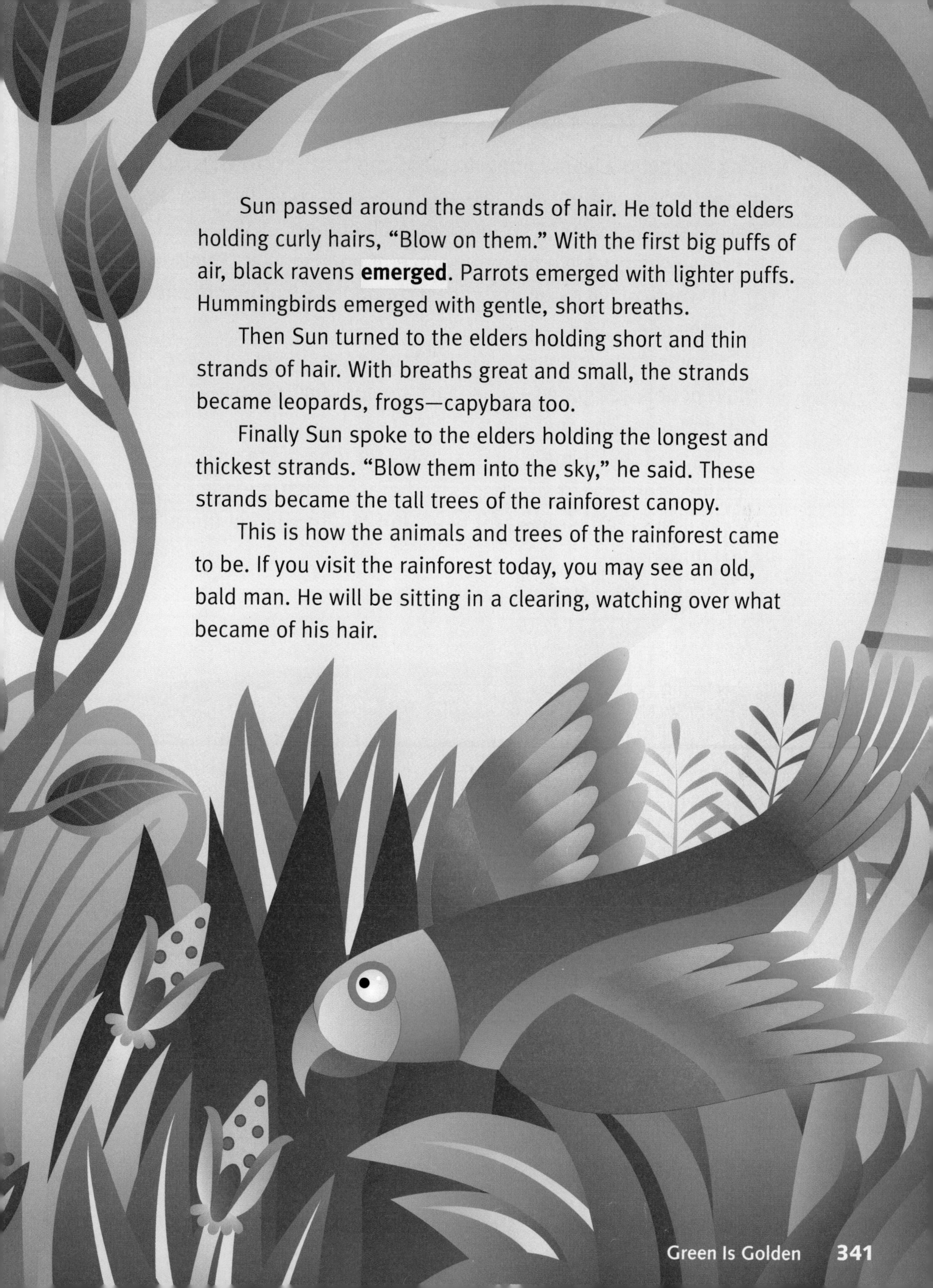

Sun passed around the strands of hair. He told the elders holding curly hairs, "Blow on them." With the first big puffs of air, black ravens **emerged**. Parrots emerged with lighter puffs. Hummingbirds emerged with gentle, short breaths.

Then Sun turned to the elders holding short and thin strands of hair. With breaths great and small, the strands became leopards, frogs—capybara too.

Finally Sun spoke to the elders holding the longest and thickest strands. "Blow them into the sky," he said. These strands became the tall trees of the rainforest canopy.

This is how the animals and trees of the rainforest came to be. If you visit the rainforest today, you may see an old, bald man. He will be sitting in a clearing, watching over what became of his hair.

Plants for Food

Long ago people learned how to plant and harvest crops, which meant that people became less migrant—they could live in one place instead of moving around in search of food.

Today plants are a primary source of nourishment. Think about what you've eaten in the past 24 hours. What plants did you consume?

People grow grains, or cereals, more than any other plant. When people eat grains—which include corn (maize), wheat, rice, and oats—they get energy.

Many of the animals humans raise for food graze on pastures. They eat fresh grasses and grasses that are dried as hay. Hogs, cattle raised for beef, and poultry are fed these plant materials.

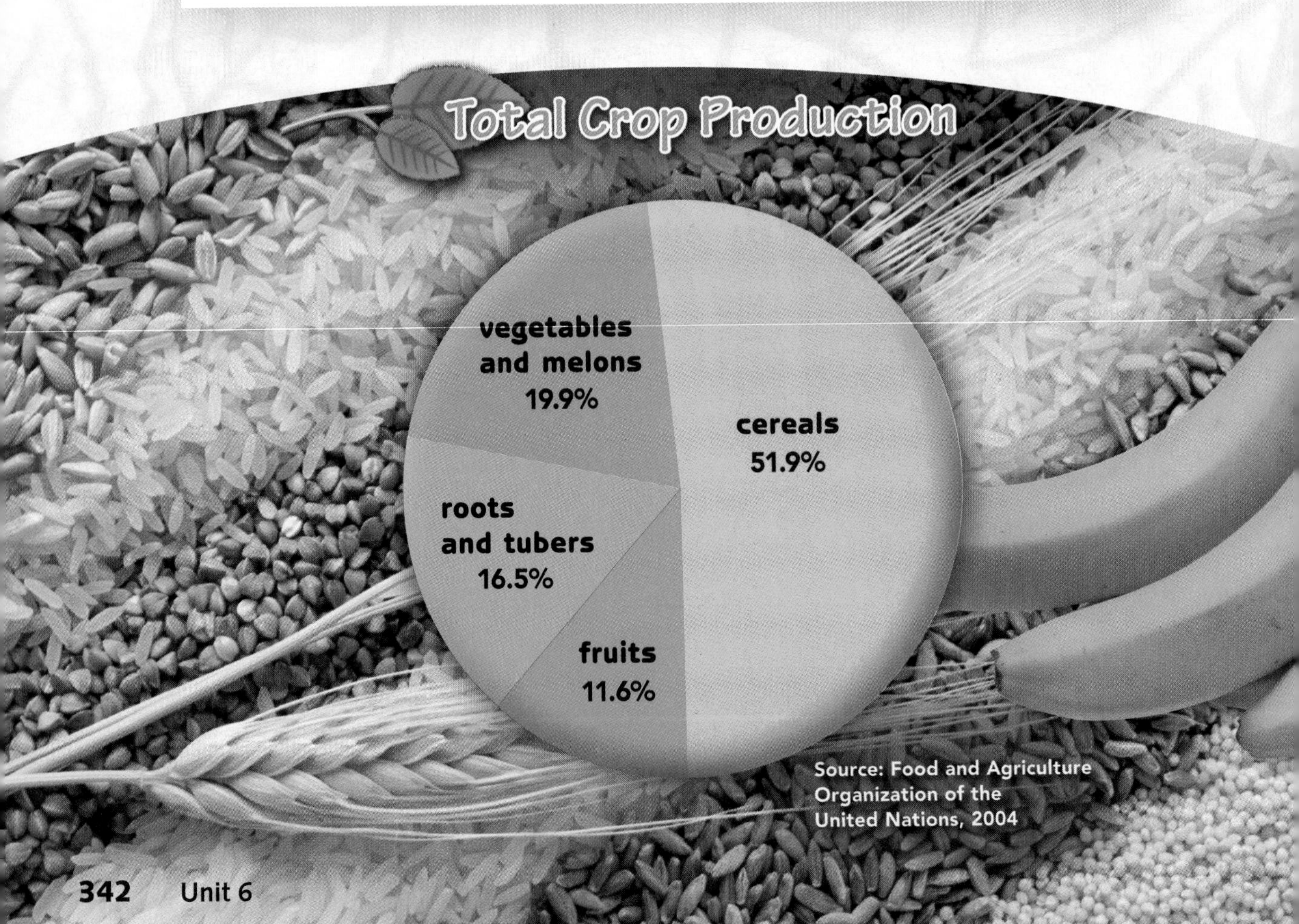

People also grow vegetables and fruits. For example, many different kinds of melons, cabbages, and squash are grown and eaten in various parts of the world. People also harvest beans and nuts. Popular foods such as coffee, tea, cola, and chocolate all begin with plants.

Where people live makes a difference in what they can grow. Apple trees grow best in temperate climates. They need a period of cold temperatures to grow well and produce fruit. Apples are an important crop in states such as New York, Washington, and Michigan. Bananas grow best in tropical climates, because they cannot produce crops in places with cold temperatures. Bananas are an important crop in some Central and South American countries. Some crops grow well in many climates. For example, even though potatoes are native to Peru, people around the world now grow different kinds of potatoes.

More Than Food

Name a product that you use, wear, or play with. Unless it is plastic, metal, or synthetic, it probably has something to do with a plant. Soap, chewing gum, spices, oils, clothing, dyes, baskets—all begin with plants.

Latex is harvested from rubber trees. Latex is used to make rubber tires for cars and other vehicles.

Medicines from Plants

This cinchona tree is located in Brazil.

Plants make many different chemicals. Over time, people have used some of these chemicals as useful medicines to fight certain illnesses. For example, poppy plants are the source of morphine. Morphine is a medicine used to relieve intense pain. Digitoxin is a medicine that comes from some kinds of foxgloves, common garden plants. This medicine is used to help regulate the rate and strength of a patient's heartbeat. The Madagascar periwinkle contains vincristine and vinblastine—two medicines used to battle some forms of cancer.

Quinine, a medicine that comes from the bark of the cinchona tree, is used to treat malaria. Cinchona trees grow in warm climates in South America and in some Asian countries. Malaria, a disease spread by mosquitoes, is one of the most widespread human diseases. Scientists have created synthetic drugs to treat malaria, but in some cases quinine still works best.

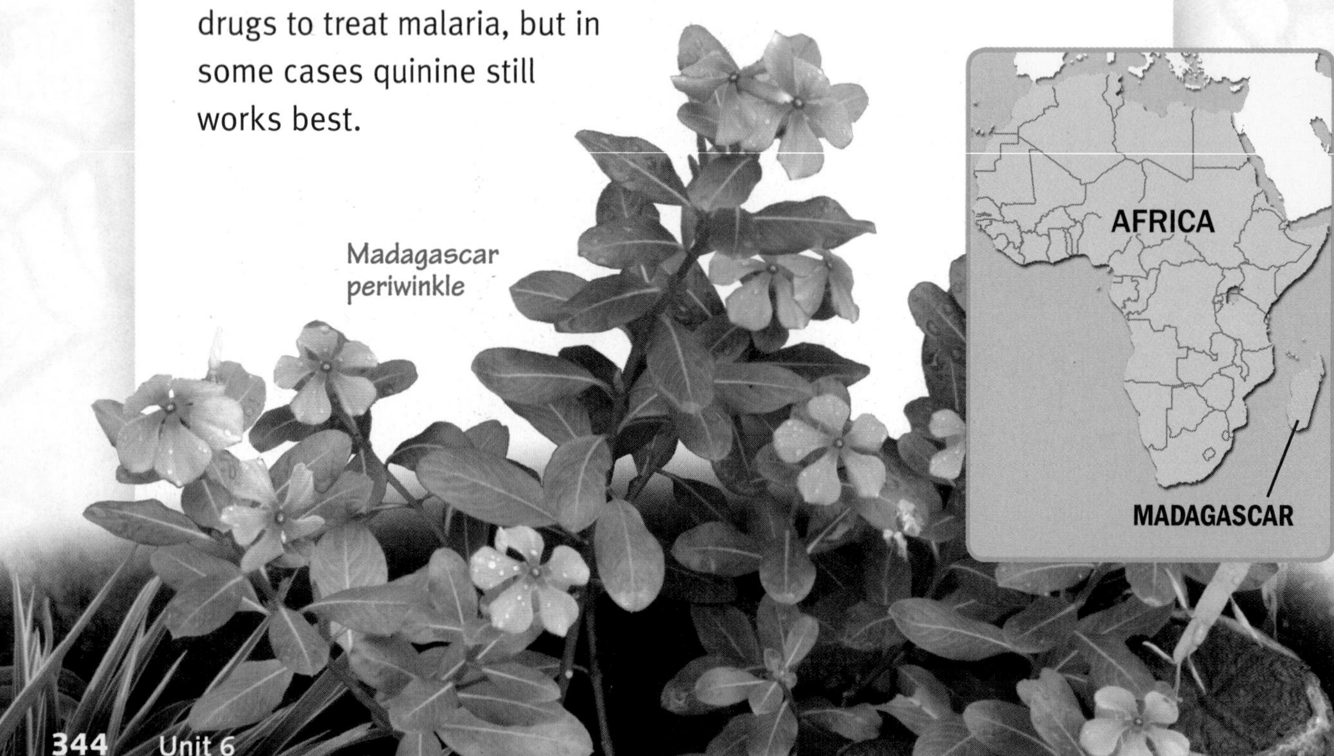

Madagascar periwinkle

Protecting the Rainforest

The rainforest is one of the most important places to explore new uses for plants. Tropical rainforests are rich with plant life. They include more than 50 percent of Earth's plant species. However, they cover only a small part of Earth's surface. Scientists **estimate** that a 4-square-mile area of a tropical rainforest may have 1,500 kinds of flowering plants and 750 kinds of trees! In fact, scientists are still looking for and studying new rainforest plants.

Such riches are a good reason to protect rainforests. If an unidentified plant dies out, we never will know how it could have been used.

The Big Ideas

Plants are part of almost every habitat on Earth, making our planet a kingdom of green. Learning about plants helps us take care of them, ourselves, and our planet.

- Plants are complex living things. Scientists group them according to their structures.
- Plants have special ways of surviving in many different, sometimes harsh, environments.
- Plants grow from seeds, which are packaged and spread in many different ways.
- Plants are vitally important to the health of every living thing on Earth.

(Answer to riddle on page 318: a watermelon)

Kate and the Beanstalk

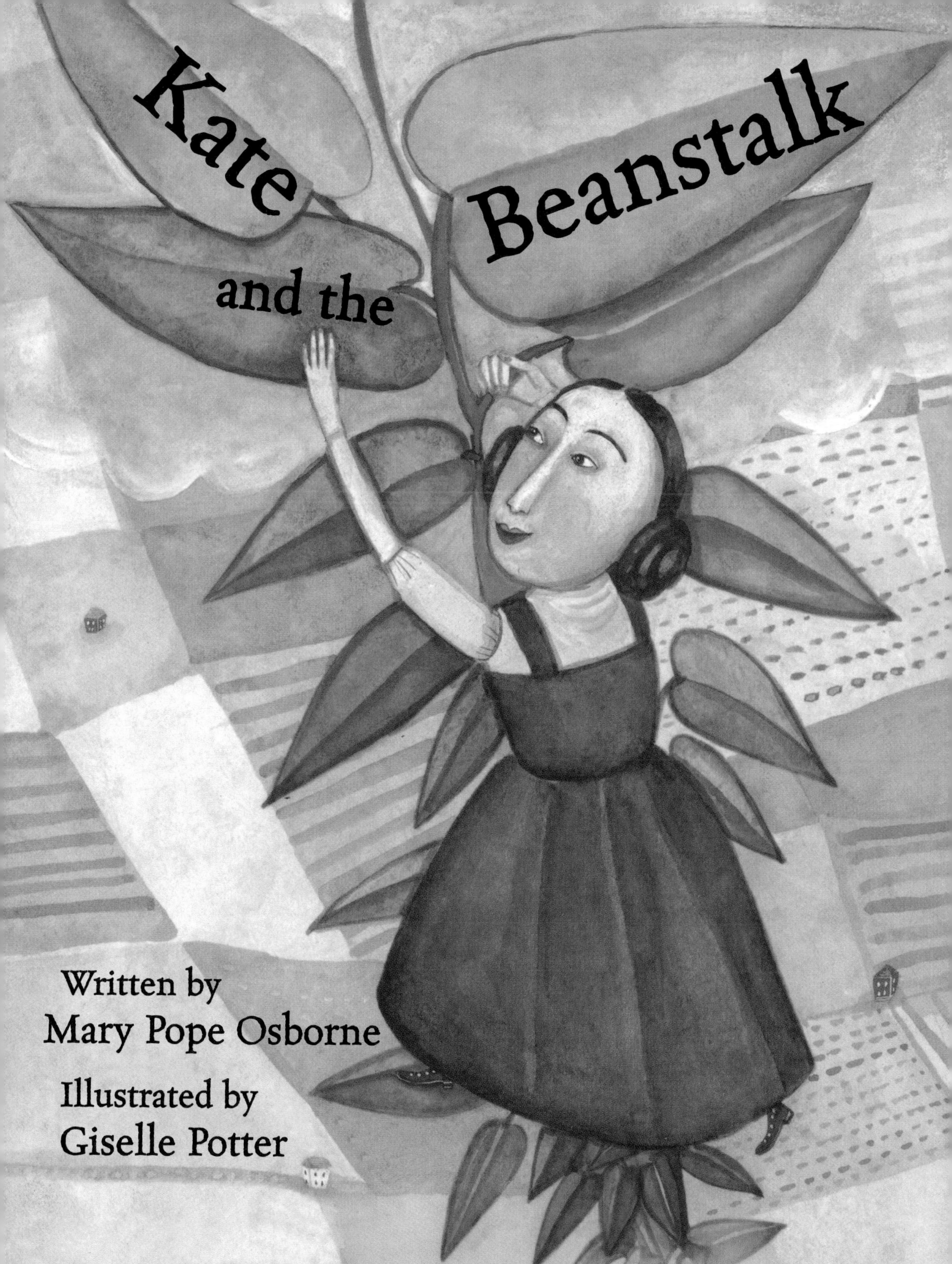

Written by
Mary Pope Osborne

Illustrated by
Giselle Potter

Long ago, a girl named Kate lived with her mother in a humble cottage. One day, after a hard winter, Kate's mother was in despair.

"We are sure to die from hunger," she said, "unless we sell our only cow to get money for food."

Kate was a plucky girl who loved to help. "Don't worry," she said, giving her mother a hug. "I'll take care of everything."

And she set out for market with their cow.

On the way, Kate met a beggar holding a small sack.

"Special beans," the beggar said in a creaky voice.

"How **extraordinary**!" said Kate when she saw them, for the brown beans shone like dark gold. "I don't think I can live without them."

"They can be yours–in exchange for your cow," said the beggar.

Without another thought, Kate traded her cow for the beans and rushed home to give them to her mother.

But to Kate's surprise, her poor mother was horrified. "Our only hope is gone!" she cried. "Now we will surely starve!" And she tossed the beans out the window.

Hungry and forlorn, Kate went to bed.

During the night, Kate couldn't sleep. She got up and crept into the moonlit garden.

She gasped. For in the darkest corner, a giant beanstalk rose into the sky. It rose higher and higher and higher still, till it disappeared behind the clouds.

"Does it never end?" whispered Kate.

Without waiting for morning, Kate began climbing the beanstalk. She climbed and climbed and climbed . . .

. . . up and up and up and up.

When Kate reached the top, light was creeping into the gray sky. Through a misty haze, she saw the most astonishing sight: Above the clouds was a countryside with fine woods, a crystal stream, a rolling sheep meadow, and a mighty castle.

As Kate stared in wonder, an old woman hobbled out of the woods.

"Hello!" said Kate. "Is that castle your home?"

"No, my dear," the woman replied. "It once belonged to a noble knight and his fair wife. They had a small infant and many treasures. But one day, a monstrous giant came to steal from them. He killed the good man and took over his castle."

"How dreadful!" said Kate.

"Fortunately, the knight's wife and baby were visiting in the valley," said the old woman. "Afraid to return home, the grieving widow stayed below to raise her child. But alas, now they are very poor and close to starving."

"That's so sad," said Kate.

"Sadder than you know, my dear," replied the old woman. She looked deeply into Kate's eyes. "Perhaps you are the one to right the terrible wrongs that have occurred."

"Me?" said Kate.

"Are you afraid?"

"I don't think so. I fear nothing when I'm doing right. How can I help?" said Kate.

"The knight had three precious treasures–a hen that lays golden eggs, a bag filled with gold coins, and the most wondrous harp in all the world," said the old woman. "If you find these and return them to the knight's widow, then she and her child will not die from hunger."

Kate took a deep breath. "I shall try," she said.

Kate bid farewell to the old woman, then strode across the sheep meadow. As she approached the castle, a giantess lunged into the early morning light.

"Help me!" the huge woman roared. "My husband makes me cook from the cock's crow to the owl's hoot! Whenever I hire servants, he gobbles them up!"

"I'll be your servant," said Kate. "But you must hide me from the giant."

Kate helped the giantess make breakfast until the sun came up. When she heard the giant coming down the hall, she trembled with fear. His footsteps sounded like the booms of a cannon.

"Hide!" whispered the giantess, and she pushed Kate into a closet.

Peeking through the keyhole, Kate watched and listened.

"Fee,

Fi,

Fo,

Fum'un,

I smell the blood of an Englishwoman.
Be she alive or be she dead,
I'll grind her bones to make my bread."

"Don't be silly," said the giantess. "You only smell the wagonload of bacon I fried for your breakfast."

"Oh," said the giant.

When the giant finished eating, he said, "Bring me the knight's hen."

The giantess brought out a small brown hen.

"Lay!" ordered the giant. And the little hen laid a golden egg.

"Ha-ha-haah!" roared the giant. "I love my lovely little stolen hen." Then he put down his head and fell asleep, snoring as loud as thunder.

Ever so quietly, Kate crept out of the closet.

She grabbed the hen and rushed from the castle. She ran across the sheep meadow to the beanstalk. Down and down and down she climbed and climbed and climbed, until she landed *kerplop* in the garden.

Kate sighed with relief. "It's better if Mother doesn't know of the danger I've been in," she whispered to the hen. "Stay here, until I can return you to the knight's poor widow."

Kate hid the hen behind a bush, then slipped back inside her house.

Kate knew she must **disguise** herself to return to the castle. That night she dressed in a wig and a beard, crept out to the moonlit garden, and climbed the beanstalk again.

Kate climbed and climbed and climbed . . .

. . . up and up and up.

In the light before dawn, Kate crossed the sheep meadow and knocked on the castle door.

When the giantess came out, she roared,

"Help me! I need a servant! The last one stole our hen and ran away!"

All happened as before. Kate helped the giantess make breakfast until the sun came up. When they heard the giant's booming footsteps and bellowing voice, the giantess hid Kate in the closet.

"Fee,
Fi,
Fo,
Fum'un,
I smell the blood of an Englishwoman.
Be she alive or be she dead,
I'll grind her bones to make my bread."

"Calm down," said the giantess. "You only smell the mountain of hash I made for your breakfast."

"Oh," said the giant.

When the giant finished eating, he said, "Bring me the knight's money bag."

The giantess brought out a bag filled with gold coins, and the giant greedily counted them.

"Ha-ha-haah!" he roared. "I love my lovely little stolen coins."

Soon the giant's head began to nod. Kate watched him fall asleep. Then she crept out and grabbed the money bag. She ran out of the castle and across the sheep meadow to the beanstalk.

Down and down and down . . .

. . . she climbed and climbed and climbed, until she landed *kerplop* in the garden.

"Goodness!" said Kate. "What a day! I must hide these coins until I can return them to the knight's poor widow."

Kate hid the money bag with the hen, then slipped back inside her house.

That night, Kate disguised herself once again and started up the beanstalk.

She climbed and climbed and climbed . . .

. . . up and up and up and up.

She ran across the sheep meadow, and just as the sun came up, she knocked on the castle door.

When the giantess came out, she grabbed Kate and cried,

"Help me!
I need a servant! The last one stole our money bag and ran away!"

Again, all happened as before. Kate helped the giantess make breakfast. Soon the giant's footsteps boomed down the hall, and the giantess hid Kate in the closet.

"Fee, Fi, Fo, Fum'un,
I smell the blood of an Englishwoman.
Be she alive or be she dead,
I'll grind her bones to make my bread."

"You old fool," said the giantess. "You only smell the sea of fish soup I made for your breakfast."

"Oh," said the giant.

When the giant finished his soup, he cried, "Bring me the knight's singing harp."

The giantess brought out a magnificent harp, the only one of its kind in the world. The harp sparkled with diamonds and rubies, and it had strings made of gold.

"Sing!" bellowed the giant.

The harp began to sing a sad, haunting song. It sang of the past, of the noble knight, his lost wife and child, of golden days and starry nights. The harp's lovely song nearly broke Kate's heart.

When the giant fell asleep, she crept out from behind the door, seized the harp, and ran away with it.

But the harp was so frightened, it sang high, fearful notes: "*Help me! Help me! Help me!*"

"Quiet!" said Kate. "I'm going to return you to the knight's poor widow!"

But the giant had already been awakened. He jumped up and with a shout, he ran after Kate.

Kate flew like the wind across the sheep meadow. She grabbed the beanstalk and started down with the harp, the giant fast on her heels.

. . . she climbed and climbed and climbed, and the giant climbed and climbed and climbed right after her.

As soon as Kate's feet touched the ground, she shouted, "Mother! Bring the ax! Hurry!"

Kate's mother ran out with the ax, and Kate grabbed it.

With one mighty blow, Kate chopped the beanstalk in two. Down and down it fell, down through the sky, and down fell the giant—*WHUMP!*—down into the garden. The ground shook like an earthquake.

Kate's mother took one look and cried out in horror, "That's the giant that killed your father!"

"My father?" asked Kate.

Before her mother could answer, a fairy approached in a chariot drawn by two peacocks.

"Greetings, brave Kate," she said. "As Queen of the Fairies, I have long wanted to avenge the treachery done to the good knight. But first I needed to know if his daughter was worthy of her inheritance. So I disguised myself as both the beggar and the old woman and sent you on your quest to your father's castle."

"My father's castle?" Kate looked at her mother, who nodded.

"I never spoke of your father after he was slain," Kate's mother said. "He would be most proud of you now."

Kate hugged her mother, and they wept for the sorrow and wonder of it all.

Then they climbed into the chariot and rose through the clouds, to the castle that was once again theirs . . .

. . . up and up and up.

Kate asked the giantess to stay on as their cook.

"Thank you for your kindness," said the giantess. "Would you like a biscuit and jam?"

"Indeed," said Kate and her mother.

And the giantess served them a biscuit as big as a cow.

UNIT 7

Foundations of Freedom

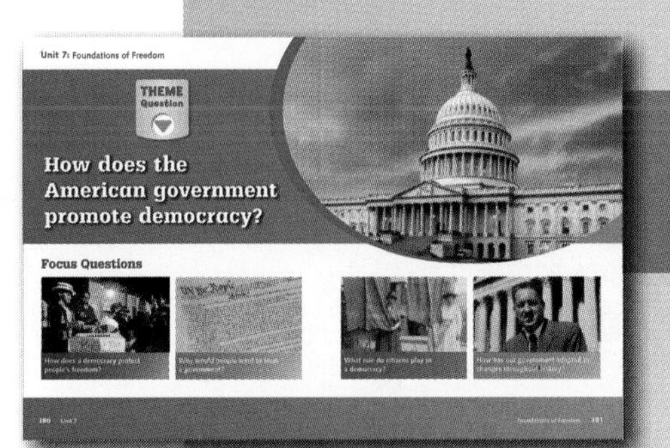

How does the American government promote democracy?

Focus Questions

How does a democracy protect people's freedom?

Why would people want to form a government?

What role do citizens play in a democracy?

How has our government adapted to changes throughout history?

A Government of, by, and for the People

by Joyce Jackson

Contents

Chapter 1

Every Vote Counts!

Have you ever voted in a mock election? In recent years some people have come up with interesting ways to predict which Presidential candidate might win an election. In 2008 a chain of stores offered customers the chance to express their choice by the color of their coffee cups. People who preferred Republican candidate John McCain took their coffee in a red cup. Those who supported Democratic candidate Barack Obama used a blue cup. By election day the stores had distributed more than 3 million cups. More people chose blue cups for Barack Obama, just as more people voted for him in the general election.

A nationwide chain of ice cream shops also held its own election—with similar results! The company developed two new flavors, one each for Senators Obama and McCain. People voted for their favorite flavor online or at their local shop. Nearly 500,000 votes were cast, and Obama defeated McCain by a margin of only two points.

Students participate in a mock election at a school in Stockholm, California.

Voters are assured some privacy when voting to guarantee the preferences they express on their ballots will remain secret.

America's Form of Government

As American citizens we have many rights—and many responsibilities. Voting is one of our most important rights and responsibilities.

Our form of government is based on **democracy**, which means "rule by the people." We vote for leaders to represent us, and those leaders make decisions and speak for us. The United States, then, is a representative democracy—that is, a republic.

At the federal, or national, level we vote for a President every four years. Senators are elected to six-year terms, although not every senator is up for re-election at the same time. The entire House of Representatives is elected every two years.

How do our elected officials know what to do? How do they make a difference in the lives of Americans? Let's find out!

The Government's Rule Book

In 4,543 words—just four pages—the writers of the Constitution described our form of government and set down the rules for running it. The Constitution describes a government with three branches, with each branch working both independently and together with the other branches. This ensures that no individual branch ever becomes too powerful.

Balancing the Branches The Framers of the Constitution limited government powers through a system of "checks and balances." The President (executive) can appoint a Supreme Court justice, for example, but the Senate (legislative) must approve him or her. Congress (legislative) can pass a law; however, the President (executive) can veto, or refuse to sign, it. If the law is passed (legislative), the Supreme Court (judicial) can declare it unconstitutional.

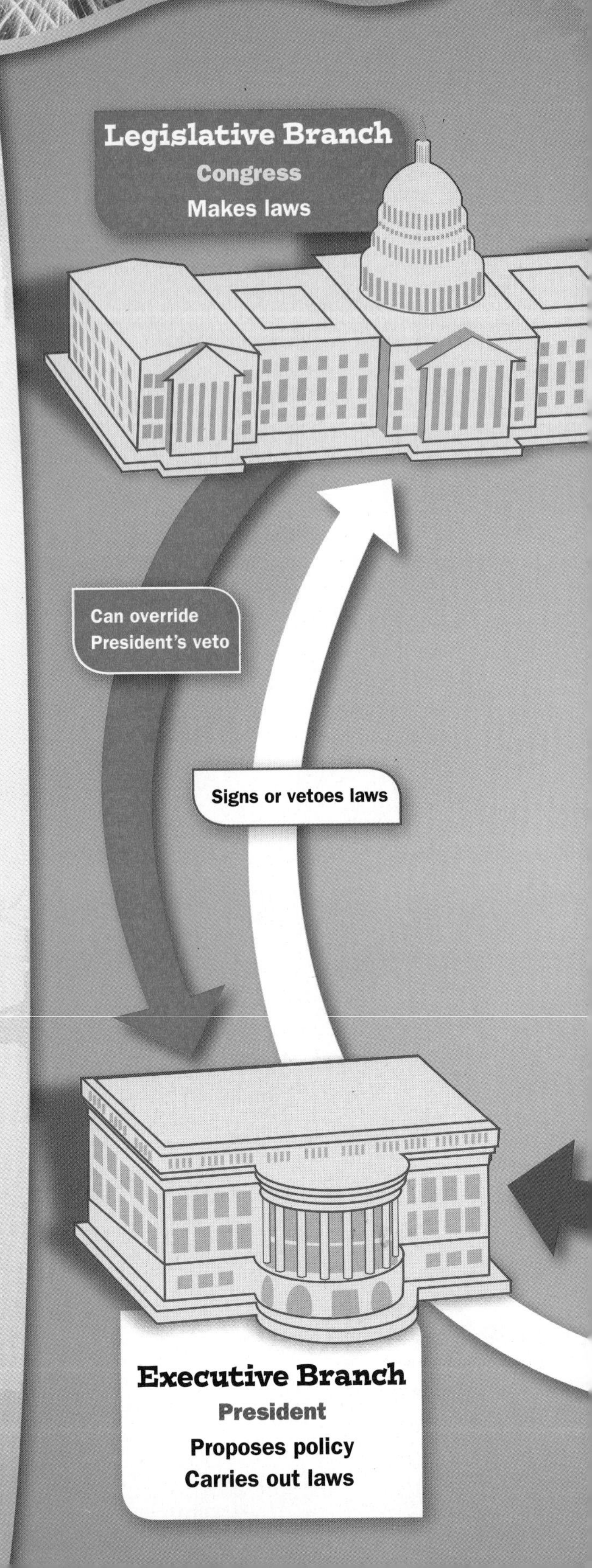

The Three Branches of Government

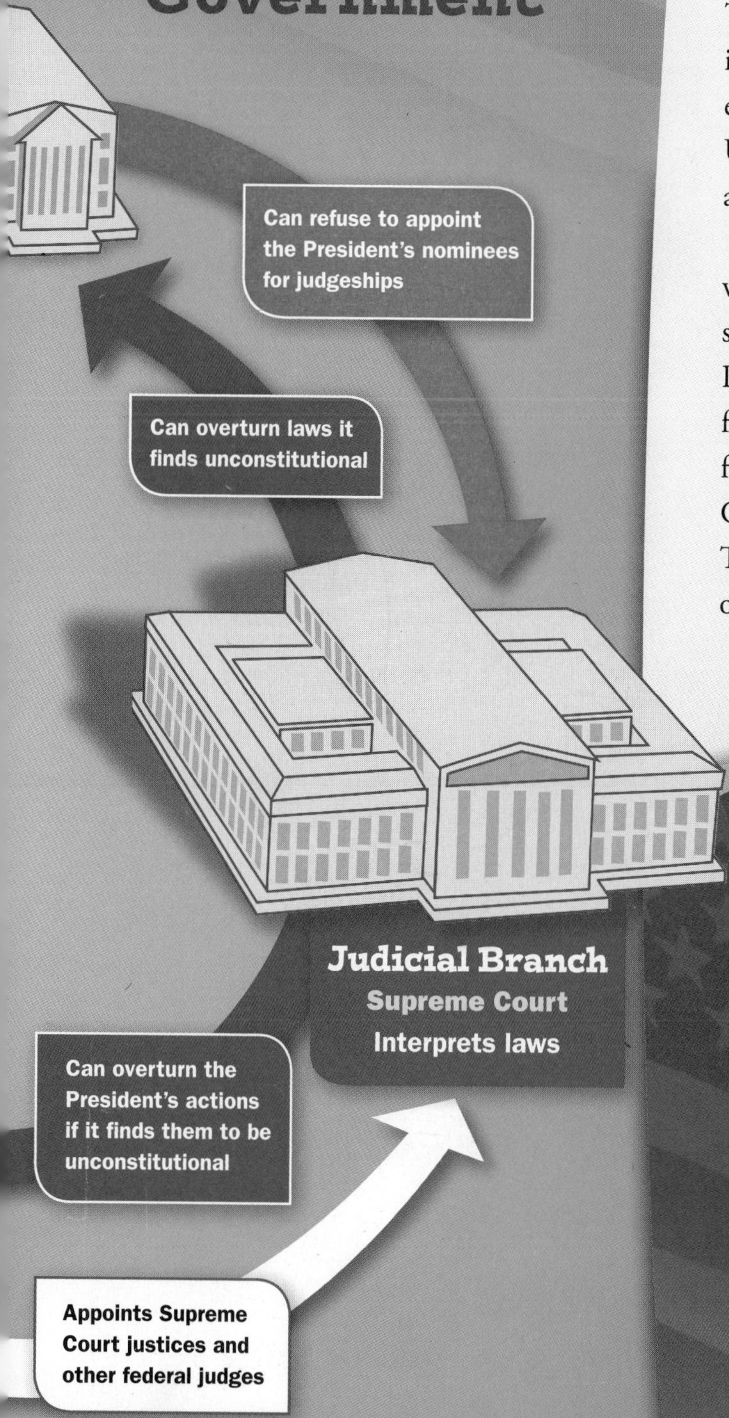

Can refuse to appoint the President's nominees for judgeships

Can overturn laws it finds unconstitutional

Judicial Branch
Supreme Court
Interprets laws

Can overturn the President's actions if it finds them to be unconstitutional

Appoints Supreme Court justices and other federal judges

The Executive Branch Many people think of the executive branch as being only the office of the President. This isn't true. The Vice President and presidential advisers, including the Cabinet, are also part of the executive branch, as are agencies such as the United States Postal Service, the Peace Corps, and the Federal Bureau of Investigation.

The Constitution tells how a President will be elected and how long he or she may serve. The Constitution also names the President's responsibilities, such as directing foreign affairs and commanding the armed forces. The President may suggest laws to Congress and enforce laws passed by Congress. The President also appoints government officials, including some judges.

The Electoral College

After fighting for independence from Britain, Americans didn't want a king for a leader, so they decided on an elected President. But how best to choose that President? If Congress chose, the President might listen to Congress more than to the people. If the people chose directly, a very popular person might seize power and then refuse to leave office. The Framers (the designers of our government) decided that electors would choose the President. Today citizens vote, but the Electoral College still officially chooses the President and Vice President.

The Legislative Branch The legislative branch is made up of the House of Representatives and the Senate, together called the Congress. The Senate has 100 members, two from each state. The number of representatives in the House is based on each state's population. While California with its large population has more than 50 representatives, some states with much smaller populations have only a single representative.

The most important job of the legislative branch is to make laws. Congress is also responsible for raising money through taxes—money that pays for programs that Congress thinks are important for the American people.

The legislative branch has other responsibilities too. It is the only branch of the federal government that can declare war, and it is responsible for raising an army and a navy. It can print or borrow money. Furthermore, this branch can suggest **amendments** to the Constitution.

These powers and others are named in the Constitution. The Constitution also tells who can be a member of Congress, how often Congress must meet, and how Congress must keep records of its work.

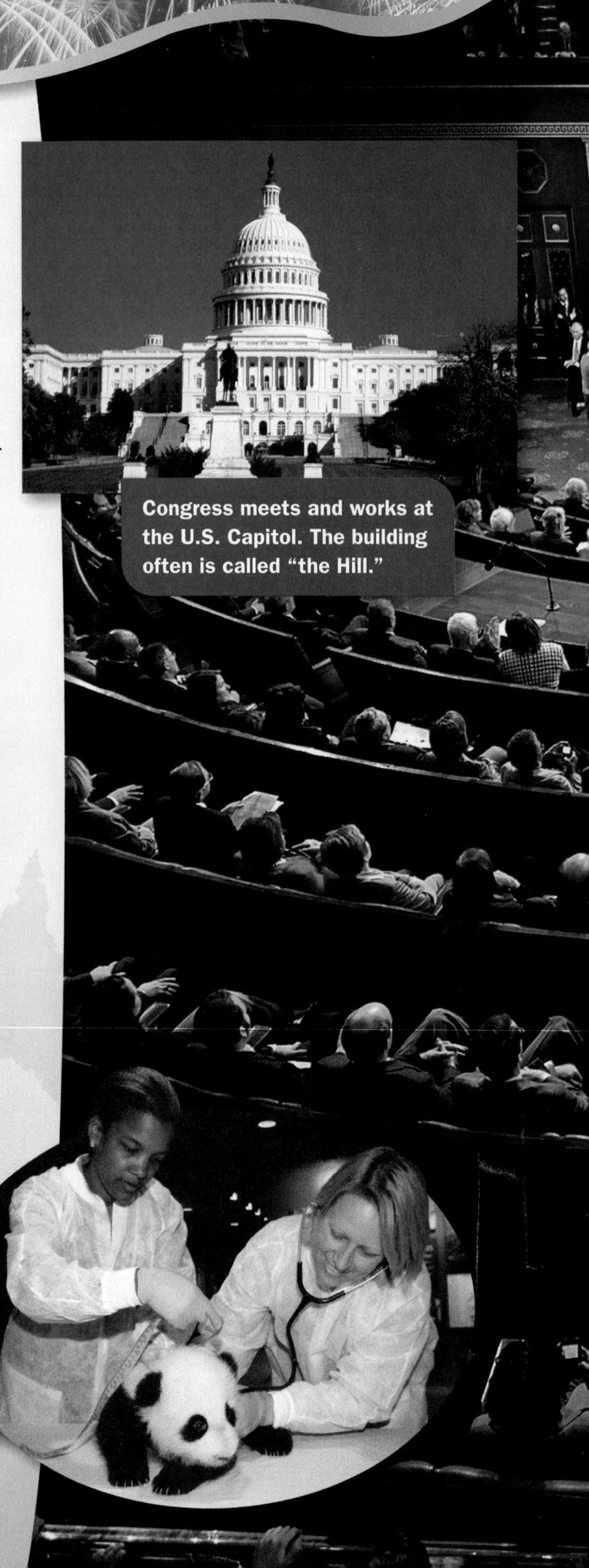

Congress meets and works at the U.S. Capitol. The building often is called "the Hill."

Besides the responsibilities that are listed in the Constitution, Congress has a wide range of other jobs. It oversees the U.S. Botanic Garden and the museums of the Smithsonian, which includes the National Zoo.

The Judicial Branch The judicial branch is the system of courts. The highest court, the Supreme Court, makes final decisions about whether laws and lower-court decisions are constitutional; that is, supported by the Constitution.

The Supreme Court is made up of a chief justice and eight associate justices, appointed by the President and approved by the Senate. These justices serve for as long as they wish; they do not have a set term of office.

Judicial Review

What can you do if you think that a law is unconstitutional? You can go to court! If a lower court, such as a federal district court, rules against you, you can appeal to a higher court—and eventually your case may reach the Supreme Court. There the justices rule on the law's constitutionality, because they have the authority to interpret the meaning of the Constitution. That authority is called judicial review, and it was developed largely by John Marshall, an early chief justice.

Making Laws

If you are wondering where laws come from, take a look in the mirror. Many laws begin with ideas from ordinary citizens like you!

For example, suppose that your class reads about a terrible accident at a railroad crossing. In a class discussion you agree that all railroad crossings should have gates—and you decide to do something about it, with the help of your legislative representatives. Here's the path that your idea would take to become a law.

Sometimes the President signs a bill that then becomes a law in a public ceremony. Often people who helped pass the law are asked to attend the signing ceremony. In this photo, President Lyndon B. Johnson signs the Civil Rights Act of 1964.

Congressional "Pork"

Many bills that sponsors introduce involve spending money. As these bills work their way through Congress, they often pick up "pork"; that is, additional projects that will be paid by the federal government (through taxes) but that benefit only one locality. Members of Congress promote these projects to benefit the people they represent. The presence of pork can attract support for a bill, but sometimes pork can kill a bill as well.

How a Bill Becomes a Law

A bill can originate in the House or Senate.

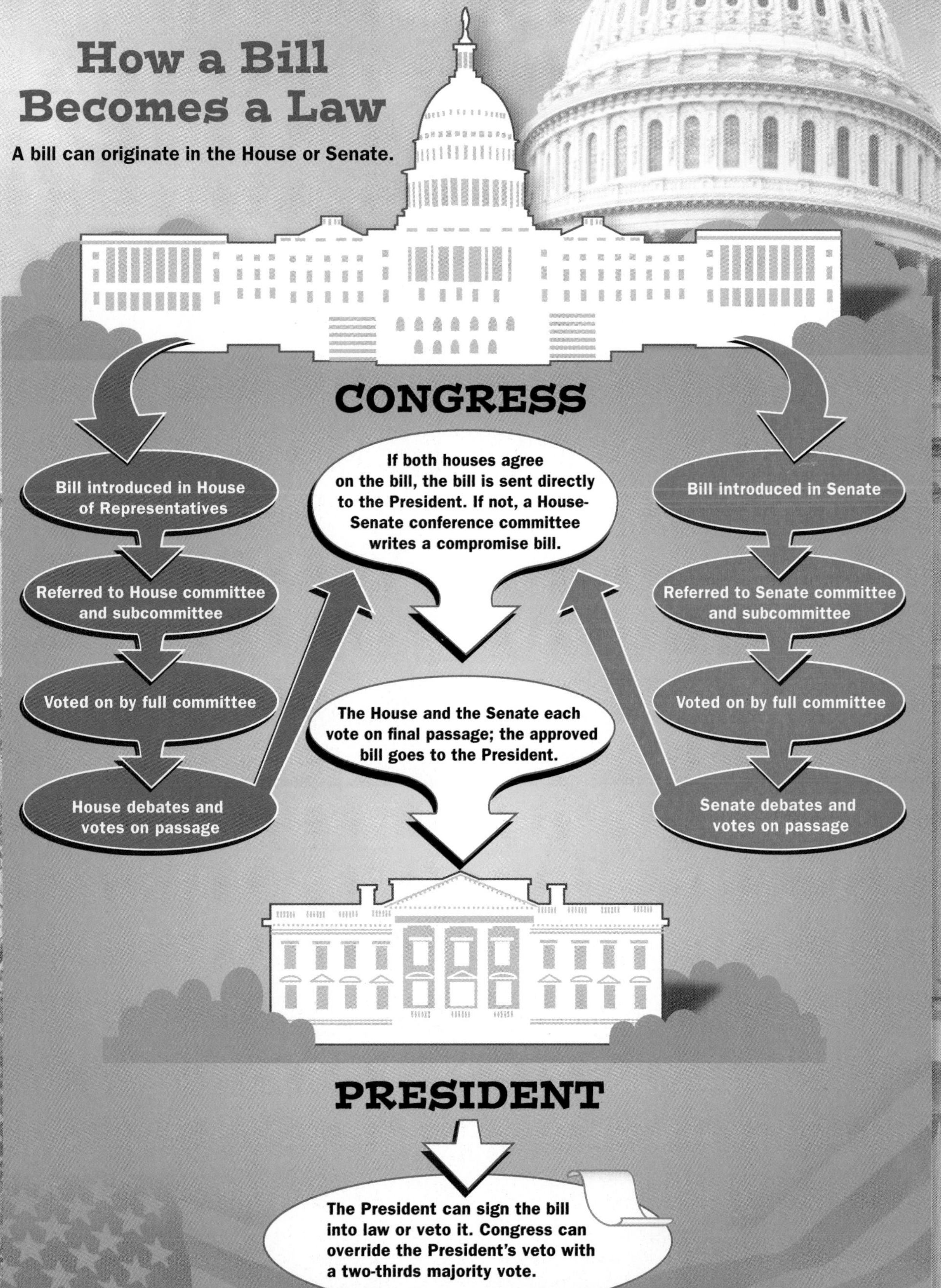

CONGRESS

- Bill introduced in House of Representatives
- Referred to House committee and subcommittee
- Voted on by full committee
- House debates and votes on passage

- Bill introduced in Senate
- Referred to Senate committee and subcommittee
- Voted on by full committee
- Senate debates and votes on passage

If both houses agree on the bill, the bill is sent directly to the President. If not, a House-Senate conference committee writes a compromise bill.

The House and the Senate each vote on final passage; the approved bill goes to the President.

PRESIDENT

The President can sign the bill into law or veto it. Congress can override the President's veto with a two-thirds majority vote.

Chapter 2

Writing the Constitution

On a cold December day in 1952, two documents were placed in helium-filled cases, inside wooden crates that were then laid on mattresses in an armored personnel carrier. An armed escort accompanied the documents on their journey from secret vaults to a public museum.

These two documents were the Declaration of Independence and the Constitution of the United States. Each year hundreds of thousands of people visit the National Archives in Washington, D.C., to see the original documents for themselves.

In the past you may have thought about the importance of the Declaration of Independence. To understand the importance of the Constitution, let's study the history that influenced the writing of this document.

We the People

Article. I.

The Framers included George Washington and Benjamin Franklin. James Madison, who has been called "the Father of the Constitution," arrived in Philadelphia carrying the rough draft of a governing document.

The Need for a Central Government

After the Revolutionary War there was a growing nation to govern, bills to pay, and foreign countries to deal with. Who would take charge, and on what authority?

The new nation's first answer was the Articles of Confederation. This document, approved in 1781, gave a lot of power to the states, which created multiple problems at a time when the nation was trying to come together. How responsive would leaders be to the need for change?

Coming Together in Philadelphia

In 1787 representatives from 12 of the 13 states met in Philadelphia and worked in secret. The representatives debated and compromised for many months. Finally they agreed on a plan: the Constitution of the United States.

The Constitution consists of seven articles that describe the government as having three branches, each with some power to overrule the others. Its articles describe how states and the federal government work together; they also explain how to amend the Constitution.

Drawing on the Past

The Constitution is based on ideas in several earlier documents and traditions. Here are a few examples.

The Magna Carta The "Great Charter" was written by a group of English barons. Angered by what they saw as abuses of their traditional rights, the barons rebelled and forced King John to sign this document in 1215. Many historians point to parts of the Magna Carta as the foundation of the constitutional rights to a trial by jury and a ban on imprisonment without a legal reason.

The Great Law of Peace Before Europeans settled North America, separate Native American Iroquois groups formed a peaceful, democratic relationship. This relationship, known as the Iroquois Confederacy, produced a democratic government called the "Great Law of Peace." Benjamin Franklin, who helped write parts of the Declaration of Independence and the Constitution, knew about the Great Law of Peace. Parallels between the Iroquois social structure and the U.S. Constitution include a government that combines local and national authority and has a two-part legislature.

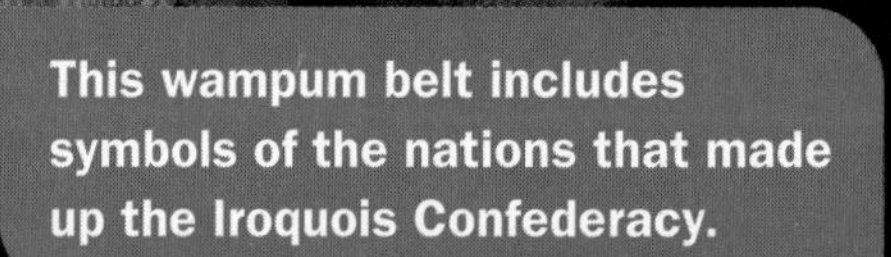

This wampum belt includes symbols of the nations that made up the Iroquois Confederacy.

N. C. Wyeth's 1939 painting *Mayflower Compact* depicted the signing of this important document, nearly 300 years after it occurred.

The Mayflower Compact In 1620 the Pilgrims on the *Mayflower* wrote an agreement called the Mayflower Compact. The Pilgrims pledged "to enact, constitute, and frame, such just and equal laws . . . for the general good of the colony; unto which we promise all due submission and obedience."

The English Bill of Rights In 1689, after a dispute with King James II, England's legislative body—Parliament—wrote a bill of rights, which was agreed to by the next king and queen. The English Bill of Rights created a constitutional monarchy, in which the ruler could not act without the approval of Parliament. The document also listed rights that later would appear in our Constitution and its amendments, such as freedom of speech, the right to a speedy and fair public trial, and a ban on cruel and unusual punishment.

Ratifying the Constitution

Article VII explains how the Constitution would become law—namely, by having nine of the thirteen states **ratify** it. The Framers felt that once nine states had ratified the document, the remaining four would follow.

Still, ratification was not an easy process. Members of the state conventions argued heatedly. Well-known Americans who had fought together for independence from Britain now fought each other over their governing document. Two schools of thought emerged. The Federalists were eager to replace the Articles of Confederation with the Constitution because they favored a strong national government. The Anti-Federalists opposed a strong federal government. They were used to making their own laws at the state level, and they worried about how that ability would change with an untested new form of government.

Completed in 1753, Independence Hall in Philadelphia was the setting for the signings of both the Declaration of Independence and the Constitution.

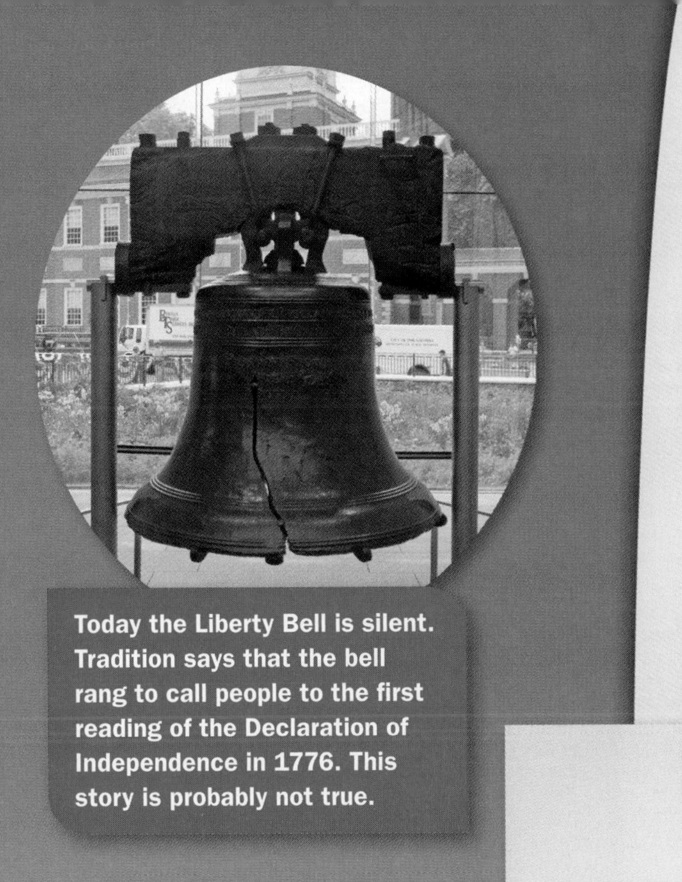

Today the Liberty Bell is silent. Tradition says that the bell rang to call people to the first reading of the Declaration of Independence in 1776. This story is probably not true.

The first state to ratify the Constitution was Delaware, in December 1787. In June 1788, New Hampshire became the ninth state to ratify it. This made the Constitution the law of the land.

Over the years the Constitution showed itself to be an equitable, or fair, document and an improvement over the Articles of Confederation. Even opponents eventually realized that the Framers had worked hard to balance federal and state powers.

Ratifying the Constitution

State	Date of Approval
Delaware	December 7, 1787
Pennsylvania	December 12, 1787
New Jersey	December 18, 1787
Georgia	January 2, 1788
Connecticut	January 9, 1788
Massachusetts	February 6, 1788
Maryland	April 26, 1788
South Carolina	May 23, 1788
New Hampshire	June 21, 1788
Virginia	June 25, 1788
New York	July 26, 1788
North Carolina	November 21, 1789
Rhode Island	May 29, 1790

Source: Jim R. McMellan, *Historical Moments: Changing Interpretations of America's Past: Volume I, the Pre-Colonial Period Through the Civil War*

Chapter 3

A Document for Change

The Constitution was written more than 200 years ago. Since then dramatic changes have occurred in the United States. Changes occurred that could not have even been imagined by the citizens who wrote the document that is still the foundation of our laws in this country.

The Framers knew that the government needed to change in response to the people. They decided that the Constitution should be amended, if the people wanted it to be changed. Despite the long hours of discussion and **compromise** that went into writing the Constitution, some people were still unhappy with it.

Visitors to the Rotunda for the Charters of Freedom can view the original documents of the Declaration of Independence, the Constitution of the United States, and the Bill of Rights.

The Anti-Federalists thought the document gave too much power to the national government at the expense of state governments. The Bill of Rights that protects our individual liberties today grew out of the dissatisfaction expressed by the Anti-Federalists.

Article V within the Constitution explains the amendment processs. A bill suggesting an amendment is proposed in Congress, which then must approve it by a two-thirds majority. Then the bill is sent to the states for approval. Three-fourths of the states must ratify the amendment for it to be constitutional.

Each amendment was ratified for a reason. Amendments have explained rights of individuals, defined citizenship, and even changed how the President and Vice President are elected. To date the Constitution has 27 amendments, and only one—the Eighteenth Amendment—has been **repealed**.

Changing the Constitution by amending it is not an easy process. The process was made to take time so people could consider the effects of the proposed change. Our Constitution has been called a "living document." It changes as our country and its people change. The original writers of this document, which ensures our freedoms and lists our duties as citizens, wrote it with change in mind.

Securing Basic Liberties

The first ten amendments to the Constitution are called the Bill of Rights. The Bill of Rights protects the basic rights of U.S. citizens. Some of the amendments were created in response to the way the colonists were treated during the Revolutionary War. The Bill of Rights guarantees, for example, that people

- have freedom of speech;
- are protected against unlawful searches;
- do not have to let soldiers live in their homes;
- have the right to a speedy and fair trial if they are accused of a crime;
- cannot be punished in ways that are cruel or unusual;
- can assemble peacefully;
- can petition the government; that is, can ask the government to change something.

People often assemble, or participate, in protests and demonstrations to bring attention to an important issue or cause.

James Madison Writes for Rights

James Madison, who would later become the fourth President of the United States, believed in a strong federal government. He spoke often in debates during the Constitutional Convention, and many of his ideas are in the plan that the Framers approved.

But the new Constitution needed help. At the state level, not everyone thought that ratifying it was a good idea. Therefore, James Madison wrote many essays in support of the Constitution that, along with essays written by Alexander Hamilton and John Jay, became part of a collection called the Federalist Papers.

One argument against ratification was that the Constitution did not list individual rights. James Madison, once elected to the House of Representatives, changed that by proposing seventeen amendments! His ideas eventually were stated in twelve amendments, ten of which were ratified as the Bill of Rights.

James Madison (1751–1836) served two terms as President of the United States.

Slavery Banned

The Constitution can be thought of as a mirror that reflects the hopes and freedoms of the people of the United States. In some cases the Constitution changes when our politics change.

On January 31, 1865, toward the end of the Civil War, the House of Representatives approved the Thirteenth Amendment after the Senate had already approved it. This amendment stated that slavery is illegal in the United States. Three-quarters of the states would need to ratify the proposed amendment before it could become part of the Constitution. This meant 27 of the 36 states would need to vote to ban slavery. This happened on December 6, 1865, when Georgia became the twenty-seventh state to ratify the amendment. Two weeks later the U.S. Secretary of State declared the amendment officially ratified, and it became part of the Constitution.

The Fourteenth Amendment was ratified in 1868. It was originally written to guarantee that all formerly enslaved persons have the same rights as other citizens. The amendment says that anyone born in the United States is an American citizen and that all citizens live under the same laws and protections.

This group of formerly enslaved men gathered at a harbor worksite shortly after Abraham Lincoln signed the Emancipation Proclamation in 1863.

Frederick Douglass Visits the White House

At one time, African Americans were not welcome at the White House, but Abraham Lincoln changed that when he met there with Frederick Douglass. Douglass, a formerly enslaved person, was a leader in the campaign to end slavery.

Lincoln said that he hated slavery and wanted to end it. The two men discussed how the emancipation, or freeing, of African American enslaved persons could happen. As they talked, Douglass, once a critic of Lincoln, became a strong supporter of the President.

Douglass was invited to a reception at the White House after Lincoln's second inauguration, in March 1865. Douglass arrived, only to be stopped twice by the police. When Lincoln heard about it, Douglass was brought in, and Lincoln announced to all that his friend Douglass had arrived.

Frederick Douglass (c. 1818–1895) said that Abraham Lincoln "was the first great man that I talked with in the United States freely, who in no single instance reminded me of the difference between himself and myself, of the difference of color. . . . "

Voting Rights for Women

The Fifteenth Amendment, ratified in 1870, said that citizens could not be kept from voting because of their race. "Citizens" really meant "male citizens." Women still were denied suffrage—the right to vote.

Some people insisted that the Fifteenth Amendment be followed immediately by an amendment granting women the right to vote, but that did not happen.

It took quite some time for women to win the right to vote. In 1848 a group of women gathered for a convention in Seneca Falls, New York, to discuss expanding the limited rights of women, including the right to vote. It was the beginning of a struggle that would last for more than 70 years.

It was the states that first gave women the right to vote. Wyoming did so first, when it was still a territory. Other states followed until the Nineteenth Amendment, covering the nation as a whole, was ratified in 1920.

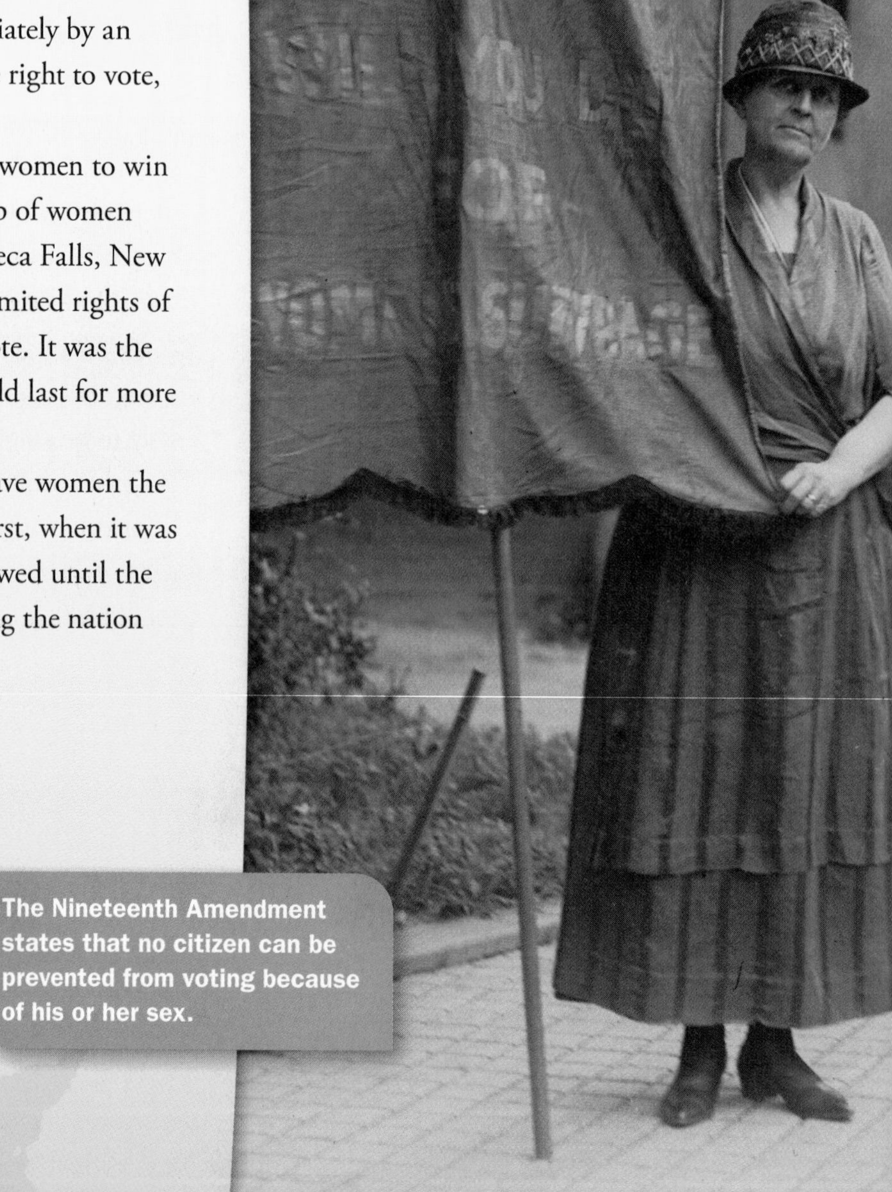

The Nineteenth Amendment states that no citizen can be prevented from voting because of his or her sex.

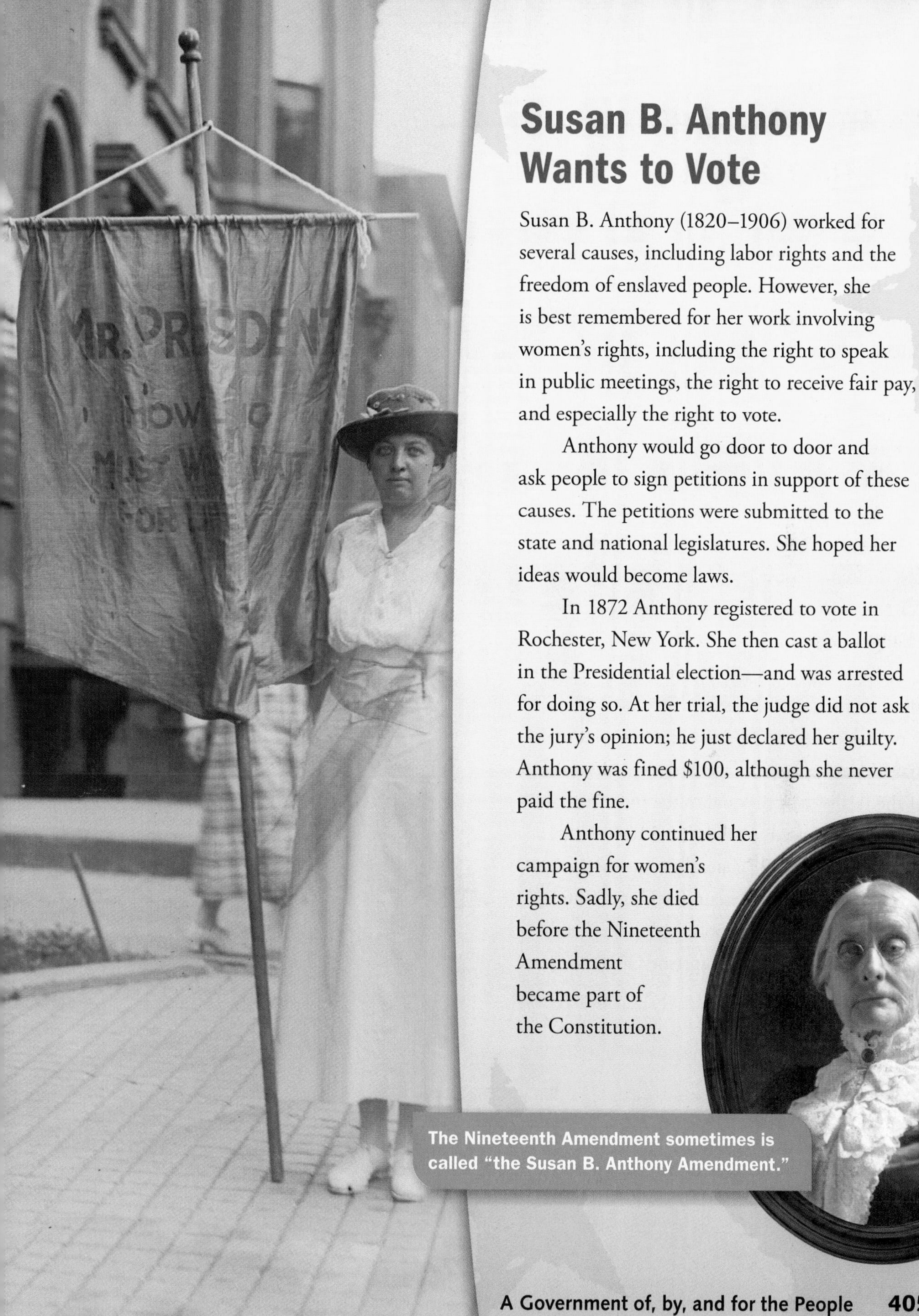

Susan B. Anthony Wants to Vote

Susan B. Anthony (1820–1906) worked for several causes, including labor rights and the freedom of enslaved people. However, she is best remembered for her work involving women's rights, including the right to speak in public meetings, the right to receive fair pay, and especially the right to vote.

Anthony would go door to door and ask people to sign petitions in support of these causes. The petitions were submitted to the state and national legislatures. She hoped her ideas would become laws.

In 1872 Anthony registered to vote in Rochester, New York. She then cast a ballot in the Presidential election—and was arrested for doing so. At her trial, the judge did not ask the jury's opinion; he just declared her guilty. Anthony was fined $100, although she never paid the fine.

Anthony continued her campaign for women's rights. Sadly, she died before the Nineteenth Amendment became part of the Constitution.

The Nineteenth Amendment sometimes is called "the Susan B. Anthony Amendment."

Change through Interpretation

People sometimes use the Constitution to create change in America without passing an amendment. Because amending the Constitution requires the approval of three-fourths of the states, it can take a long time. People often appeal to the judicial branch of the government to effect change. The Supreme Court of the United States is the ultimate decider of the meaning of our laws. The justices can decide on whether a law contradicts the Constitution or is supported by it. In effect the Supreme Court interprets the Constitution for our citizens. Sometimes the interpretation changes over time.

For example, in 1896, the Supreme Court decided the case of *Plessy v. Ferguson*. The Court declared that it was constitutional to have separate facilities for African Americans if the facilities were equal to the ones that white people used. At that time the idea of "separate but equal" generally required African Americans to use different drinking fountains, building entrances, schools, and more. It took almost 60 years for the Supreme Court to change this decision.

This photo, taken before the landmark Civil Rights Act of 1964 was signed into law, shows how segregation was instituted under the policy of "separate but equal."

Thurgood Marshall Argues for Equality

Thurgood Marshall, a lawyer, asked the Supreme Court to look at the Fourteenth Amendment again. He wanted the Court to understand why separate was not equal.

Marshall argued the 1954 Supreme Court case *Brown v. Board of Education of Topeka*. In this case, Marshall showed that the African American schools were not as good as, or equal to, the all-white schools. He argued that this was a violation of the promise of equal protection given to all people by the Fourteenth Amendment.

The Supreme Court agreed with Marshall. Even though this case was about schools, it affected many other areas of American life. The Court's decision meant that **discrimination** was illegal. Marshall's argument helped strengthen the rights of all Americans, not just African Americans. It showed how rights named in the Constitution could be extended based on changes in our society.

COLORED
WAITING ROOM
INTRASTATE PASSENGERS

In 1967 Thurgood Marshall (1908–1993) became the first African American member of the Supreme Court.

Change Over Time

The Constitution changes with the writing of new amendments, and it changes when our politicians and courts interpret it to reflect the needs of the people of this country in modern times. For example, in the nineteenth century and into the early years of the twentieth century, children—some younger than ten years of age—worked long hours. Often the jobs they had were dangerous. Some children worked in mines and mills. Others walked the streets of American cities selling newspapers and other items. They didn't earn much money, were mistreated, and were sentenced to lives of low-paying jobs because many did not attend school while they worked.

Change occurred slowly regarding the rights of children. In the 1930s Franklin Roosevelt signed the Fair Labor Standards Act. This act, in part, changed the ways children were treated in the workplace. Today laws regulate the ways children can work and the amount of schooling they must receive if they do work.

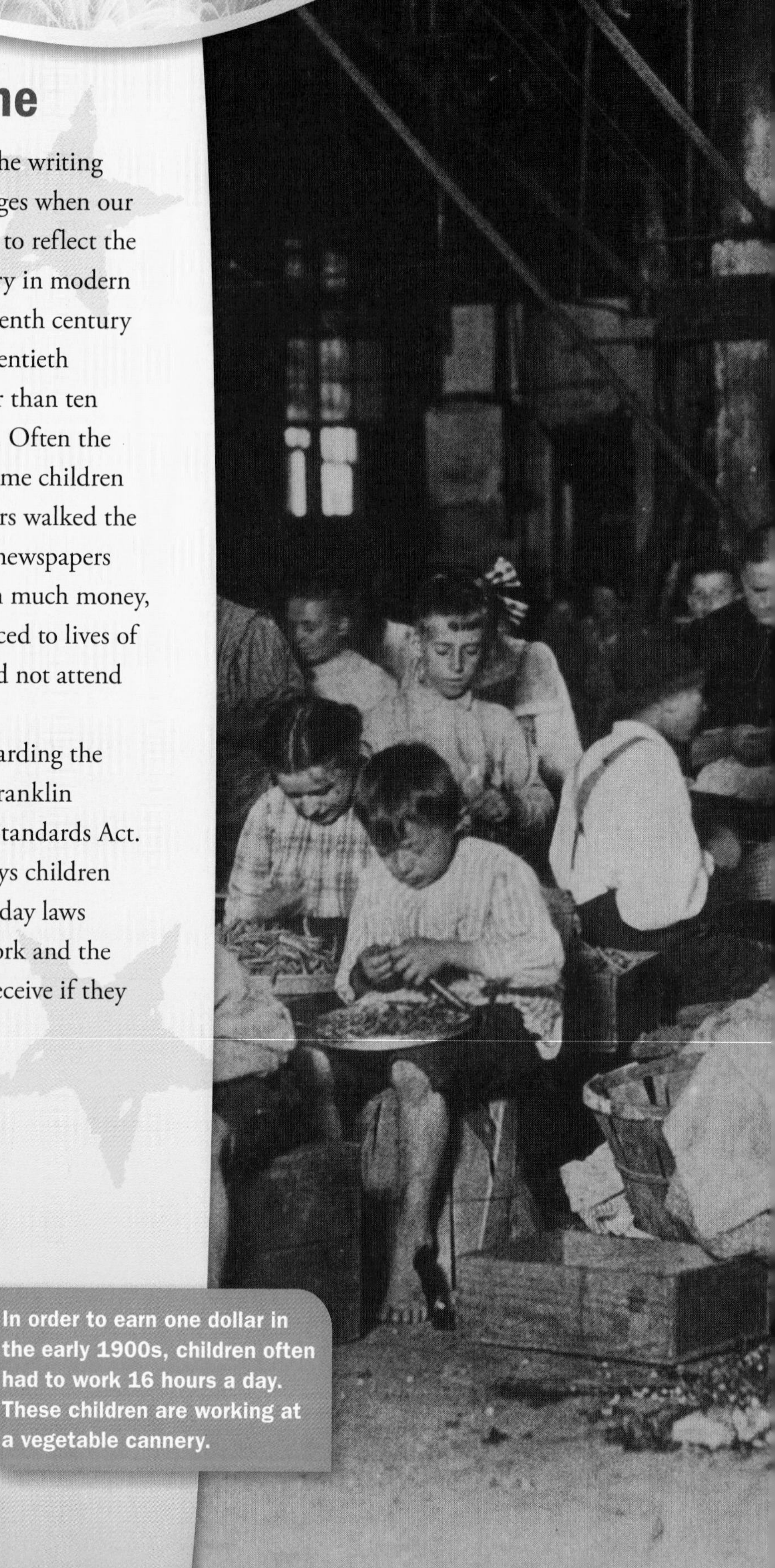

In order to earn one dollar in the early 1900s, children often had to work 16 hours a day. These children are working at a vegetable cannery.

Dennis Chavez Works for Change

As a teen, Dennis Chavez (1888–1962) dropped out of school in New Mexico to help support his family. Still, he wanted to learn. He taught himself about politics and history at the Albuquerque Public Library. Later he traveled to Washington, D.C., to work and earned a law degree from Georgetown University.

Chavez's personal experiences and his belief in the Constitution led him to a career of defending people's rights. He started in local politics and soon became a state representative. In 1930 he was elected to represent New Mexico in Washington, D.C. He served in the House of Representatives and then in the Senate for the rest of his life. He was the first Hispanic senator from New Mexico.

Chavez supported legislation that allowed thousands of people to keep their homes during the economic depression of the 1930s. He supported an equal rights amendment to the Constitution. He fought for a commission that would end discrimination in employment. The commission was not formed, but Chavez's ideas became part of later civil rights laws. Chavez served as a senator until his death on November 18, 1962.

Dennis Chavez (1888–1962) once said, "If the Constitution is worth anything, . . . fair employment practices are correct and necessary."

Many people worked hard to create the Constitution of the United States. It is an enduring document because it was written by the Framers to protect people's liberties and guarantee certain individual rights. It is a document of great power. In fact, the Constitution has inspired other countries seeking to create a democratic government.

What do you think is the most important part of the Constitution?

What are some ways in which you might support the ideas in the Constitution?

SEVEN MILES TO FREEDOM

THE ROBERT SMALLS STORY

Robert Smalls's dreams of freedom began in his hometown of Beaufort, South Carolina, the largest town on a cluster of plantation islands down the coast from Charleston. He was born there in 1839 in the slave quarters on the McKee family's property.

Robert's mother was a house servant, and when he was about six years old Robert also began working in the McKee household. He brushed Master McKee's horse, carried his hunting bow, and baited his fishing hook. Good-spirited and talkative, Robert was the master's favorite.

As a favored house servant, Robert had an easier life than most slaves. Even so, from the time he was a young boy, he witnessed the evils of slavery. At neighboring plantations he saw slaves whipped until they were bloody, punished for the simplest things– getting to the fields a few moments late, missing a patch of weeds, not working fast enough. In town Robert watched boys and girls his own age sold like animals on the auction block.

Although the McKees were kind to him, Robert grew to hate slavery. More and more he wished to be free.

In 1851, when Robert was twelve, the McKees sent him to live and work in Charleston. All day and into the night he waited tables and made deliveries to rooms at the **elegant** Planter's Hotel. Robert earned five dollars a month but had to give the money to his master.

Anytime Robert wasn't working he headed to the waterfront. He watched the boats of all shapes and sizes, fascinated by how they could sail anywhere in the world.

Robert liked talking to the workers on the ships. In hushed voices they told him stories about "Up North," where *all* people were free to learn to read and write. Free to keep the money they earned. Free to make their own decisions. Robert's eyes lit up with hope. Someday he would have those freedoms too.

Eager to spend more time at the waterfront, Robert got permission from Master McKee to work at the docks loading and unloading cargo from ships. Robert worked hard. He was smart and dependable, and by age fifteen he was foreman of a crew, directing men twice his age.

Eventually Robert grew to dislike the routine of the job, so he began working in the shipyard, making and rigging sails. Robert enjoyed testing the sails on boats in the water, and he learned to navigate narrow channels, gliding carefully past hidden rocks. His boss boasted that Robert had the makings of a wheelman, the title given to African American boat pilots in the South.

When Robert was seventeen he met Hannah Jones, a Charleston hotel maid who was the slave of Samuel Kingman. Robert loved Hannah's sparkling eyes and sharp intelligence, and wanted to spend his life with her. In order to marry and live together, the couple worked out agreements with their masters. Robert and Hannah would find their own jobs. Every month Robert would give McKee fifteen dollars, and Hannah would give Kingman seven dollars. Any other money the couple earned would be their own.

Robert and Hannah married on December 24, 1856, and in February 1858, their first child, Elizabeth, was born. As Robert held the tiny bundle, he was saddened by the realization that Elizabeth did not belong to them. She was the property of Hannah's master. So Robert made a deal to buy his wife's and daughter's freedom for eight hundred dollars. Although Robert was still enslaved, the arrangement would allow Hannah and Elizabeth to go wherever he went.

Robert and Hannah didn't know how they would save that much money, but they were going to try.

In the evenings, by candlelight, Hannah sewed garments for the wealthy women of Charleston while Robert studied charts and maps of the harbor, rivers, creeks, and channels. He noted the location of every reef, sandbar, and current.

Soon Robert was expertly navigating the waterways, delivering boats to plantations all along the coast. During summers, he worked as a sailor on a coastal schooner. His dedication and skill earned him a reputation as one of the best boat handlers in Charleston.

After three years Robert and Hannah had saved seven hundred dollars. The couple were close to their goal, but a storm was brewing in the nation.

By the spring of 1861, Charleston was at the eye of the storm. For a long time, northern and southern states had been arguing about slavery. As the country expanded west, southerners wanted slavery allowed in the new territories. Northerners did not. In 1860 Abraham Lincoln, who opposed the spread of slavery, was elected president. South Carolina responded by breaking away from the United States. Several other southern states followed. Together, they formed the Confederate States of America. The northern states remained the United States of America, or the Union.

The Confederacy quickly took charge of many military forts in the South, but the Union kept control of Fort Sumter in Charleston Harbor. On April 12, 1861, a battle for Fort Sumter ended in the fort's **surrender** to the Confederacy. A civil war between the North and South had begun.

For slaves such as Robert and Hannah war brought uncertainty, but also hope. If the North won, slavery would end.

Commercial boat traffic in and out of Charleston Harbor slowed to a trickle. Soon there was no work for Robert in the shipyard. In July he took a job as a deckhand on the *Planter*, a 147-foot, wood-burning steamer. The boat once hauled cotton but had been converted into an armed Confederate ship for carrying soldiers, equipment, and supplies.

All that summer on the *Planter* Robert helped build up Confederate defenses in the harbor and along the coast. He laid mines, destroyed a lighthouse, and built new forts. But in his heart Robert wanted the Union to win the war.

Robert's navigational skills and knowledge of the waterways impressed the *Planter's* officers. He was promoted to wheelman, a position of trust and honor. Now responsible for steering the boat, Robert learned the secret steam whistle signals for passing the harbor's many forts.

In late 1861 freedom suddenly grew closer for Robert and Hannah. The Union navy captured Port Royal, just down the coast from Charleston. A Union fleet set up a blockade at the entrance to Charleston Harbor. Looking through the captain's field glasses, Robert could see the northern ships. The Union lines and freedom were within reach–only seven miles away.

This gave Robert renewed hope and determination, as did the birth of his son, Robert Jr. Now more than ever, Robert knew he had to find a way to freedom, for himself and his growing family.

When the opportunity finally came, it started with a joke. One evening the boat's white officers went ashore to spend the night, even though this was against military rules. Jokingly, one of the crew plopped the captain's straw hat on Robert's head. Robert crossed his arms and strutted about just like the short, strongly built captain. Everyone laughed. Given Robert's similar build, the resemblance was amazing.

Suddenly Robert became serious and told the men to keep the joke to themselves. He had an idea.

Robert shared his plan with Hannah. On a night when the officers were ashore, he and the crew would steal the *Planter.* Their families would hide at a nearby wharf and be picked up on the way. Wearing the captain's hat and responding with the secret steam whistle signals, Robert would trick the fort guards into letting the ship pass. He would sail the *Planter* out to the Union fleet and to freedom.

Hannah asked him what would happen if they were caught. Robert told her they would probably be shot. Hannah was quiet for a moment, and then agreed to go along. She too was willing to risk her life and the lives of their children for a chance at freedom.

Robert explained the plan to his crewmates and made them promise to keep it secret. He also told them that if something went wrong, they would sink the ship rather than allow themselves to be captured. If it didn't go down fast enough, they would all clasp hands and jump overboard. The men agreed. They trusted Robert, and they too yearned for freedom.

The timing was left to Robert. He had to choose the right moment.

Day after day Robert watched and listened. In the spring of 1862, an opportunity arose. The *Planter's* crew was to move four cannons guarding a river southwest of Charleston to a fort being built in the harbor. The captain wanted the move completed by dark on Monday, May 12. The officers planned to go ashore that night and stay until morning.

Robert realized this was the chance he had been waiting for.

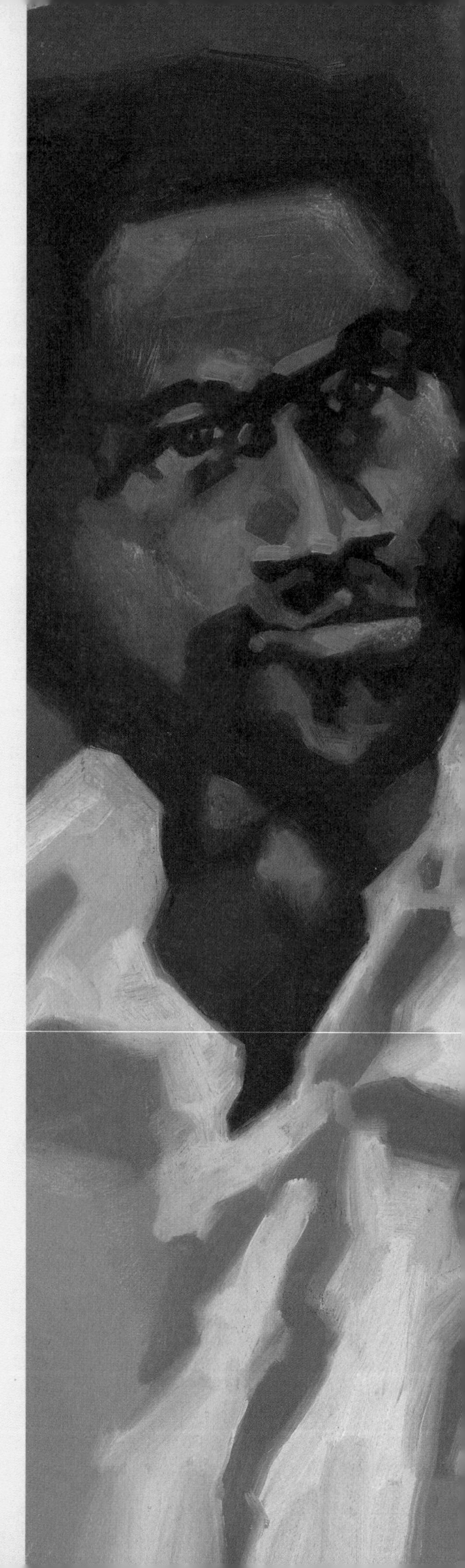

On May 12 the *Planter* traveled to the river to transfer the cannons. Robert and his crewmates knew how valuable these weapons would be to the Union. They planned to delay the delivery of the cannons and escape with them.

The men purposely worked slowly. They fumbled knots and dropped lines. By the time all four cannons were on board it was late afternoon. Robert's plan was working. Delivery to the fort would have to wait until morning.

Robert's mind raced as he guided the *Planter* back to its dock in the harbor. The time for the escape was nearing. Throbbing with anticipation, he was careful not to let his excitement show.

Finally the officers went ashore, trusting Robert to have the boat ready for an early start in the morning.

Robert immediately gathered the crew and went over the plan once more. Then the men sprang into action, loading stacks of firewood on deck to power the steam boilers and double-checking every instrument. Robert put on a white ruffled shirt, a dress jacket, and the captain's wide-brimmed straw hat.

It was three o'clock in the morning by the time a full head of steam hissed in the boilers. The Confederate and South Carolina flags were raised to the top of the mast. In the pilothouse Robert gripped the wheel as he backed the *Planter* away from its dock. The ship coasted upstream a short way and stopped. A rowboat stole from the *Planter* to fetch the families of the crew from a boat they had hidden in since nightfall.

Robert peered uneasily at the dark water, waiting for the rowboat to return with its precious load. After a few long minutes, it appeared. In pin-drop quiet the families boarded and were led below deck.

With everyone safely aboard, Robert started down the harbor. He blew the whistle to leave the dockside, and it was answered. Fighting a strong urge to rush, Robert eased the ship cautiously into the open water. He had to stay calm. His family and the others on board were all counting on him. Robert's patience paid off. The shore guard saw the *Planter* leave but did not stop it.

The *Planter's* paddle wheels cut through the dark water with a steady churn. Castle Pinckney and Fort Ripley were passed easily. Fort Johnson loomed ahead, its walls bristling with cannons. His palms sweaty, Robert reached for the cord of the steam whistle. He blew the secret signal and prayed. The lookout signaled back: *All right.* Robert breathed a sigh of relief.

As the ship neared the **massive** walls of Fort Sumter, Robert saw that dawn was breaking. The *Planter* had lost time bucking the incoming tide. In the early-morning light the lookout might be able to tell that Robert was not the captain. An anxious crewmate told Robert to make a dash for freedom. But Robert knew that if the *Planter* sped by the fort, cannons would be fired on them, smashing the ship to pieces. He continued at the slow, even speed the guards expected.

Robert asked a crewmate to take the wheel. He pulled down the captain's straw hat to shadow his face and stood at the window of the pilothouse. Under his dress jacket Robert's heart thumped loudly. Mimicking the captain, he folded his arms across his chest. Then, slowly, Robert sounded the signal.

WOOOOO, WOOOOO, WOO!

From the pilothouse to the engine room to the hold, bodies tensed. The response was taking too long. . . . Finally, the *Planter* received the signal to pass. Robert mopped sweat from his brow. There were only a few more miles to go and one more fort to pass.

Fort Moultrie came up quickly, and the *Planter* passed without trouble. Robert kept the same deliberate pace until the ship was out of range of the last Confederate gun. Then he ordered FULL STEAM AHEAD! Clouds of black smoke belched from the smokestack. The boat surged forward, its paddle wheels whisking the water white.

A Confederate lookout saw the burst of speed through his field glasses. When the ship headed out to sea, he knew something was wrong. Frantically the lookout signaled an alert. Lights flashed and flickered, but it was too late. No Confederate guns could reach the *Planter* now.

The Union ships and freedom waited just ahead, but the *Planter* still was not safe. From the beginning Robert had worried most about these final moments. Union sailors would be prepared to fire on any boat coming from Charleston. Robert had to convince them not to shoot. Ordering the flags lowered and Hannah's best white sheet raised as a sign of surrender, Robert sailed toward the *Onward*, the nearest ship of the Union fleet. In the early morning fog, the Union lookout couldn't see the white sheet. He saw only a big boat speeding through the haze and mist. He thought it was a Confederate ship coming to ram them.

The lookout shouted an alarm. The *Onward* turned, pointing a row of guns at the *Planter.* Leaning hard on the wheel, Robert swung the boat around. With the turn the white sheet caught the wind and flapped open in the ocean breeze. Suddenly a Union sailor cried out that he saw a white flag.

The *Onward's* captain ordered the gunners to hold their fire and instructed the *Planter* to come alongside.

Men, women, and children ran out onto the deck of the *Planter*. Robert, standing straight and proud, stepped forward and raised the captain's hat high in the air. He shouted that he had brought the Union a load of Confederate cannons.

When the *Onward's* surprised captain climbed aboard, Robert told him he thought the *Planter* might be of some service to "Uncle Abe" Lincoln. Then Robert turned the Confederate ship and its cannons over to the Union navy.

The white sheet was lowered. As the *Planter's* crew and their families gazed up, the Union flag rose skyward. Robert and Hannah held their children close, their hearts full of hope. On this morning of a new day, they were on their way to freedom.

AFTERWORD

While the South fumed over the loss of the *Planter*, the North praised Robert Smalls as a national hero. *The New York Herald* declared his action "one of the most heroic and daring adventures since the war commenced." Robert was employed as a civilian pilot for the Union navy. He met with President Lincoln, and helped convince him to let African Americans enlist in the Union army. Robert also spoke to crowds in the North to gain aid for former slaves.

On December 1, 1863, Robert had another risky adventure aboard the *Planter*. He was piloting the ship for the Union when it came under intense fire in South Carolina. The captain of the *Planter* ordered Robert to surrender the boat, then hid in the coal bunker. Knowing the crew of former slaves could be killed if captured, Robert quickly took the wheel, steering the ship to outrun the Confederates. For his bravery Robert was named as the *Planter's* new captain, making him the first African American captain of a United States vessel.

Throughout the war Robert piloted several Union ships, taking part in seventeen battles. During these years Hannah gave birth to the couple's second daughter, Sarah. Sadly, their son, Robert Jr., died of smallpox.

Robert and his family remained in Beaufort after the war. He purchased the McKee house, where he had once been a slave, and learned to read and write. In 1868, along with seventy-six African Americans and forty-eight whites, Robert helped write a new democratic state constitution. The document included his proposal for the creation of South Carolina's first free system of public schools for all children. Robert also won a seat in the state legislature, where he fought for equal rights for African Americans, and became active in the state militia, rising to the rank of major general.

Robert was elected to the United States Congress in 1875. During his five terms, he called for the elimination of race discrimination in the army, introduced a petition to give women the right to vote, and fought against the policy of separate railroad cars for African Americans. When Robert's congressional career came to an end, he was appointed the collector of customs in Beaufort, holding the position for nearly twenty years. Hannah died in 1883. Robert later remarried and had another son.

In 1895 South Carolina revised its state constitution, legally restricting the right of African Americans to vote–a right that was granted by an amendment to the United States Constitution in 1870. As one of only six African American delegates at the 1895 convention, Robert argued eloquently to preserve his people's right to vote. Still, this right was all but taken away by the limitations placed on it. Robert and other African American delegates refused to sign the document to adopt these changes. With African American rights slipping away, Robert continued to fight unfair laws, giving speeches and reaching out to members of the United States Congress for support.

In his later years Robert often visited with African American students in Beaufort. He told them about the accomplishments of their people and stressed the importance of education. Robert died in 1915 at the age of seventy-five. His funeral was the largest ever held in Beaufort.

The United States Army christened the *Major General Robert Smalls* in 2004. This ship is the first army vessel ever named after an African American.

UNIT 8

Standing Up for What's Right

How can you stand up for what's right?

Focus Questions

Why do people stand up for freedom and rights?

What can we do to make the world a better place?

Why can it be so hard to stand up for what's right?

How have children made a difference by standing up for what's right?

Changing the World

"Never doubt that a small group of thoughtful, committed citizens can change the world. Indeed, it's the only thing that ever has."

Margaret Mead (1901–1978), anthropologist

One Dream at a Time

Contents

CHAPTER 1

Caring Begins with Asking Questions

This unit is all about making a difference by standing up for what's right. But what does "standing up for what's right" mean?

You may have heard about people whose words and actions have helped others. Time and time again, people of all ages have been moved to take action to make life better for those who are sick, poor, or oppressed.

Taking action isn't always easy; for example, it may cost money or require a lot of organizing. It's even more difficult when people don't grasp the importance of the work, or when they respond, "We've never done that kind of thing before."

What motivates people to "stand up for what's right"; that is, to care about people and places, even when doing so is difficult? Motivation often begins with a question.

Mother Teresa won the Nobel Peace Prize for her work in helping people in need in India and around the world.

Jackie Robinson became an inspiring figure when he broke Major League Baseball's color barrier. He made his debut with the Brooklyn Dodgers on April 15, 1947.

How Would That Make Me Feel?

Anthony Leanna asked that question as he watched his grandmother undergo treatment for cancer. At the same time he met other cancer patients and saw how their medical treatments often caused them to lose their hair.

Anthony thought about these people and imagined himself in their place; then he founded Heavenly Hats, a nonprofit organization that collects and distributes new hats to cancer patients. From asking people in his Wisconsin town to donate hats, Anthony went on to write to hat companies, and hats soon came pouring in from many places—even from as far away as Australia!

The program has grown quickly, and Anthony has been pleased to see its effect on the people it helps. The hats are fun to get and they provide warmth and comfort. They also represent hope and show that people care. So far Heavenly Hats has donated more than 350,000 new hats of many styles to patients.

A Word from Anthony

Anthony Leanna tells other young people, "I have learned not to sit by and do nothing when you see a problem just because you think there is nothing that you can do. I learned to have the courage to ask for help . . . You do not have to be an adult, strong, or rich to give; you just need to have a cause and a big heart."

Anthony started Heavenly Hats in 2001, when he was just ten years old!

Can We Make This Place Safer?

We have all probably heard of a bully who picks on people for no good reason. Bullying is a serious problem in many schools. It distracts kids from learning and prevents them from doing their best.

A bullying problem was creating stress on the playground at Whitefriars School in England. A group of ten- and eleven-year-olds who wanted to stop the bullying organized themselves and asked: *What can we do to stop the bullies and make kids feel safe on our playground?*

The monitors identify and **mediate** problems between students and speak to students who misbehave. In addition, they organize games for the younger children and make sure no one who wants to play is left out.

Students apply to become monitors, and although it's now seen as a cool job, this wasn't always the case. When the program began in 2008, their peers didn't listen to the monitors and left playground equipment out to be picked up. However, the monitors earned the respect of other students by showing their determination to make a difference. Today the playground at Whitefriars School is a safe and welcoming place for all students.

The Whitefriars Playground Monitors received the Anne Frank Award, given to "young people and educators who have shown great personal strength, moral courage, and determination to stand up for what is right."

Can We Clean Up This Place?

Pigeon Creek in the state of Washington was terribly polluted not long ago. The salmon that used to spawn there no longer did. In fact, kids who lived near the creek had never seen any fish there!

Fifth graders at Jackson Elementary School in the town of Everett, Washington, asked: *What can we do about Pigeon Creek? Can we clean up the creek so that salmon will be able to live there again?*

The kids took on the challenge with gusto. They enthusiastically organized their school and people in their community to clean up Pigeon Creek. The kids also used a school aquarium to raise fish from eggs that they got from the state hatchery. Like excited parents, the whole school watched and cheered as the eggs hatched and grew into young fish. Finally the fish were released into the now-clean Pigeon Creek. The kids wondered if the fish would return to spawn.

After two years the salmon did return! Classes continue to raise fish eggs in their school aquarium. Each spring the kids release the young fish into Pigeon Creek.

The story of Pigeon Creek eventually became international news. Schools from as far away as Japan set up similar programs in an effort to clean up the environment.

How Can I Help Hungry People?

In the late 1930s, Dan West, an Indiana farmer, was working in Spain on a **relief** project, helping people who were suffering because of the Spanish Civil War. As he distributed cups of milk to hungry children, he thought, *These children don't need a cup; they need a cow.*

West started a program that gives animals to families in need. The program started in Puerto Rico and is now working in more than 50 countries worldwide, including Ukraine, Senegal, China, and Peru. The animals—cows, goats, sheep, chickens, rabbits, and bees, for example—provide families with the opportunity to feed themselves. Families are also often able to breed these animals and raise more of them for food or for sale. Furthermore, they sometimes can make and sell butter, cheese, honey, woolen goods, and other products.

People who receive an animal must promise to "pass on the gift." This means that they must give an animal, such as a calf, to another person in need and teach that person how to take care of it.

Today, West's program is called Heifer International. Schoolkids, adults, and other groups give money to buy an animal. Donors can even choose which animal they want to buy! The animals give people a source of food and a way to feed themselves in the future.

Don't be fooled by the word "International"; this organization also has projects in the United States. In eastern Kentucky, for example, many people used to work in coal mines; however, in recent years many people have lost their jobs. Heifer International is helping these people start small farms to sustain themselves. Its Appalachia Program helps communities teach their kids how to farm. Students are learning how to raise and market goats, bees, poultry, vegetables, and red-claw crayfish. The students then teach adults how to do the same!

Take Your Pick!

In 2009, donors to Heifer International could choose from a wide variety of animal gifts:

Sample Price List

Animal	Price
Heifer	$500
Water buffalo	$250
Llama	$150
Sheep or goat	$120
Trio of rabbits	$60
Honeybees	$30
Flock of chicks, ducks, or geese	$20

Some farmers in the program prefer raising goats instead of cows. Goats can be easier to manage, and goat milk can be used to make cheese, yogurt, and even soap.

CHAPTER 2 Kids in History: Newsies Make a Difference

Today most people can have newspapers delivered, can buy papers from a street stand as they go to or from work, or can read electronic newspapers online. But in the late 1800s, newspapers hired "newsies" to go out onto city streets and sell papers to passersby. The shouts of "Extra! Extra! Read all about it!" were commonly heard just a few generations ago.

Newsies often were teenage boys (and sometimes girls); however, some newsies were as young as six years old. They would buy newspapers in bundles of 100 from a newspaper's office for 50 cents and sell them for a penny apiece. They worked hard, sometimes late into the night, to sell all of their papers; the newspaper office would not buy back unsold papers. Many of these kids needed money to help their families. Others had no family and used the money to pay for housing or food.

It was not uncommon for newsies to be working past midnight, even in bad weather, trying to sell all of their newspapers.

A Problem for the Newsies

In 1898 two major newspapers, the *New York World* and the *New York Morning Journal*, raised the price of newspaper bundles to 60 cents—an increase of 20 percent! Despite the dramatic increase, this was not a problem for the newsies at first. The Spanish-American War was going on, and headlines about the fighting attracted a news-hungry public. After the war, however, the *New York World* and the *New York Morning Journal* kept the price at 60 cents. This created a **dilemma**: without headlines about the war, newspapers weren't selling as well, and the newsies began to lose money.

To get a better deal from these two newspapers, in 1899 the newsies decided to strike. They agreed to stop working until they received better wages. Five thousand kids attended a meeting—so many that the meeting hall could not hold them all. Overflow attendees gathered in the street, and those inside the hall passed news outside to them.

Newsies would earn about 30 cents a day.

A Tough Choice

The decision to strike was a difficult one. All the newsies needed to agree to strike for it to be effective, and it wasn't easy to give up the money that they earned every day. Despite the challenge, the newsies banded together in solidarity and put an embargo, or ban, on selling the *Journal* and the *World*.

Newsies gathered around Brooklyn, protesting and blocking traffic. They prevented papers from being sold, and they held demonstrations in front of the newspaper offices.

And the other papers? They wrote gleefully about the strike, and the *World* and the *Journal* received more negative attention. As these papers reported on the strike leaders, often quoting them, the public learned about newsies such as Kid Blink (a young boy with an eye patch), Spot Conlon (leader of the Brooklyn newsies who often wore suspenders), and Boots McAleen.

Brooklyn Bridge

> **Help us in our struggle to get a fair play by not buying The Journal or The World. Help us! Do not ask for The World or The Journal.**
>
> **—Newsboys' Union.**

Flyers such as this were handed out by the newsies to gain support, as reported by the *New York Times*, July 23, 1899.

Results of the Strike

Some people were annoyed by the strike, but many sympathized with the newsies. The newsies received letters of encouragement from state senators and union leaders. Supporters gave the newsies money to help offset the loss of earnings.

The strike ended with a compromise: the two newspapers refused to drop their prices, but they agreed to buy back unsold papers. The success of the strike in New York led other working kids to strike against their employers in other cities.

Although not all such strikes were successful, they gradually made people aware of the issues that working kids in the United States faced. Laws were eventually passed to regulate working ages and work environments for kids.

Support for the Newsies

Stories like this from the *New York Times* helped sway people to support the newsies.

July 24, 1899
"The striking newsboys in pursuit of their efforts to receive better terms for selling The Evening Journal and Evening World have planned a mass meeting to be held tonight in Irving Hall, 214 Broome Street, for a general discussion of their grievances . . . Senator Sullivan has in a signed letter to the strikers' Executive Committee, expressed his deep sympathy with the boys, and has promised to be present tonight to address the meeting."

July 26, 1899
"There was a meeting last night to begin a movement for the permanent improvement of the condition of the newsboys . . . Fourteen men and four women attended . . . They find that there are in Greater New York 2,500 newsboys, ranging in age from six to sixteen years, and that, apart from the lodging houses, there is no systematic effort to regulate or help them."

CHAPTER 3

Rosa Parks: Mother of the Civil Rights Movement

On December 1, 1955, a tired forty-two-year-old seamstress climbed the rear steps of the Cleveland Avenue bus in Montgomery, Alabama. Some say that she was tired after working all day; she would say that she was tired of being treated as a second-class citizen.

As she rode the bus that evening, Rosa Parks was reminded of that status. She had paid her fare at the front of the bus and then had walked to the rear entrance and boarded. Then she watched as a white man got on, knowing that because the bus was full, she would have to give up her seat to him.

And because she was tired—from work and from the unfairness of the situation—she sat. When the bus driver demanded that she move, she didn't. When he warned her that she was going to be arrested, Rosa Parks acknowledged the warning but still refused to leave her seat.

Today people can sit anywhere they choose on public transportation, but in the past that was not always the case. Rosa Parks's famous action in 1955 paved the way for equal treatment of all people.

Becoming Rosa Parks

Rosa Louise McCauley was born on February 4, 1913, in Tuskegee, Alabama. Her mother was a schoolteacher; her father, a carpenter. Rosa grew up in a place where "White Only" signs were common and where African Americans had separate schools, separate water fountains, separate swimming pools, and separate seating in theaters and other public buildings.

Rosa McCauley married Raymond Parks on December 18, 1932. They both were active in the National Association for the Advancement of Colored People (NAACP), an organization that worked against inequality. Rosa Parks was her chapter's secretary and a youth leader. She also helped the Voters League register African Americans, remembering that she had twice been denied the right to vote because of unfair voting practices that targeted African Americans in some of the Southern states. Through these activities she learned to stand against injustice.

In an interview about her work with the NAACP, Parks said that she wanted "to let it be known that we did not wish to continue being second-class citizens."

Arrested!

When Rosa Parks was arrested for refusing to give up her seat, she spoke with E. D. Nixon, a colleague from the NAACP. Nixon told her that with her permission they could fight segregation on the buses with her case. With that Rosa Parks decided to challenge the law that required segregation on buses.

There was no time to waste, as her court date was set for Monday, December 5. Civil rights workers quickly organized a boycott of the buses in the city. Handbills asked all African Americans to not take the bus that Monday; instead, they should walk to work or stay home. African Americans who owned cabs agreed to pick up passengers at the bus stops for the same price as a bus fare. Since 70 to 75 percent of the bus ridership was African American, few people rode that Monday!

On the day of the boycott, Rosa Parks stood in court; she was convicted and fined.

Dr. Martin Luther King Jr. planned the boycott along with Rosa Parks and other leaders of the Civil Rights Movement.

Meeting Martin Luther King Jr.

The first meeting of the Montgomery Improvement Association (MIA) was held on the evening of December 5, the same day as Parks's court date. As Dr. Martin Luther King Jr., who became the organization's president, spoke about this milestone moment, he echoed the feeling that had motivated Rosa Parks: "There comes a time that people get tired."

The success of the one-day boycott led to a unanimous decision that it should be extended. There were many roadblocks. The bus company would not **negotiate** with the MIA to end the boycott. Violence erupted against the leaders of the MIA, and its leaders were arrested. Through it all, African Americans continued to refuse to ride the buses. They refused for 381 days.

Alternate Transportation

The taxi service did not last long, because city officials threatened legal action against cab drivers who charged less than the minimum cab fare (45 cents instead of the 10-cent bus fare). The MIA set up a complex system of "private taxis"—people who owned cars and were willing to provide transportation. In the weeks that followed, that system also was attacked, with police arresting drivers and passengers for minor causes. Some auto insurance companies also dropped coverage of African Americans. Still, the boycott continued.

Ending the Boycott

In 1954 the Supreme Court overturned the idea that schools could be "separate but equal," saying that segregated schools, by their very nature, were unfair to African American children. African Americans in Montgomery wanted to use the same logic; that is, they wanted to show that segregation on the city buses was "separate but equal" and therefore illegal. They fought their way through the federal courts and won. The city finally appealed the case to the Supreme Court, and on November 13, 1956, the Court agreed that segregation on buses was also unconstitutional.

Rosa Parks, whose simple act of refusing to leave her seat started the boycott, showed that African Americans working together could bring about change. Today she is remembered as the Mother of the Civil Rights Movement.

Rosa Parks was photographed sitting on an integrated bus after the boycott ended on December 21, 1956.

Civil Rights Movement Timeline

1954 — Decision in *Brown v. Board of Education* declares "separate but equal" unconstitutional

1955 — Rosa Parks arrested; Montgomery Bus Boycott begins

1956 — Segregation on public buses declared unconstitutional

1957 — Central High School in Little Rock, Arkansas, desegregated

Not Just a Dream

On August 28, 1963, a march and rally for civil rights, organized in part by Dr. Martin Luther King Jr., was held in Washington, D.C. The speech Dr. King delivered that day inspired the nation and continues to have an impact decades later.

Most people are very familiar with the section of Dr. King's speech in which he tells of his dream that one day Americans of all races will live together in peace. However inspiring this part of the speech has become, it was only one part of the famous speech he delivered that day.

Ralph Abernathy, who worked with Dr. King, later said that the March on Washington showed "that people were coming together . . . It made it clear that we did not have to use violence to achieve the goals which we were seeking."

Dr. King prefaced the description of his dream with a stark assessment of life in the United States. One aim of his speech was to dramatize the "shameful condition" of the lives of African Americans. He spoke of "chains of discrimination," of some African Americans living in an "island of poverty," and of people not being allowed to vote, or their votes being meaningless.

Rosa Parks's simple act seemed to be that of a person tired after a long day's work, but it was much more. Dr. King's speech described racial problems in America. His words challenged all Americans to deal with these problems. Both actions achieved a higher purpose.

1960
Sit-in held at Woolworth's in North Carolina to desegregate lunch counters

1963
About 200,000 people gather for the March on Washington

1964
President Lyndon B. Johnson signs the Civil Rights Act

CHAPTER 4 One Dream Inspires Others

Who or what inspires you? Many people are inspired by situations in their lives or by what they see happening in their world, while other people take **inspiration** from the work, dedication, and words of others. Although Dr. Martin Luther King Jr. died in 1968, his words have inspired many people to action!

Nonviolence Doesn't Mean Inaction

Dr. King encouraged people to fight injustice in nonviolent ways—for example, by holding sit-ins, boycotts, marches, and demonstrations. In the 1960s King and others worked to end racial segregation. People have used these same kinds of methods to work for other kinds of changes, such as improving working conditions and making our planet a better place to live. Two of these people are Cesar Chavez and Wangari Maathai (wan-GAH-ree mah-DY).

Dr. King on Nonviolence

Dr. King often wrote about nonviolence. He once called nonviolence "a powerful and just weapon . . . which cuts without wounding and ennobles the man who wields it. It is a sword that heals."

Worlds Apart

Cesar Chavez and Wangari Maathai were born on different continents in different decades, but their early lives were not dissimilar. Chavez was born in 1927 in Yuma, Arizona, into a family that owned a farm and a small grocery store. During the days, his aunts, uncles, and cousins worked on the family farm.

Maathai was born in 1940. Like Chavez, she was born into a world of gardens—only hers were in the highlands of Kenya, in Africa. Maathai grew up amongst rolling hills, fields, trees, and streams of sparkling clean water.

Both Chavez and Maathai enjoyed learning at school. Maathai had an advanced formal education and earned several degrees, beginning with one in biology. Chavez, however, faced discrimination from some of his teachers, was punished for speaking Spanish, and never finished high school. He continued to learn by teaching himself.

Cesar Chavez

Wangari Maathai

Disasters!

Early in their lives, both Chavez and Maathai experienced something that was terrible but that led them into a life of action.

A terrible drought hit the southwestern United States in 1937, and the Chavez family lost their farm. Along with many other people, the Chavez family packed up and moved to California. There, at the age of ten, Chavez became a migrant worker—someone who travels from farm to farm, finding employment by picking whatever fruits and vegetables are in season.

Chavez and other migrant workers were treated badly. Farm owners made workers spend long days in the fields, without breaks, doing demanding work for little pay. People who complained often were fired or beaten. The migrant workers seemed to be powerless against the injustices of the farm owners.

A farmer supervises a crew of migrant workers as they pick onions. Workers live in barracks and earn a living moving from one farm to another.

In 1963, while Maathai was in college in the United States, Kenya became an independent country. However, many people continued to live in poverty and suffer from malnutrition.

Shortly after returning to Kenya to earn her graduate degree, Maathai noticed the farming industry was changing. Forests were being cleared for commercial farming. Without trees to hold the soil in place, land was eroding. Streams were drying up as well. In short, the land was becoming a desert. As a result, small farmers had no firewood to cook with; their goats had little grass to eat and so gave little milk; their families were going hungry. Worst of all, much like America's migrant workers, they seemed powerless to change what was happening.

With little rain, few plants will grow well. Over time this can cause an area that once produced crops to become desert.

Working for Change

Both Maathai and Chavez wanted to change things; both got to work by talking to people, one at a time.

Chavez's ideas were put to the test in 1965 when his organization, the National Farm Workers Association, joined a strike—a *huelga*—against a landowner in Delano, California, who treated his workers unfairly. Chavez began by speaking with other migrant workers. He told them that they could change their situation and that they could do so without using violence.

A few months later, in 1966, Chavez organized a march. He led protesters to the state capital in Sacramento, more than 300 miles away. Along the way they told others of their **plight**. Many people stepped up in support of better working conditions for farm workers. In time the peaceful march was successful: Chavez brought about the first labor contract for farm workers in the United States.

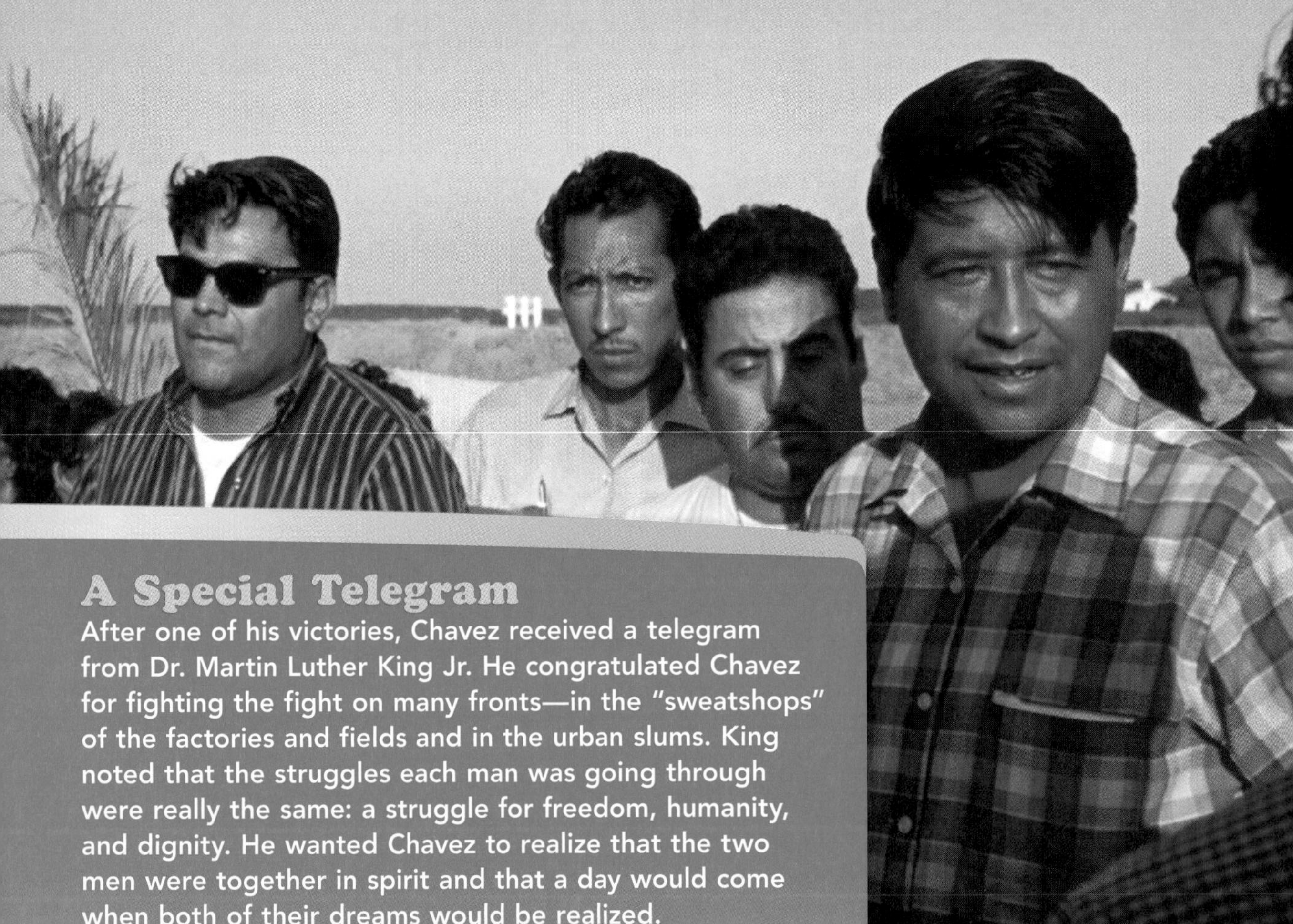

A Special Telegram

After one of his victories, Chavez received a telegram from Dr. Martin Luther King Jr. He congratulated Chavez for fighting the fight on many fronts—in the "sweatshops" of the factories and fields and in the urban slums. King noted that the struggles each man was going through were really the same: a struggle for freedom, humanity, and dignity. He wanted Chavez to realize that the two men were together in spirit and that a day would come when both of their dreams would be realized.

Maathai began her fight for change by speaking with women in the villages of Kenya. She listened to them and realized that by cutting down trees for firewood, the villagers themselves were part of the dilemma. Maathai knew how to fix things: plant more trees!

In 1977 Maathai started the Green Belt Movement. One part of this movement is the Billion Tree Campaign—a plan to plant a billion trees all over the world. As part of this campaign, millions of trees have been planted in her native Kenya. The work continues today.

Maathai, who was awarded a Nobel Peace Prize in 2004, believes that "When we plant trees, we plant the seeds of hope."

More Alike Than Different

Chavez and Maathai turned out to be more alike than different! They both have helped make the world a better place: Chavez gave poor people a voice, and Maathai is still showing people how to take better care of their environment. Both people have inspired others to do the same.

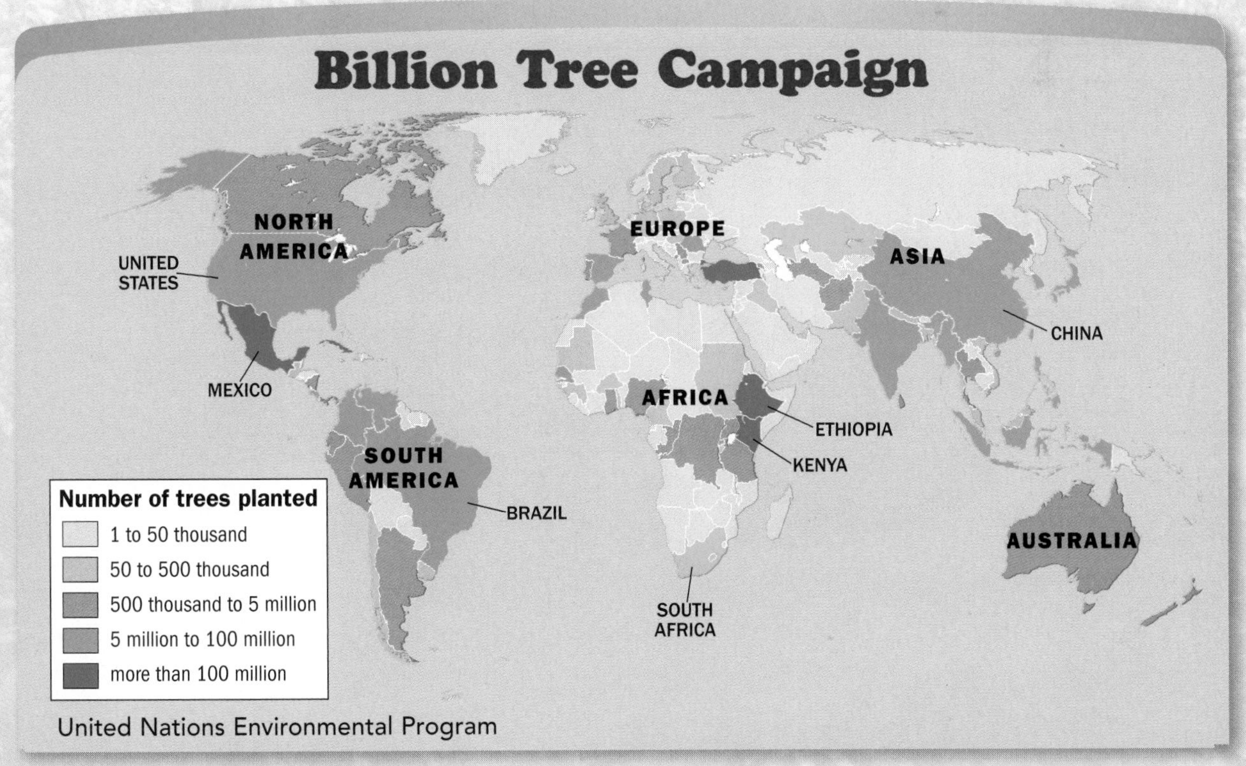

CHAPTER 5

Your Dream Is Calling!

Poets often have been inspired by others. They also can inspire us to do great things. Here are some poems about finding the confidence to change the world.

I Can

I can
be anything
I can
do anything
I can
think
anything
big
or tall
OR
High or low
W I D E
or narrow
fast or slow
because I
CAN
and
I
Want
TO!

Mari Evans

Where?

Where after all do human rights begin?
In small places close to home
Such are the places
Where every man, woman and child
Seeks equal justice
Equal opportunity
Equal dignity

Eleanor Roosevelt

The Flag Goes By

HATS off!
Along the street there comes
A blare of bugles, a ruffle of drums,
A flash of color beneath the sky:
Hats off!
The flag is passing by!

Blue and crimson and white it shines,
Over the steel-tipped, ordered lines.
Hats off!
The colors before us fly;
But more than the flag is passing by.

Sea-fights and land-fights, grim and great,
Fought to make and to save the State:
Weary marches and sinking ships;
Cheers of victory on dying lips;

Days of plenty and years of peace;
March of strong land's swift increase;
Equal justice, right and law,
Stately honor and reverend awe;
Sign of a nation, great and strong
To ward her people from foreign wrong:
Pride and glory and honor,—all
Live in the colors to stand or fall.

Hats off!
Along the street there comes
A blare of bugles, a ruffle of drums;
And loyal hearts are beating high:
Hats off!
The flag is passing by!

Henry Holcomb Bennett

Sum It Up

About 2,500 years ago, the Chinese philosopher Confucius noted, "To see what is right and not do it is want [lack] of courage." As you have read, it often takes a great deal of courage to stand up for what is right!

Over time many people—including students like you—have taken on the challenge of standing up for what is right. Anyone can take a stand against injustice, whether in the form of unsafe playgrounds, dirty streams, or unfair treatment of people. Just open your eyes to what's around you—and you just might change the world!

Who in this unit has inspired you? What do you think you would have done in that person's situation?

In your opinion, what are some of the things that are worth standing up for? Why?

PASSAGE TO FREEDOM

The Sugihara Story

Written by Ken Mochizuki

Illustrated by Dom Lee

Afterword by Hiroki Sugihara

There is a saying that the eyes tell everything about a person.

At a store, my father saw a young Jewish boy who didn't have enough money to buy what he wanted. So my father gave the boy some of his. That boy looked into my father's eyes and, to thank him, invited my father to his home.

That is when my family and I went to a Hanukkah celebration for the first time. I was five years old.

In 1940, my father was a diplomat, representing the country of Japan. Our family lived in a small town in the small country called Lithuania. There was my father and mother, my Auntie Setsuko, my younger brother Chiaki, and my three-month-old baby brother, Haruki. My father worked in his office downstairs.

In the mornings, birds sang in the trees. We played with girls and boys from the neighborhood at a huge park near our home. Houses and churches around us were hundreds of years old. In our room, Chiaki and I played with toy German soldiers, tanks, and planes. Little did we know that the real soldiers were coming our way.

Then one early morning in late July, my life changed forever.

My mother and Auntie Setsuko woke Chiaki and me up, telling us to get dressed quickly. My father ran upstairs from his office.

"There are a lot of people outside," my mother said, "We don't know what is going to happen."

In the living room, my parents told my brother and me not to let anybody see us looking through the window. So, I parted the curtains a tiny bit. Outside, I saw hundreds of people crowded around the gate in front of our house.

The grown-ups shouted in Polish, a language I did not understand. Then I saw the children. They stared at our house through the iron bars of the gate. Some of them were my age. Like the grown-ups, their eyes were red from not having slept for days. They wore heavy winter coats—some wore more than one coat, even though it was warm outside. These children looked as though they had dressed in a hurry. But if they came from somewhere else, where were their suitcases?

"What do they want?" I asked my mother.

"They have come to ask for your father's help," she replied. "Unless we help, they may be killed or taken away by some bad men."

Some of the children held on tightly to the hands of their fathers, some **clung** to their mothers. One little girl sat on the ground, crying.

I felt like crying, too. "Father," I said, "please help them."

My father stood quietly next to me, but I knew he saw the children. Then some of the men in the crowd began climbing over the fence. Borislav and Gudje, two young men who worked for my father, tried to keep the crowd calm.

My father walked outside. Peering through the curtains, I saw him standing on the steps. Borislav translated what my father said: He asked the crowd to choose five people to come inside and talk.

My father met downstairs with the five men. My father could speak Japanese, Chinese, Russian, German, French, and English. At this meeting, everyone spoke Russian.

I couldn't help but stare out the window and watch the crowd, while downstairs, for two hours, my father listened to frightening stories. These people were refugees—people who ran away from their homes because, if they stayed, they would be killed. They were Jews from Poland, escaping from the Nazi soldiers who had taken over their country.

The five men had heard my father could give them visas—official written permission to travel through another country. The hundreds of Jewish refugees outside hoped to travel east through the Soviet Union and end up in Japan. Once in Japan, they could go to another country. Was it true? the men asked. Could my father issue these visas? If he did not, the Nazis would soon catch up with them.

My father answered that he could issue a few, but not hundreds. To do that, he would have to ask for permission from his government in Japan.

That night, the crowd stayed outside our house. Exhausted from the day's excitement, I slept soundly. But it was one of the worst nights of my father's life. He had to make a decision. If he helped these people, would he put our family in danger? If the Nazis found out, what would they do?

But if he did not help these people, they could all die.

My mother listened to the bed squeak as my father tossed and turned all night.

The next day, my father said he was going to ask his government about the visas. My mother agreed it was the right thing to do. My father sent a message by cable. Gudje took my father's written message down to the telegraph office.

I watched the crowd as they waited for the Japanese government's reply. The five representatives came into our house several times that day to ask if an answer had been received. Any time the gate opened, the crowd tried to charge inside.

Finally, the answer came from the Japanese government. It was "no." My father could not issue that many visas to Japan. For the next two days, he thought about what to do.

Hundreds more Jewish refugees joined the crowd. My father sent a second message to his government, and again the answer was "no." We still couldn't go outside. My little brother Haruki cried often because we were running out of milk.

I grew tired of staying indoors. I asked my father constantly, "Why are these people here? What do they want? Why do they have to be here? Who are they?"

My father always took the time to explain everything to me. He said the refugees needed his help, that they needed **permission** from him to go to another part of the world where they would be safe.

"I cannot help these people yet," he calmly told me. "But when the time comes, I will help them all that I can."

My father cabled his superiors yet a third time, and I knew the answer by the look in his eyes. That night, he said to my mother, "I have to do something. I may have to disobey my government, but if I don't, I will be disobeying God."

The next morning, he brought the family together and asked what he should do. This was the first time he ever asked all of us to help him with anything.

My mother and Auntie Setsuko had already made up their minds. They said we had to think about the people outside before we thought about ourselves. And that is what my parents had always told me—that I must think as if I were in someone else's place. If I were one of those children out there, what would I want someone to do for me?

I said to my father, "If we don't help them, won't they die?"

With the entire family in agreement, I could tell a huge weight was lifted off my father's shoulders. His voice was firm as he told us, "I will start helping these people."

Outside, the crowd went quiet as my father spoke, with Borislav translating.

"I will issue visas to each and every one of you to the last. So, please wait patiently."

The crowd stood frozen for a second. Then the refugees burst into cheers. Grown-ups embraced each other, and some reached to the sky. Fathers and mothers hugged their children. I was especially glad for the children.

My father opened the garage door and the crowd tried to rush in. To keep order, Borislav handed out cards with numbers. My father wrote out each visa by hand. After he finished each one, he looked into the eyes of the person receiving the visa and said, "Good luck."

Refugees camped out at our favorite park, waiting to see my father. I was finally able to go outside.

Chiaki and I played with the other children in our toy car. They pushed as we rode, and they rode as we pushed. We chased each other around the big trees. We did not speak the same language, but that didn't stop us.

For about a month, there was always a line leading to the garage. Every day, from early in the morning till late at night, my father tried to write three hundred visas. He watered down the ink to make it last. Gudje and a young Jewish man helped out by stamping my father's name on the visas.

My mother offered to help write the visas, but my father insisted he be the only one, so no one else could get into trouble. So my mother watched the crowd and told my father how many were still in line.

One day, my father pressed down so hard on his fountain pen, the tip broke off. During that month, I only saw him late at night. His eyes were always red and he could hardly talk. While he slept, my mother massaged his arm, stiff and cramped from writing all day.

Soon my father grew so tired, he wanted to quit writing the visas. But my mother **encouraged** him to continue. "Many people are still waiting," she said. "Let's issue some more visas and save as many lives as we can."

While the Germans approached from the west, the Soviets came from the east and took over Lithuania. They ordered my father to leave. So did the Japanese government, which reassigned him to Germany. Still, my father wrote the visas until we absolutely had to move out of our home. We stayed at a hotel for two days, where my father still wrote visas for the many refugees who followed him there.

Then it was time to leave Lithuania. Refugees who had slept at the train station crowded around my father. Some refugee men surrounded my father to protect him. He now just issued permission papers—blank pieces of paper with his signature.

As the train pulled away, refugees ran alongside. My father still handed permission papers out the window. As the train picked up speed, he threw them out to waiting hands. The people in the front of the crowd looked into my father's eyes and cried, "We will never forget you! We will see you again!"

I gazed out the train window, watching Lithuania and the crowd of refugees fade away. I wondered if we would ever see them again.

"Where are we going?" I asked my father.

"We are going to Berlin," he replied.

Chiaki and I became very excited about going to the big city. I had so many questions for my father. But he fell asleep as soon as he settled into his seat. My mother and Auntie Setsuko looked really tired, too.

361
FWAGEN

Back then, I did not fully understand what the three of them had done, or why it was so important.

I do now.

AFTERWORD

Each time that I think about what my father did at Kaunas, Lithuania in 1940, my appreciation and understanding of the incident continues to grow. In fact, it makes me very emotional to realize that his deed saved thousands of lives, and that I had the opportunity to be a part of it.

I am proud that my father had the courage to do the right thing. Yet, his superiors in the Japanese government did not agree. The years after my family left Kaunas were difficult ones. We were imprisoned for 18 months in a Soviet internment camp; and when we finally returned to Japan, my father was asked to resign from diplomatic service. After holding several different jobs, my father joined an export company, where he worked until his retirement in 1976.

My father remained concerned about the fate of the refugees, and at one point left his address at the Israeli Embassy in Japan. Finally, in the 1960s, he started hearing from "Sugihara survivors," many of whom had kept their visas, and considered the worn pieces of paper to be family treasures.

In 1969, my father was invited to Israel, where he was taken to the famous Holocaust memorial, Yad Vashem. In 1985, he was chosen to receive the "Righteous Among Nations" Award from Yad Vashem. He was the first and only Asian to have been given this great honor.

In 1992, six years after his death, a monument to my father was dedicated in his birthplace of Yaotsu, Japan, on a hill that is now known as the Hill of Humanity. In 1994, a group of Sugihara survivors traveled to Japan to re-dedicate the monument in a ceremony that was attended by several high officials of the Japanese government.

The story of what my father and my family experienced in 1940 is an important one for young people today. It is a story that I believe will inspire you to care for all people and to respect life. It is a story that proves that one person can make a difference.

Thank you.

Hiroki Sugihara

Comprehension Strategy Handbook

How will this handbook help me?

Each page of this handbook will help you choose and use comprehension strategies while you read. Comprehension strategies are tools you can use to help you understand what you read:

Ask and Answer Questions
Determine Important Information
Make Connections
Make Inferences
Make Predictions
Monitor Comprehension
Summarize
Visualize

How do I use the handbook?

The **box** at the top of each page will remind you what each strategy is and help you decide if you want to use it.

The **steps** will remind you exactly what you need to do.

The **tip** will show you a way to keep track of information as you read.

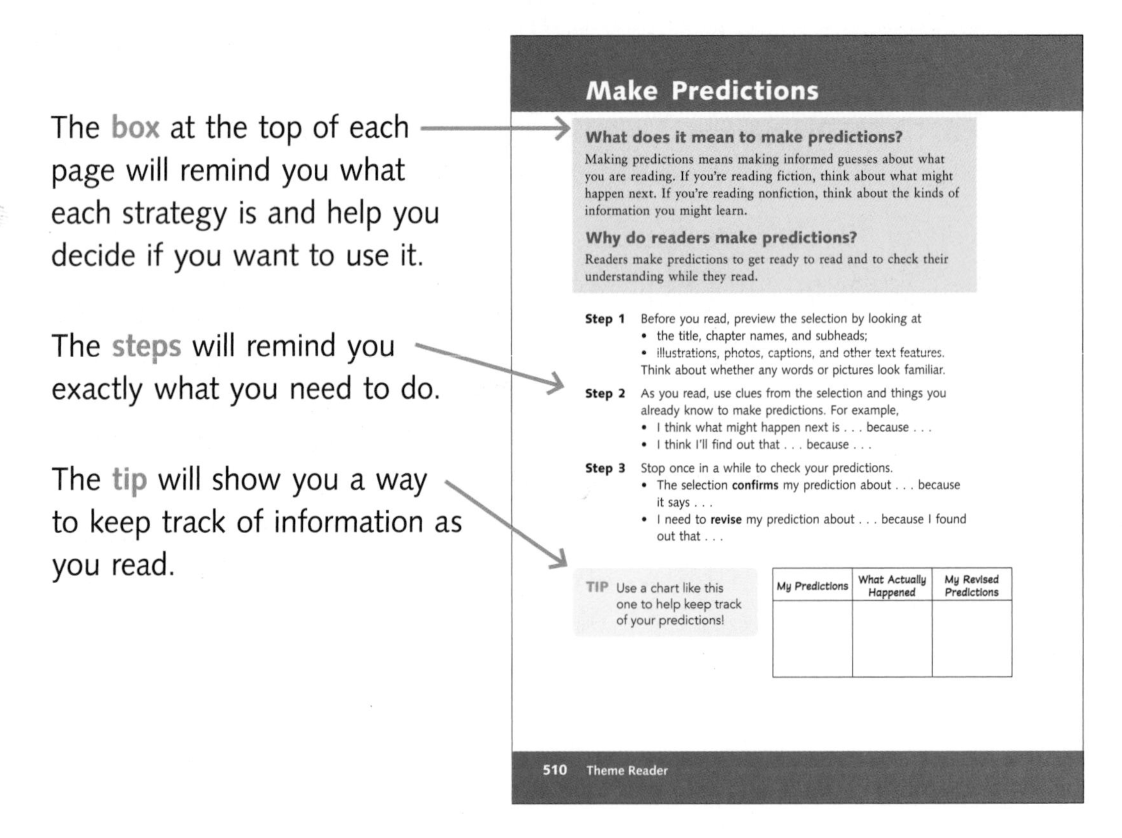

Make Predictions

What does it mean to make predictions?
Making predictions means making informed guesses about what you are reading. If you're reading fiction, think about what might happen next. If you're reading nonfiction, think about the kinds of information you might learn.

Why do readers make predictions?
Readers make predictions to get ready to read and to check their understanding while they read.

Step 1 Before you read, preview the selection by looking at
- the title, chapter names, and subheads;
- illustrations, photos, captions, and other text features.

Think about whether any words or pictures look familiar.

Step 2 As you read, use clues from the selection and things you already know to make predictions. For example,
- I think what might happen next is . . . because . . .
- I think I'll find out that . . . because . . .

Step 3 Stop once in a while to check your predictions.
- The selection **confirms** my prediction about . . . because it says . . .
- I need to **revise** my prediction about . . . because I found out that . . .

TIP Use a chart like this one to help keep track of your predictions!

My Predictions	What Actually Happened	My Revised Predictions

510 Theme Reader

Can I use multiple strategies?

Yes! Experienced readers use more than one strategy at a time. Read this paragraph to see how each strategy helps you notice and understand different things.

Rani pushed the door open slowly. **Creeaaak!** She peered down the stairs into the pitch-black darkness of the basement. *Should I really be doing this?* She took a deep breath and swallowed hard.

"He-hello?" she called timidly. Her voice was barely a whisper.

There was no answer. Then she heard it again! *What was that noise?* It sounded almost like a giggle.

Rani crept quietly down the stairs, grasping the railing and feeling for each step in front of her, counting as she went. One, two, three, four . . . finally her foot hit the last step. She reached for the light switch, but something grabbed her arm! She squeezed her eyes shut and began to scream when all of a sudden—

"Surprise! Happy birthday to you . . . " her friends began to sing.

Visualize I can really picture this scene in my mind. It gives me the chills!

Make Predictions I've read stories like this before! I think that giggle means her friend is hiding down there.

Make Connections Wow, is she brave! I would never walk into a dark room like that!

Check Predictions Aha! I knew it was going to be her friends!

Ask and Answer Questions

What does it mean to ask and answer questions?

Readers ask themselves questions before, during, and after reading. Sometimes there are questions someone else asks at the end of a selection. Readers find answers in the selection, from their own experiences, or both!

Why do readers ask and answer questions?

Asking and answering questions helps readers check their understanding. It helps them think more deeply about the selection so that they better understand it.

Step 1 **Before You Read** As you preview the selection, ask questions to activate prior knowledge and set purposes for reading. For example,

- What is this selection going to be about?
- What do I already know about this topic?
- Is this picture going to be important?

Step 2 **As You Read** Continue asking questions about things you don't understand or things you'd like to find out more about. Keep reading to look for answers to your questions.

Step 3 **After You Read** Are there any questions you have not yet answered? Is there anything new you wonder about now that you have finished reading?

TIP Keep track of your questions in a chart like this one. When you find the answer, write it down! If you don't find the answer, write down other places you could look for it.

Questions	*Did you find the answer?*		
	Yes	No	Need more information
	✔		

Determine Important Information

What does it mean to determine important information?

Fiction and nonfiction selections include many details that make the writing interesting. But the most interesting ideas may not always be the most important. Determining important information means figuring out the big ideas in the selection.

Why do readers determine important information?

Separating the big ideas from the details helps readers understand the important information the author wants them to know.

Step 1 Look for key words. Key words may be
- in the title, chapter names, and subheads;
- boldface or highlighted;
- repeated in many parts of the selection.

Step 2 Look at the text features. They could be clues about the important ideas in that chapter.

Step 3 Carefully read the first and last sentences in each paragraph. Authors often put important information here.

Step 4 Stop after each section and ask questions.
- What is the most important idea of this section?
- Can I pick out a sentence that tells the most important idea?
- Which information is interesting but not that important?

TIP Use a chart to help you determine important information as you read. Write the big ideas in the left column. Write the supporting details in the right column.

Big Ideas	Supporting Details

Make Connections

What does it mean to make connections?

Readers make connections when something they read reminds them of other things they know. Readers make connections to their own experiences, to other things they have read, and to what they know about the world around them.

Why do readers make connections?

Readers understand a selection better when they can find ways to connect it to things they already know.

Step 1 Before you read, preview the selection and look for words, pictures, or ideas that are familiar to you. Ask yourself:

- What do I already know about this topic?
- What else have I read about this topic?

Step 2 When you read a part of the selection that reminds you of something, stop and jot it down.

- **Text-to-Self** Does it remind you of your own experiences?
- **Text-to-Text** Does it remind you of something else you have read?
- **Text-to-World** Does it remind you of something you know about the world?

Step 3 Think about how the connection you made helps you better understand the selection.

TIP Use sticky notes to record connections you make! Label them like this:
S = self
T = other texts you've read
W = the world

__S:__ This character reminds me of my friend Brian. They both get into trouble, but they mean well.

__T:__ I read an article online about this! It also talked about how birds fly.

__W:__ I don't think the character understands that it's hard for everyone to make friends sometimes.

Make Inferences

What does it mean to make inferences?

Readers make inferences by using what they know to fill in information that is not stated in the selection.

Why do readers make inferences?

Authors don't always include every detail, so readers need to make inferences. Readers understand a selection better when they add what they already know to the information on the page.

Step 1 As you read, pause to ask yourself:
- What information is the author giving me?
- What other information do I need to understand this?

Step 2 Think about what you already know.
- Think about your own experiences.
- Recall other books you have read about the topic.
- Think about the world around you.

Step 3 Use what you know to better understand the information in the selection.

TIP You can also make inferences to figure out unfamiliar words and understand text features. Use a chart like this one to help you.

What I read in the text:	+	What I know about this:	=	Inference:

Make Predictions

What does it mean to make predictions?

Making predictions means making informed guesses about what you are reading. If you're reading fiction, think about what might happen next. If you're reading nonfiction, think about the kinds of information you might learn.

Why do readers make predictions?

Readers make predictions to get ready to read and to check their understanding while they read.

Step 1 Before you read, preview the selection by looking at
- the title, chapter names, and subheads;
- illustrations, photos, captions, and other text features.

Think about whether any words or pictures look familiar.

Step 2 As you read, use clues from the selection and things you already know to make predictions. For example,
- I think what might happen next is . . . because . . .
- I think I'll find out that . . . because . . .

Step 3 Stop once in a while to check your predictions.
- The selection **confirms** my prediction about . . . because it says . . .
- I need to **revise** my prediction about . . . because I found out that . . .

TIP Use a chart like this one to help keep track of your predictions!

My Predictions	What Actually Happened	My Revised Predictions

Monitor Comprehension

What does it mean to monitor comprehension?

Experienced readers pay attention not only to *what* they read but also to *how* they read. They recognize when they don't understand something. When their comprehension is breaking down, they use fix-up strategies.

Why do readers monitor comprehension?

At some point, all readers have trouble understanding something they read. Monitoring comprehension helps readers notice when they don't understand something and figure out how to fix it.

Step 1 Pause and ask yourself: Do I understand? Try to summarize what you just read. If you can summarize it, keep reading.

Step 2 If you are not sure you understand, use a fix-up strategy.

- **Reread** the section.
- **Keep reading** to see if the author explains further.
- **Slow down** so you don't miss important information.
- **Speed up**—reading one word at a time makes it difficult to put ideas together.
- **Use the images** to see if they *show* what the text *says*.
- **Seek help** from a dictionary; ask someone to help you.

Step 3 Ask yourself again: Do I understand? If not, try another fix-up strategy.

TIP Follow the arrows to help you decide what to do when you get stuck!

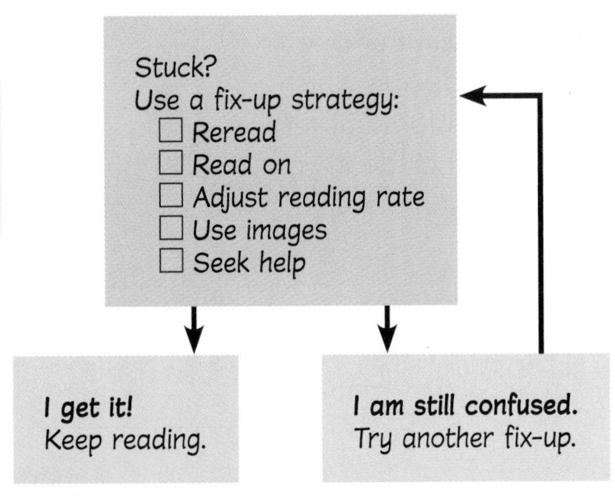

Summarize

What does it mean to summarize?

Summarizing means using your own words to explain the most important ideas of a selection you have read. A summary of a nonfiction text tells the most important information. A summary of a story tells who the main characters were and what happened to them.

Why do readers summarize?

Readers summarize to check their understanding and to help them remember what they have read. Readers might stop as they read to summarize part of the text. They might also summarize the entire text once they have finished reading.

Step 1 When you finish a paragraph, chapter, or selection, stop and think about the most important ideas. Make a list.

Step 2 Look over the list and cross out details that are interesting but not that important.

Step 3 Think of a topic sentence that tells the main idea. Ask yourself: What is this paragraph or selection mostly about?

Step 4 Use your list to write sentences that explain the big ideas.

TIP Use a chart like this one to decide which information to include in your summary.

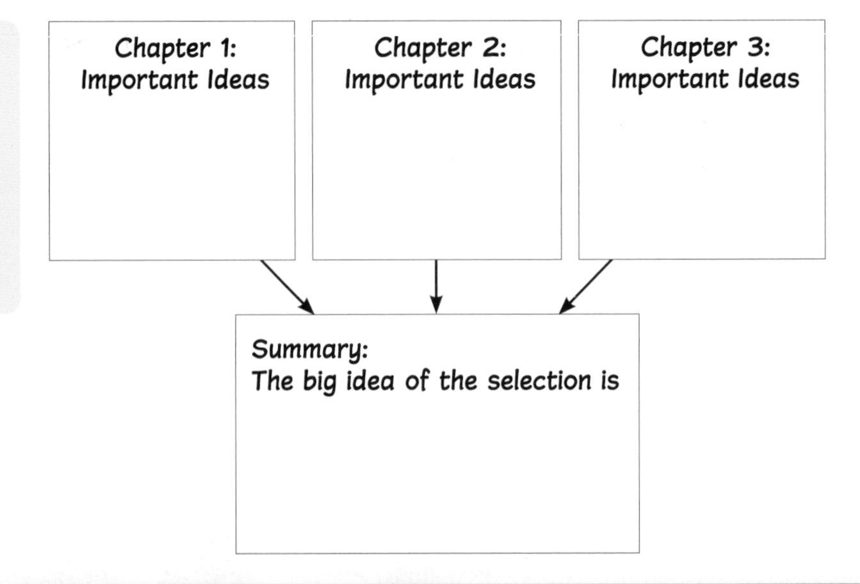

Visualize

What does it mean to visualize?

When readers visualize, they use the words on the page to create pictures in their minds. Readers picture the people, places, and things the author describes.

Why do readers visualize?

Visualizing helps readers see, feel, and hear what the author describes. When readers visualize, they can imagine being a part of the story.

Step 1 Look for clues in the selection that signal it might be a good time to visualize:

- Descriptive words
- Actions
- Comparisons

Step 2 Think about your own experiences. Use the selection and your own ideas to create a picture in your mind.

Step 3 As you read on, use new information from the selection to add to or revise your mental picture.

TIP You can draw pictures to help you visualize!

Words from the Selection	The Picture in My Mind

Strategies at a Glance

Use this chart to help you decide which strategies to use.

Ask and Answer Questions Do you find yourself wondering about something you read? Asking and answering questions helps build understanding.
Determine Important Information Which ideas are important, and which ones are supporting details? Figuring out what is important will help you better understand the selection.
Make Connections Does something you read remind you of your own experiences? Does it remind you of something else you have read or something in the world?
Make Inferences Did the author leave out some information? Sometimes readers need to "fill in the blanks" by using what they already know. Making inferences helps you make sense of what you read.
Make Predictions Are you wondering what is going to happen next? Make a prediction and then check it as you read.

Monitor Comprehension
Not sure you understand something? Stop and check your understanding. Then try using a fix-up strategy, such as rereading, using images, or reading on.

Summarize
Can you sum up what you just read using your own words? Try summarizing to help you remember what you have read.

Visualize
Is the author using descriptive words or figurative language? Use the words to make a picture in your mind.

Glossary

Pronunciation Key			
a	b**a**t	oi	t**oy**
ā	**a**pe	ou	sh**ou**t
air	**air**	ŏŏ	b**oo**k
ä	p**a**rk	ōō	m**oo**n
e	l**e**t	s	**s**un
ē	**e**asy	sh	pre**ss**ure
i	**i**f	th	**th**e, **th**ing
ī	l**ie**	u	n**u**t
îr	d**ear**	ûr	c**ir**cle
k	**c**ause	ə	**a**go
o	l**o**t	ər	moth**er**
ō	g**o**	′	primary stress
ô	**a**ll	′	secondary stress

abroad (ə brôd′) *adv.* outside one's country;

The researcher traveled abroad to learn about European history. **271**

abundant (ə bən′ dənt) *adj.* plentiful; more than enough;

We made many salads with last year's abundant vegetable crop. **134**

admire (əd mīr′) *v.* to look at with appreciation;

The parents admire the pictures at the school art show. **310**

amendment (ə mend′ mənt) *n.* a formal change that is made according to specific procedure;

A majority of the classes voted for the amendment to the student constitution. **388**

analyze (a′ nə līz′) *v.* to study something carefully or to find out what something is made of;

Lior and Elena like to analyze paintings. **73**

artifact (är′ ti fakt′) *n.* an item made by a person that is of historical or cultural importance;

That mask is an interesting African artifact. **132**

befriend (bi frend′) *v.* to become a friend to someone;

Maria and Michael befriend all the newcomers to our building. **107**

celebrate (se′ lə brāt′) *v.* to honor or observe a special event or day;

We celebrate July Fourth by displaying the flag. **183**

circulate (sûr′ kyə lāt′) *v.* to move around freely;

The breeze will circulate the air in my bedroom. **198**

climate (klī′ mət) *n.* the average weather conditions of a place or region throughout the year;

The climate in Arizona is hot and dry during the summer. **208**

clung (klung) *v.* past tense of *cling*: to stick closely;

We clung to our parents in the large crowd. **480**

compromise (kom′ prə mīz′) *n.* an agreement to give up something in order to settle an issue;

Our compromise was that we got to stay up later if we washed the dinner dishes. **398**

constitution (kon′ stə tōō′ shən) *n.* the principles and ideas that govern a country, state, organization, or other group;

The club leaders voted to accept the constitution. **156**

cooperate (kō o′ pə rāt′) *v.* to work together;

Jenna and I cooperate to get our chores done quickly. **10**

courage (kûr′ ij) *n.* bravery; the strength to overcome fear;

It took courage to dive off that high diving board. **185**

culture (kul′ chər) *n.* a group of people with the same background and ways of thinking about and doing things;

Tea is a common drink for her culture. **16**

deliver (di li′ vər) *v.* to take or carry to a particular person or place;

I deliver groceries to Mr. Hain every Tuesday. **81**

democracy (di mo′ krə sē) *n.* a government that is run by the people;

A democracy allows its citizens to choose its leaders by voting. **385**

devastation (de′ və stā′ shən) *n.* destruction; ruin;

The devastation from the tornado affected the whole town. **214**

dilemma (də le′ mə) *n.* a difficult problem;

My dilemma is that I want to have a paper route but don't like to wake up early. **453**

disappointment (dis′ ə point′ mənt) *n.* the feeling of being let down or frustrated;

My brother's tears showed his disappointment to everyone in the room. **165**

discrimination (dis kri′ mə nā′ shən) *n.* the unfair difference in treatment of someone;

Not hiring a person because of his or her religion is discrimination. **407**

disguise (dis gīz′) *v.* to change appearance in order to hide one's identity;

The twins plan to disguise themselves as ghosts on Halloween. **362**

dispersal (di spûr′ səl) *n.* the breaking up and scattering of something, such as seeds;

Bird droppings help in seed dispersal. **338**

diversity (di vûr′ sə tē) *n.* difference; variety;

The players from all over the country give our team great diversity. **222**

dormant (dôr′ mənt) *adj.* not active;

There have been no eruptions from the dormant volcano in 200 years. **195**

eager (ē′ gər) *adj.* wanting to do something very much;

We were eager to go to the movie on opening day. **52**

ecologist (i ko′ lə jist) *n.* someone who studies how living things relate to their environment;

The ecologist taught my class that all living things are connected. **224**

economy (i ko′ nə mē) *n.* the way a country or other government produces and uses money, goods, services, and resources;

The U.S. economy depends on things such as farming and manufacturing. **155**

elegant (e′ li gənt) *adj.* very fine;

That elegant flower arrangement makes the table more beautiful. **414**

emerge (i mûrj′) *v.* to come out or to come into view;

The sun will emerge after that cloud passes by. **341**

emigrate (e′ mə grāt ′) *v.* to leave one's country and live in another;

Hari's aunt will emigrate from India and come to live in Connecticut. **266**

encourage (in kûr′ ij) *v.* to urge on someone or something;

I will encourage my cousin to finish his art project. **496**

estimate (es′ tə māt) *v.* to guess or form an opinion by reasoning;

They estimate that there were 150 people in the crowd. **345**

examine (ig za′ mən) *v.* to look at and check closely;

The doctor will examine my throat. **320**

expedition (ek′ spə di′ shən) *n.* a journey or trip made for a specific purpose, or the people making that journey;

The expedition to the mountaintop took two weeks. **86**

extraordinary (ek strôr′ də ner′ ē) *adj.* very unusual;

That bird's feathers have extraordinary colors. **350**

famine (fa′ mən) *n.* a serious lack of food in an area;

When food crops don't grow, a famine can occur. **20**

gaze (gāz) *v.* to look at something for a long time;

I could gaze at the stars all night. **38**

generation (jen′ ə rā′ shən) *n.* a step in a family from an ancestor down, as from parent to child;

It is one generation from my parents to my sister and me. **22**

germinate (jûr′ mə nāt′) *v.* to begin growing from a seed;

We will water the seeds regularly so that they germinate. **335**

haze (hāz) *n.* smoke, mist, or dust in the air;

The smog created a haze over the mountains. **354**

immigrant (i′ mə grənt) *n.* someone who comes to another country to live there permanently;

Marcia's grandmother arrived in the United States as an immigrant in 1950. **266**

incident (in′ sə dənt) *n.* an event or something that happens;

The fire drill was an incident that interrupted classes. **52**

inspiration (in′ spə rā′ shən) *n.* the creation of a good feeling that may lead to a creative idea or positive action;

The inspiration for my poem came from reading about Rosa Parks. **462**

intimidating (in ti′ mə dā′ ting) *adj.* being able to frighten;

The intimidating roar of the lion scared me. **258**

massive (ma′ siv) *adj.* very big; large and solid;

That massive vehicle uses a lot of gasoline. **434**

mediate (mē′ dē āt′) *v.* to help two or more sides reach an agreement;

Our principal helps mediate disagreements between students. **448**

mentor (men′ tôr′) *n.* a coach, tutor, or trusted counselor;

A mentor can help you learn to make good decisions. **13**

mission (mi′ shən) *n.* a special job or task;

Their mission was to help control the spacecraft. **108**

navigate (na′ və gāt′) *v.* to sail or steer a course on or through something;

Airplane pilots must learn to navigate their aircraft safely. **75**

negotiate (ni gō′ shē āt′) *v.* to discuss in order to reach an agreement;

The two lawyers will negotiate a settlement of the case. **459**

nutrient (nōō′ trē ənt) *n.* something needed by living things for life and growth;

Iron is an important nutrient found in wheat. **320**

ozone (ō′ zōn) *n.* a gas similar to oxygen;

The ozone layer is important to the health of Earth. **232**

patriot (pā′ trē ət) *n.* a person who loves, defends, and supports his or her country;

I believe that everyone who supported the American Revolution was a patriot. **149**

permission (pər mi′ shən) *n.* official approval;

My mom gave us permission to stay up later than usual. **486**

perspective (pər spek′ tiv) *n.* a point of view;

Elian's special perspective shows in the music he writes. **28**

pioneer (pī ə nîr′) *n.* someone who is one of the first to settle in a region;

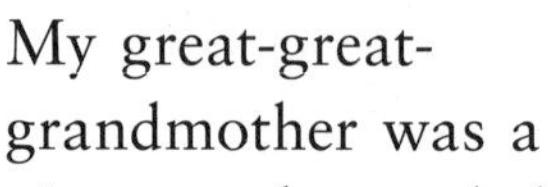

My great-great-grandmother was a pioneer who settled in Nebraska. **264**

plight (plīt) *n.* a sad or dangerous situation;

The plight of homeless animals has inspired me to volunteer at a shelter. **466**

poverty (po′ vûr tē) *n.* a lack of money; the situation of being poor;

A family that lives in poverty has little money for food. **271**

pronounce (prə nouns′) *v.* to make the sound of a word or letter;

Some words are more difficult to pronounce than others. **306**

prosper (pros′ pər) *v.* to do very well and to be successful;

Andrea's parents worked hard to help their business prosper. **143**

ratify (ra′ tə fī′) *v.* to approve or to agree officially;

The senators will ratify the change to the bill. **396**

rebellion (ri bel′ yən) *n.* an armed fight against a government or other authority;

The colonists staged a rebellion against the British governor. **149**

relief (ri lēf′) *n.* aid given in times of trouble or danger;

The relief supplies included bottled water and bags of rice. **450**

repeal (ri pēl′) *v.* to officially do away with something;

The City Council will repeal the law against outdoor seating at restaurants. **399**

research (ri sûrch′) *n.* the act of studying in order to learn facts;

Mom's research is about the history of Guatemala. **87**

resource (rē′ sôrs′) *n.* a material that a place or country uses to support itself;

Our town's river is a valuable resource. **143**

seep (sēp) *v.* to spread slowly;

The tiny hole in the window shade will let some light seep in. **205**

similar (si′ mə lər) *adj.* almost alike;

The house next door is similar to mine, but it is a different color. **22**

slump (slump) *v.* to fall or sink suddenly;

I saw him slump in his seat when the monster appeared on the movie screen. **308**

species (spē′ shēz) *n.* a group of plants or animals that have similar characteristics;

All dog breeds belong to one species. **91**

stable (stā′ bəl) *adj.* not easily changed or moved;

The price of corn has remained stable all summer. **211**

substance (sub′ stəns) *n.* a certain kind of material;

The countertop has a rough substance in it. **92**

surrender (sə ren′ dər) *n.* the act of yielding or giving up;

The surrender of the army was quick. **423**

survey (sər′ vā) *n.* the measurement of land to show its boundaries;

The survey team measured the size of the land for the new skyscraper. **105**

temperate (tem′ prət) *adj.* neither too cold nor too hot;

Spring is usually a temperate season. **328**

triumph (trī′ əmf) *v.* to achieve a victory or great success;

Our baseball team will triumph at today's game. **278**

Index

Acknowledgments

Photo Credits

6 (bl) ©Mark Saltz/Associated Press, (br) ©Photodisc/Getty Images; **6-7** (t) ©Play for Peace; **7** (bl) ©Lars Klove Photo Service/Getty Images, (br) ©Absodels/Getty Images; **8-9** ©Leland Bobbe/Corbis; **10** ©Mark Saltz/Associated Press,(br) ©kozvic49/Shutterstock; **11** (b) ©Danuta Otifnowski, (cr) ©www.daveyhearn.com; **12** (t) ©www.daveyhearn.com, (bl) ©C. Squared Studios/Getty Images, (tl) ©kozvic49/ Shutterstock; **13** ©Stuart O'Sullivan/Getty Images; **14** (b) ©Play for Peace; **14-15** ©Play for Peace; **16-17** (b) ©Peter Adams/Panoramic Images; **18** (inset) ©Trinh Le Nguyen/ Shutterstock; **18-19** ©The McGraw-Hill Companies, Inc./Barry Barker, photographer; **19** (t) ©WizDate, Inc./Shutterstock, (br) ©Image Source/PunchStock; **20** ©Cora Reed/Shutterstock; **21** (b) ©Ned Frisk/Getty Images, (bl) ©Photodisc/Getty Images, (tr) ©PhotosIndia.com/Getty Images; **21** (tl) ©Ingram Publishing/Fotosearch; **22** ©Lars Klove Photo Service/Getty Images; **28** ©Carmen Lomas Garza, (b) ©The McGraw-Hill Companies Inc./Ken Cavanagh Photographer; **29** ©Carmen Lomas Garza, ©The McGraw-Hill Companies Inc./Ken Karp Photographer; **30** ©Carmen Lomas Garza; **31** ©Carmen Lomas Garza; **32** ©ClearView Images/Alamy; **33** ©Absodels/ Getty Images; **34-35** ©Fotocromo/Shutterstock; **35** (tr) ©Danita Delimont/Alamy; **36** ©Robert Michael/Corbis; **55** (cr) ©The Hidden Ocean, Artic 2005 Exploration, (b) ©Mike Kemp/Getty Images; **68** (bl) StockTrek/Getty Images, (br) ©Library of Congress/DAL; **69** (bl) ©Jeremy Potter/NOAA, (br) ©NASA, (t) ©NASA; **70-71** (bkgrd) ©Photodisc/Getty Images; **72** (b) ©Corbis/SuperStock; **72-73** (bkgrd) ©K-PHOTOS/Alamy; **72-73** (t) ©INTERFOTO Pressebildagentur/Alamy; **73** (tr) ©Alamy Images; **74-75** (bkgrd) ©Gerard Lodriguss/Photo Researchers, Inc.; **76** (b) ©North Wind Picture Archives/Alamy; **76-77** (b) ©Library of Congress; **77** (cr) ©Stockbyte/Getty Images, (t) ©Charles Marie Rigobert Bonne/Getty Images; **78** (inset) ©Johnson Space Center/NASA, (bkgrd) ©StockTrek/Getty Images; **79** (b) ©NASA, (t) ©NASA, (tc) ©Nasa, (b) ©I. Glory/Alamy; **80** (b) ©Library of Congress/DAL, ©James Darell/Getty Images; **80-81** (b) ©reggieworld.com/Jupiterimages, (t) ©Photodisc/ Getty Images; **81** (t) ©Richard Warehm Fotografie/Alamy; **82** (cr) ©IBM Research, (b) ©Mike Kemp/Getty Images; **83** ©Courtesy of Vreseis Limited; **84** (tr) ©Photodisc/Getty Images, (cl) ©Jiri Pavlik/Shutterstock, (l) ©Digital Vision/Getty Images; **85** (b) ©Lana Langlois/Shutterstock, (c) ©Getty Images, (t) ©Royalty-Free/Corbis; **86-87** (bkgrd) ©Ian MacDonald/NOAA, (t) ©Joseph Becker/Shutterstock; **87** (inset) ©Jeremy Potter/NOAA; **88** (inset) ©The Hidden Ocean, Artic 2005 Exploration, NOAA-OE; **88-89** (bkgrd) ©Sue Flood/ Getty Images; **89** (inset) ©The Hidden Ocean, Artic 2005 Exploration; **90** ©The Hidden Ocean, Artic 2005 Exploration; **91** (tl) ©Hidden Ocean 2005 Expedition: NOAA Office of Ocean Exploration, (tc) ©Hidden Ocean 2005 Expedition: NOAA Office of Ocean Exploration, (tr) ©Hidden Ocean 2005 Expedition: NOAA Office of Ocean Exploration, (b) ©Hidden Ocean 2005 Expedition: NOAA Office of Ocean Exploration; **92** ©Chris Mattison/Alamy; **92-93** (t) ©Photodisc/Getty Images; **93** (t) ©I. Glory/Alamy, (c) ©David Hancock/AFP/Getty Images; **94** ©Chase Jarvis/Uppercut Images/Getty; **95** (bkgrd) ©Cranston, Bob/Animals Animals - Earth Scenes - All Rights Reserved.; **96** (inset) ©Nasa; **96-97** (bkgrd) ©StockTrek/Getty Images; **98** ©Stockbyte/Getty Images; **128** (bl) ©Marina Dodis/Getty Images, (br) ©Library of Congress; **129** (bl) ©Library of Congress, (br) ©Corbis, (t) ©Brand X Pictures/PunchStock; **130-131** ©Digital Vision/ Getty Images; **132** (b) ©National Museum of the American Indian/Smithsonian; **133** (b) ©Ingram Publishing/AGE Fotostock, (t) ©National Museum of the American Indian/ Smithsonian; **134-135** ©Kevin Miller/Getty Images; **135** (b) ©Richard Schlecht/Getty Images; **136-137** ©Marina Dodis/ Getty Images; **138** (b) ©North Wind/North Wind Picture Archives; **138-139** (bkgrd) ©Danita Delimont/Alamy; **139** (b) ©The Granger Collection, New York; **140-141** ©The Granger Collection, New York; **142** (t) ©The Granger Collection, New York; **143** (b) ©After G. Bramati/Getty Images, (t) ©The Granger Collection, New York; **144-145** ©Library of Congress; **146** (inset) ©The Granger Collection, New York; **146-147** (bkgrd) ©Maurice Savage/Alamy; **147** (inset) ©North Wind/Nancy Carter/North Wind Picture Archives; **148-149** ©LOOK Die Bildagentur der Fotografen GmbH/Alamy; **149** (b) ©The Granger Collection, New York, (frame) ©Getty Images; **150-151** ©Corbis; **151** (inset) ©DarleneBordwell.com; **152-153** (t) ©The Granger Collection, New York, (bkgrd) ©William Owens/Alamy, (frame) ©Photodisc/Getty Images; **154** (t) ©National Archives and Records Administration; **154-155** (bkgrd) ©The Granger Collection, New York; **156-157** ©Corbis; **158** ©Getty Images; **190** (bl) ©J.D. Girggs/U.S. Geological Survey, (br) ©Digital Stock/Corbis; **190-191** (t) ©Pixtal/AGE Fotostock; **191** (br) ©Jan Martin Will/Shutterstock, (bl) ©Creatas/Punchstock; **192-193** ©Digital Vision/Getty Images; **194** (tc) ©J.D. Girggs/U.S. Geological Survey; **194-195** (b) ©Greg Vaughn/Alamy, (t) ©Dr. Parvinder Sethi, (bkgrd) ©PhotoLink/Getty Images; **195** (t) ©Science Source/Photo Researchers; **196** (b) ©Josiah Davidson/Getty Images; **197** (tr) ©Peter French/AGE Fotostock, (b) ©SuperStock, Inc./SuperStock, (tl) ©Getty Images/Stringer; **198** (b) ©David Noton Photography/Alamy; **198** (t) ©Dorling Kindersley; **200-201** (bkgrd) ©Pete Oxford/Minden Pictures/ National Geographic Images; **201** (b) ©Robert E. Wallace/U.S Geological Survey,(c) ©Herman Emmet/Photo Researchers, Inc.; **202** ©Phil Degginger/Alamy; **203** (tr) ©Michael Newman/ PhotoEdit, (tl) ©McGraw-Hill Companies, Inc./Ken Karp Photographer, (c) ©The McGraw-Hill Companies, Inc./Ken Cavanagh Photographer; **204** (b) ©Mike Read/Alamy, (t) Digital Vision; **205** (b) ©Associated Press; **206** (b) ©Digital Stock/Corbis, (t) ©David R. Frazier Photolibrary, Inc./Alamy; **206-207** (t) ©Mike Kipling Photography/Alamy; **208** (t) ©Creatas/Punchstock; **208-209** (b) ©Peter Lillie; Gallo Images/ Corbis; **209** (t) ©Karen Kasmauski/Science Faction; **210** (b) ©Dennis Novak/Getty Images, (bkgrd) ©Brand X Pictures/ PunchStock; **210-211** (bkgrd) ©Lester Lefkowitz/Corbis; **212** (c) ©M.R. Campbell/USGS Photographic Library, (b) ©Blase Reardon/USGS Photographic Library, (t) ©Digital Vision; **212-213** ©Associated Press; **214** (b) ©Associated Press; **214-215** (bkgrd) ©Michael Routh/Alamy; **215** (t) ©Stephen St. John/Getty Images; **216** (b) ©Associated Press; **217** (b) ©SuperStock, Inc./SuperStock, (t) ©Don Farrall/Getty Images; **218-219** (bkgrd) ©Jan Martin Will/Shutterstock; **219** (br) ©Blend Images/Veer, (t) ©Stuart O'Sullivan/Getty Images, (bl) ©Dana White/PhotoEdit; **220** ©Pixtal/AGE Fotostock; **221** (t)

©Corbis/PunchStock, (b) ©Royalty-Free/Corbis, (bkgd) ©DAJ/Getty Images; **222** (dragonfly) ©Ablestock/Jupiter Images, (bl) ©Image Source,(tr) ©Photos.com/Jupiter Images,(tr) ©ANP, (cl) ©Kristy-Anne Glubish/Design Pics/Corbis, (c) ©Royalty-Free/Corbis, (tl) ©Digital Archive Japan/Alamy; **223** (tr) ©Royalty-Free/Corbis,(br) ©IT Stock Free/Alamy, (c) ©Brand X Pictures/PunchStock; **224** ©Photos.com/Jupiter Images; **225** (t) ©Photodisc/Getty Images, (b) ©Photos.com/Jupiter Images; **226** (tr) ©Robert Marien/Corbis, (tl) ©Creatas/PunchStock, (c) ©Robert Barber/Painet; **227** (tl) ©Brand X Pictures/PunchStock, (tr) ©Digital Vision/Punchstock, (b) ©Digital Vision/PunchStock; **228** (tr) ©Digital Vision/PunchStock, (br) ©Charles Smith/Corbis, (bl) ©Photodisc/Getty Images, (tl) ©Kent Knudson/PhotoLink, (r) ©Steve Hamblin/Alamy; **229** ©Xavier GallegoMorell/Shutterstock; **230** (t) ©Ingram Publishing/Alamy, (b) ©Johnny Johnson/Photographer's Choice/Getty Images; **231** ©Karl Ammann/Digital Vision/Getty Images; **232** ©Ingram Publishing/SuperStock; **233** (tl) ©Scientifica/Visuals Unlimited/Getty Images, (t) ©Digital Vision/PunchStock, (b) ©Comstock Images/Alamy; **234** (banana) ©Burke Triolo Productions/Getty Images, (orange) ©Goodshoot Image/Jupiter Images, (b) Liquidlibrary ©Jupiterimages; **235** ©Photos.com/Jupiter Images; **236** (t) ©Aleksander Bolbot, (b) ©Christoph Weihs; **237** ©Tim McCabe,USDA Natural Resources Conservation Service; **238** (tl) ©Christophe Testi, (r) ©liquidlibrary/Jupiter Images, (inset) ©Jack Hollingsworth/Getty Images; **239** (t) ©Ben Osborne/Stone/Getty Images, (b) ©Benjamin Howell, (t) ©Comstock Images/Jupiter Images; **240** (c)©Creatas/PunchStock, (b) ©ImageState/PunchStock, (bcr) ©Digital Vision/Getty Images, (bcl) ©Andy Rouse/the Image Bank/Getty Images; **241** ©Photos.com/Jupiter Images; **242** (banana) ©Photos.com/Jupiter Images, (paper) ©Photodisc/Getty Images, (milk) ©The McGraw-Hill Companies, Inc./Ken Cavanagh photographer, (cig butt) ©Photodisc Collection/Getty Images, (trash bag) ©Stockbyte/PunchStock, (crushed can), ©Chris Curtis/Shutterstock, (plastic rings) ©Stockxpert/Jupiter Images, (foam cup) ©design56/Shutterstock (tbr) ©prism68/Shutterstock **243** (tr) ©liquidlibrary/Jupiter Images, (tbl) ©Masterfile, (tl) ©PhotoAlto/Punchstock, (marble) ©Comstock Images/Jupiter Images; **244** (l) ©Stockdisc/Getty Images; **243** (b) ©Masterfile; **244** (r) ©J. Gatherum/Shutterstock; **245** ©Masterfile; **246** (l) ©kabby/Shutterstock, (br) ©Jeff Gynane/Shutterstock; **247** (t) ©Michael Rubin/Shutterstock, (b) ©Warren Gretz/Courtesy of NREL; **248** ©Vespasian/Alamy; **249** (b) ©MaxFX/Shutterstock, ©Colin Stitt/Shutterstock; **252** (t) ©Green Belt Movement.org, (b) ©Green Belt Movement.org **254** (br) ©Getty Images (bl) ©Hulton Archive/Getty Images; **254-255** (t) ©Royalty-Free/Corbis; **255** (bl) ©Cosmo Condina/Getty Images, (br) ©Hulton Archive/Getty Images; **256** (tr) ©Bettmann/Corbis (tl) ©Underwood & Underwood/Corbis; **256-257** ©Library of Congress; **257** (r) ©Photodisc/Getty Images; **258** (t) ©North Wind Picture Archives/Alamy; **258-259** (c) ©North Wind Picture Archives/Alamy, (b) ©Photodisc/Punchstock; **259** (t) ©The London Art Archive/Alamy; **260** (b) ©Hulton Archive/Getty Images; **261** (b) Digital Vision/Getty Images; **262-263** (bkgrd) ©Bettmann/Corbis, (t) ©The Granger Collection, New York; **263** (bl) ©Hulton Archive/Getty Images, (br) ©Photodisc/Getty Images; **264** (b) ©Photodisc/Getty Images; **264-265** (bkgrd) ©Bettmann/Corbis, (t) ©Greg Ryan/Alamy; **266** (c) ©Hulton-Deutsch Collection/Corbis; **266-267** (bkgrd) ©The Granger Collection, New York; **268** (c) ©Underwood & Underwood/Corbis; **268-269** (t) ©Wolfgang Kaehler, (bkgrd) ©Corbis; **269** (b) ©Paul Taylor/Getty Images; **270-271** (bkgrd) ©Lee Foster/Alamy; **271** (t) ©Mike Booth/Alamy; **272** (b) Royalty-Free/Corbis; **272-273** (t) ©Cosmo Condina/Getty Images, (bkgrd) ©Michael Ventura/Alamy; **273** (b) ©Bettmann/Corbis; **274** (c) ©Bettmann/Corbis; **274-275** (bkgrd) Eyewire/Photodisc; **275** (b) ©Photodisc/Getty Images; **276** (t) ©Studio Photogram/Alamy; **276-277** (bkgrd) ©Getty Images; **278** (t) ©Time & Life Pictures/Getty Images; **278-279** (bkgrd) ©Associated Press; **280-281** (bkgrd) ©AFP/Getty Images; **281** (b) ©Associated Press; **282** (b) ©Time & Life Pictures/Getty Images; **282-283** (bkgrd) ©Library of Congress; **283** (t) ©Associated Press; **284** ©Russell Kord/Alamy; **316** (bl) ©Dr. Brad Mogen/Getty Images, (br) ©DEA/G. Bellani/Getty Images; **316-317** (t) ©Stephen Reynolds; **317** (bl) ©Bill Beatty/Getty Images, (br) ©Robert Frerck/Stone/Getty Images; **318-319** ©©Bill Tarpening/USDA; **320-321** (bkgrd) ©Brand X Pictures/PunchStock; **321** (l) ©Dr. Brad Mogen/Getty Images, (r) ©MedicalRF.com/Getty Images; **322** (inset) ©Mark Lewis/Getty Images; **322-323** (bkgrd) ©Comstock/PunchStock; **323** (t) ©Sabine Scheckel/Getty Images, (b) ©Photodisc/Getty Images; **324** (t) ©Ingram Publishing/AGE Fotostock, (b) ©Graham Oliver/Alamy; **326-327** (bkgrd) ©Kyle Cornforth/Edible Schoolyard, (t) ©Ingram Publishing/Alamy; **327** (c) ©Katie Standke; **328** ©DEA/G. Bellani/Getty Images; **329** (l) ©Craig K. Lorenz/Photo Researchers, Inc., (r) ©David Boag/Alamy; **330-331** (bkgrd) ©Flowers galore/Den Reader/Alamy; **331** (b) ©Photodisc/Getty Images; **332-333** (bkgrd) ©Creatas Images/PunchStock; **333** (l) ©Marvin Dembinsky Photo Associates/Alamy, (r) ©Gareth McCormack/Alamy; **334-335** (bkgrd) ©Bryan & Cherry Alexander Photography/Alamy; **335** (bl) ©Nigel Cattlin/Alamy, (bc) ©Mark Boulton/Photo Researchers, Inc. (br) ©blickwinkel/Alamy, (t) ©Global Crop Diversity Trust/epa/Corbis; **336** (t) ©Michael Duva/Getty Images; **336-337** (b) ©Bill Beatty/Getty Images; **337** (c) ©Malcolm Case-Green/Alamy; **338-339** (bkgrd) ©Angelo Cavalli/Getty Images; **339** (br) ©Andrew Darrington/Alamy, (tl) ©Stone Nature Photography/Alamy, (bl) ©Scott Camazine/Photo Researchers, Inc., (tr) ©Brand X Pictures/Getty Images; **342-343** (bc) ©Comstock/JupiterImages, (bkgrd) ©Photick-Image and Click/Alamy Images **343** (b) ©Robert Frerck/Stone/Getty Images; **344** (t) ©Zeno Elea/Alamy, (b) ©Steffen Hauser/botanikfoto/Alamy; **345** ©Brian Bailey/Getty Images; **346** Katerina Havelkova/Shutterstock; **380** (br) ©Jupiterimages/Comstock Images/Alamy, (bl) ©Associated Press; **380-381** (t) ©BrandXPictures/PunchStock; **381** (bl) ©Library of Congress, (br) ©Hank Walker/Stringer/Time & Life Pictures/Getty Images; **382-383** Joe Sohm/Visions of America, LLC/Alamy; **384** (tr) ©PunchStock/ImageSource; **384-385** (bkgrd) ©Associated Press; **385** (b) ©Associated Press; thru out (fireworks) ©Eyewire(Photodisc)/PunchStock; thru out (flag) ©Eyewire(Photodisc)/PunchStock; **388** (t) ©MedioImages/Corbis, (b) ©Associated Press; **388-389** (bkgrd) ©Chip Somodevilla/Getty News/Getty Images; **390** ©Bettmann/Corbis; **391** (bkgrd) ©BrandXPictures/PunchStock, (bkgrd) ©The McGraw-Hill Companies, Inc.; **392** (b) ©Gregg Newton/Corbis; **392-393** (bkgrd) ©The Granger Collection, New York; **393** (b) ©Jupiterimages/Comstock Images/Alamy; **394** (b) ©The Granger Collection, New York; **394-395** (bkgrd) ©The Granger Collection, New York; **395** (b) ©Royalty-Free/Corbis; **396-397** (bkgrd) ©Ron and Patty Thomas/Photographer's Choice/Getty Images; **397** (t) ©Masterfile; **398** (b) ©National Archives and Records Adminstration (Public); **398-399** (bkgrd) ©Michael Ventura/Alamy; **400** (b) ©Associated Press; **400-401** (bkgrd) ©Associated Press, (bkgrd) ©Jeff Greenberg/AGE Fotostock; **401** (b) ©The Granger Collection, New York; **402-403** (bkgrd) ©Bettmann/Corbis; **403** (b) ©Royalty-Free/Corbis; **404-405** (bkgrd) ©Library of Congress; **405** (b) ©Franes Benjamin Johnston/Corbis, (frame) ©C Squared Studios/Getty Images;

Photo Credits, cont.

406-407 (bkgrd) ©Bettmann/Corbis; **407** (b) ©Hank Walker/Stringer/Time & Life Pictures/Getty Images; **408-409** (bkgrd) ©The Granger Collection, New York; **409** (b) U.S. Senate Historical Office, (frame) ©C Squared Studios/Getty Images; **410** (t) ©Purestock/PunchStock, (b) ©Richard Levine/Alamy; **442** (bl) ©Lewis Hine/Library of Congress, (br) ©Don Cravens/Time Life Pictures/Getty Images; **442-443** (t) ©Associated Press; **443** (br) ©Arthur Schatz/Time Life Pictures/Getty Images, (br) ©JBryson/istockphoto/Getty Images; **444-445** ©Digital Vision Ltd./SuperStock; **446** (b) ©Tim Graham/Alamy; **446-447** ©MLB Photos via/Getty Images, (bkgrd) ©Jack Hollingsworth/Getty Images; **447** (b) ©Courtesy of Heavenly Hats Foundation, Inc.; **448** (b) ©Alison Bagley; **448-449** (bkgrd) ©Lars Niki; **449** (b) ©Sidnee Wheelright; **450-451** ©Courtesy of Heifer International; **452-453** ©Lewis Hine/Library of Congress; **453** (b) ©Corbis, (bkgrd) ©Royalty-Free/Corbis; **454-455** ©J.S. Johnston/Corbis; **456** (tl) ©Associated Press; **456-457** (bkgrd) ©Justin Sullivan/Getty Images; **457** (c) ©Larry Downing/Getty Images; **458-459** (b) ©Don Cravens/Time Life Pictures/Getty Images, (bkgrd) ©Associated Press; **460** (c) ©Bettman/Corbis; **460-461** (bkgrd) ©Associated Press; **461** (t) ©Associated Press; **462-463** (b) ©Micheline Pelletier/Corbis, (bkgrd) ©PNC/Photodisc/Getty Images; **463** (b) ©Arthur Schatz/Time Life Pictures/Getty Images; **464** (b) ©Associated Press; **464-465** (bkgrd) ©Nic Bothma/epa/Corbis; **466** ©Ted Streshinsky/Corbis; **467** (t) ©William Campbell/Sygma/Corbis; **468** ©Joson/zefa/Corbis, (t) ©Photodisc/Getty Images; **469** ©JBryson/istockphoto/Getty Images; **470-471** ©Richard Levine/Alamy.

Art Credits

The McGraw-Hill Companies, Inc. would like to thank the following illustrators for their contributions: Christiane Beauregard, S. G. Brooks, Ortelius Design, Julia Green, Karen Minot, Luciana Navarro, Robert Schuster, Silver Editions/©The McGraw-Hill Companies, Inc.

Text Credits

Brothers by Yin, illustrations by Chris Soentpiet. Text copyright © 2006 by Keiko Yin. Illustrations © 2006 by Chris Soentpiet. Published by arrangement with Philomel Books, a division of Penguin Young Readers Group, a member of Penguin Group (USA) Inc. All rights reserved.

From *How Tía Lola Came to Visit/Stay*. Copyright © 2001 by Julia Alvarez. Published by Dell Yearling and in hardcover by Alfred A. Knopf Children's Books, a division of Random House, New York. Reprinted by permission of Susan Bergholz Literary Services, New York, NY, and Lamy, NM. All rights reserved.

"I Can" from *Singing Black* by Mari Evans, published by Reed Visuals, 1979. Reproduced by permission of the author.

I, Matthew Henson: Polar Explorer. Text copyright © 2008 by Carole Boston Weatherford. Illustrations copyright © 2008 by Eric Velasquez. Reprinted by permission of Walker Books. All rights reserved.

Kate and the Beanstalk by Mary Pope Osborne, illustrated by Giselle Potter. Text copyright © 2000 by Mary Pope Osborne. Illustrations copyright © 2000 by Giselle Potter. Reprinted by arrangement with Atheneum Books For Young Readers, an Imprint of Simon & Schuster Children's Publishing Division. All rights reserved.
2001 Notable Children's Book

Passage to Freedom: The Sugihara Story. Text copyright © 1997 by Ken Mochizuki. Illustrations copyright © 1997 by Dom Lee. Afterword copyright © 1997 by Hiroki Sugihara. Permission arranged with Lee & Low Books Inc., New York, NY 10016.
1998 Notable Children's Book

Planet Patrol: A Kid's Action Guide to Earth Care by Marybeth Lorbiecki, illustrated by Nancy Meyers. Text copyright 2005 by Marybeth Lorbiecki. Illustrations copyright 2005 by Nancy Meyers. Two-Can Publishing. Used by permission of Cooper Square Publishing LLC, Lanham, MD.

Seven Miles to Freedom: The Robert Smalls Story. Text copyright © 2008 by Janet Halfmann. Illustrations copyright © 2008 by Duane Smith. Permission arranged with Lee & Low Books Inc., New York, NY 10016.

The Buffalo Jump by Peter Roop, illustrations by Bill Farnsworth. Text copyright © 1996 by Peter Roop. Illustrations copyright © 1996 by Bill Farnsworth. Used by permission of Cooper Square Publishing, LLC, Lanham, MD.

This Land Is Your Land, Words and music by Woody Guthrie. TRO © Copyright 1956 (Renewed), 1958 (Renewed), 1970 (Renewed), 1972 (Renewed) Ludlow Music, Inc. New York, NY. International Copyright Secured. Made in U.S.A. All Rights Reserved Including Public Performance For Profit. Used by Permission of TRO.

"To You" from *The Collected Poems of Langston Hughes* by Langston Hughes, edited by Arnold Rampersad with David Roessel, Associate Editor. Copyright © 1994 by The Estate of Langston Hughes. Used by permission of Alfred A. Knopf, a division of Random House, Inc.

"We are Trees/Somos árboles" from *From the Bellybutton of the Moon* by Francisco X. Alarcón. Poems Copyright © 1998 by Francisco X. Alarcón. Reprinted with permission of the publisher, Children's Book Press, San Francisco, CA www.childrensbookpress.org.

"Where?" by Eleanor Roosevelt as appeared in *Hour of Freedom: American History in Poetry,* compiled by Milton Meltzer. Used by permission of the Estate of Eleanor Roosevelt.